Though the

HEAVENS FALL

To order additional copies of
Though the Heavens Fall,
by Mikhail P. Kulakov, Sr.,
with Maylan Schurch,
call **1-800-765-6955**.

Visit us at
www.reviewandherald.com
for information on other Review and Herald® products.

Though the
HEAVENS
FALL

MIKHAIL P. KULAKOV, SR.,
WITH MAYLAN SCHURCH

REVIEW AND HERALD® PUBLISHING ASSOCIATION
Since 1861 | www.reviewandherald.com

The author assumes full responsibility for the accuracy of all facts and quotations as cited in this book.

This book was
Edited by Penny Estes Wheeler
Copy Edited by James Cavil
Designed by Trent Truman
Cover illustration: Flag: © istockphoto.com/bkindler;
                    Soviet soldiers: © istockphoto.com/wagnerm25
Interior/Photo insert designed by Heather Rogers
Typeset: Bembo 10.5/12.5

PRINTED IN U.S.A.

12   11   10   09   08   5   4   3   2   1

Review and Herald Cataloging Service
    Kulakov, Mikhail Petrovich, 1927-   .
        Though the heavens fall, by Mikhail P. Kulakov with Maylan Schurch.

        1. Kulakov, Mikhail Petrovich, 1927-   2. Seventh-day Adventists—Russia.
    I. Schurch, Maylan, 1950-   II. Title [B]

ISBN 978-0-8280-2366-5

Dedicated to

the blessed memory of those thousands of
God's faithful men and women, prisoners of conscience,
who sacrificed their lives for the gospel of Christ
in the forced-labor camps of the Soviet Union.

Acknowledgments

Being infinitely grateful to God for innumerous blessings, including the very fruitful (in all senses of the word) contacts with His people and organizations, I want to acknowledge those who inspired this book and made valuable contributions to it:

My parents; my beloved wife, Anna; and our six children and the same number of children-in-law. You have surrounded me with your love, and supported me in my efforts to share God's love with others.

The worldwide Seventh-day Adventist Church family. You provided me with a secure spiritual foundation from which I could build a home and a ministry.

Holy men and women of the church. Your exemplary dedication to Jesus and His cause has been a great source of my inspiration.

Mark Finley, a personal friend and the former speaker/director of It Is Written International Television. Upon hearing me share my stories at one of the It Is Written meetings, you urged me to write this book, personally interviewing me to get these stories on tape.

Penny Pederson, the devout member of the Lakeview SDA Church in Georgia. You typed a considerable part of the manuscript.

Alex Swiridoff, my relative and friend. You helped me to translate into English some of my notes for the book that were previously written in Russian.

Diane and Howard Peth, the dedicated members of the Vista SDA Church in southern California. You were the first readers of my initial drafts and have been my wise advisers.

Maylan Schurch, pastor of the Bellevue SDA Church, and my coauthor. Your gift as a writer, your indefatigable persistence, and your experience in book production made this book possible.

Contents

Foreword

When I first visited Eastern Europe in 1982, the Communist ideology was deeply entrenched in every aspect of society. As I met with numerous Adventist pastors and church members one single thought impressed me repeatedly: Their lives reflected a depth of Christianity forged in the crucible of suffering that was rare in the democratic West.

When I first met Mikhail Kulakov in Moscow a decade later, this thought struck me again: *Here is a spiritual giant of sterling character.* Mikhail's knowledge of the Bible, His love for people, and his commitment to the Adventist message and movement were apparent in all of our conversations. As our friendship developed, he continued to share more freely his lifelong struggle for religious freedom in the former Soviet Union. His years in prison only deepened his faith. He served a God who was fully capable of strengthening him in the darkest moments of his life.

Mikhail's faith was not the sugarcoated faith of the wealth-and-prosperity gospel so prevalent today. It was not a superficial faith commanding God to do what *he* wanted; it was a constant seeking after what *God* wanted with his life. His faith was a confident trust in a God who was with him every moment of his life. The more he shared his story with me, the more convinced I became that it was a story that needed to be told. It is a story that must be preserved for future generations.

Adventist youth in the West especially know little of suffering. This inspiring story will lift their vision. Yet the story of this courageous warrior of the cross calls for a deeper dedication to Christ by people of all ages. It calls for a spiritual renewal in each of our lives. It invites us to spend more time in prayer and the study of the Word.

When I first met Mikhail Kulakov, he was reluctant to share the details of his story. There were at least two reasons for this. First, he is a humble man and did not want to exalt himself. Second, the Soviet believers knew all too well the consequences of saying too much. However, with the passing of time and because of the changing political climate in the former Soviet Union, I have urged him to share the saga of his life with others. As I spent many hours interviewing him, I found myself being caught up in the story. At times tears flooded my eyes; at other times I smiled. And more than once I felt like falling on my knees and praising God.

In the later years of his life as the leader of our work in the former Soviet Union, Pastor Kulakov has had to make some very difficult decisions. Not everyone, even among his colleagues, agreed with those decisions. Leaders sometimes must stand tall, alone. In this book you will read the story of a spiritual giant who was willing to make the difficult decisions he believed were right for the cause of God.

Mikhail Kulakov's life has had a profound impression on my life. I am closer to God today because of our friendship, and I am confident that you will draw closer to the Savior as you read the story of my dear friend.

In the days ahead, when the crisis really breaks for God's people at the end-time, we all will gather renewed courage from God's heroes of faith such as Mikhail Kulakov. May your life be filled with the faith of your Master as you read these pages.

Mark Finley
General Vice President
General Conference of Seventh-day Adventists
Silver Spring, Maryland

CHAPTER 1: Arrest!

In October of 2006 Great Britain's Queen Elizabeth made her first-ever royal visit to Riga, Latvia. International media crews descended on the small Baltic country and followed Her Majesty everywhere. But the popular Russian network NTV chose an intriguing centerpiece for the monarch's historical visit: the replica of a Siberian corrective labor camp barracks, where Latvian political prisoners were confined during the Soviet period.

I was lucky enough to be able to watch TV images of the queen's tour, and as I saw the cameras move through the barracks my chest tightened. Even though I knew what I was seeing was only an exhibit in Riga's Museum of the Occupation of Latvia, I could not stop my heart reaction. I'd known the reality firsthand. After my arrest in Latvia, I spent years in barracks like these, and nearly six decades later I could still taste the prisoners' food I'd been served. I could still feel those plank beds beneath me.

How I came to spend time there, I think, provides a snapshot of what life was like for practicing Christians in the Stalinist Soviet Union. Let me tell you the story.

As the summer of 1947 began, I graduated from art school in Ivanovo, a big industrial city about 180 miles northeast of Moscow. Ordinarily, an educated young man like me—even in the Soviet Union—could look toward his future with at least a modest amount of confidence.

But "ordinarily" didn't apply to my family and me, at least in one sense. Two years earlier my father, Ivanovo's Seventh-day Adventist pastor, had been arrested and was doing penal labor in a corrective labor camp in the Komi Republic, more than 600 miles to the northeast. In addition to my studies I'd tried, in his absence, to carry on his pastoral work. But at every turn I could feel the heavy menace of a disapproving government.

"We need to move," I told my mother and brothers. "Dad's arrest has made it tough for all of us. The KGB is watching us like wolves."

Mom finally agreed. "After all," she said, "when the apostle Paul was persecuted, he moved to a new area. But where shall we go?"

"One of my friends has heard of an opening for an art teacher in Daugavpils," I said.

Mom frowned. *"Latvia?"*

I nodded. "If we go 600 miles east, it might get the local KGB off our backs."

So that summer I left for Daugavpils to find a place for us to live, and a little later my mother and three brothers joined me. Daugavpils was a small provincial town, but its multinational population made it an interesting place to live, and since everybody spoke Russian as the state language we had few communication problems. We joined the local Adventist group of believers, and did our best to help Pastor Yanis Oltinsh in his cautious search for people who hungered to know the Lord.

Delighted to find a bona fide—and young—art graduate on their doorstep, the local department of education immediately put me to work teaching drawing classes at two different high schools, one of them filled with Polish students. I loved my job, though the recently-fought World War II had drained away the funds that otherwise would have been spent for art supplies and textbooks. Even drawing tools were in short supply.

"As you leave," I would tell the students at the end of each class period, "please place your instruments here on my desk." They would file forward, and I would collect the rulers and triangles and French curves into my carrying case for the next class's use.

One afternoon in my eleventh form (high school junior) class at the Polish school I made my usual request, and the students obediently filed past me. But suddenly I noticed that one of the girls, who had large, beautiful eyes, still sat in her seat, her head bent over one of my triangles. Assuming she hadn't heard me, I approached her.

"Marina," I said, "may I have that, please?"

Suddenly I realized her head was bent because she was writing something on the triangle itself. Startled, she glanced up and blushed. I held out my hand, and she shyly turned those huge eyes upon my face as she handed me the tool. I tipped it toward me and saw her carefully penciled words:

I fell in love with you the first time you came to our class. Please do not laugh at me. I simply cannot control myself. I love you now and will love you always.

I do not know who was more embarrassed, she or I!

I've told you that my family and I weren't "ordinary," and here's where our differentness was a strength. God used my wise Christian mother to save me from many foolish mistakes with the opposite sex.

"Boys," she would say to her four sons, *"never be motivated only by your emotions.* You must also use good judgment, illuminated by the Word of God." Sometimes we would shuffle our feet, wondering when the lecture would be over, but we listened.

"All our gifts and abilities—everything we have, and everything we are—has been given to us by our Creator," she would continue, "to serve Him and our neighbors. Do you understand?"

"Yes, Mom." We'd heard this speech many times, always delivered in the most solemn tones.

"And it is a sin," she added, "to use these blessings and privileges for personal indulgence."

"What's 'personal indulgence'?"

"To please only yourself," she explained.

Once, years before, two girls who were sisters had become infatuated with me at the same time (the younger was named Sonya, and I'll tell you more about her in a future chapter). When Mom learned about this, she immediately got me alone, and her tone was even more somber, and her words carefully chosen.

"Misha," she said, using the affectionate nickname for Mikhail, "you must deal in a noble way with people who are immature or unbalanced in their emotions. You will never forgive yourself if you misuse the affection that people have toward you. Remember the story of David? He was thirsty, and his soldiers overheard him talking about how much he longed for the water of a Bethlehem well. They broke through enemy lines, risking their lives to get that water for him. But he valued their generous devotion so highly that he refused to indulge in any personal satisfaction."

Even though I was a little embarrassed to be having a conversation like this, I listened carefully. She was putting this issue in a way I'd never considered before.

"Be prudent like Joseph," she insisted. "Keep yourself unsoiled. Save your thoughts and affections for the special girl the Lord has prepared for you. You will be greatly rewarded." I praise God both for my mother's words and for giving me the common sense to listen to them, no matter how difficult it sometimes was.

And now, my head spun as I turned away from Marina's desk. But Mom's counsel had steadied my emotions. And it's a good thing—because of what happened on a sunny March day barely three weeks later.

On that day I was again in my classroom, chatting with some students during break time. Suddenly the school's head of studies, a stout Jewish woman with black curly hair, came into the room, and paused, staring at me. I could see her throat moving as she swallowed twice.

I gave her a second glance. *Something's wrong,* I decided. *She's nervous. Her hands are shaking.*

She moved toward me. "Why aren't you on your break?"

Some of the students glanced at her, and then at me.

"I *am* on break," I told her. "I was just talking with—"

"Why aren't you on your break?" she repeated in a trembling voice. And then, more softly: "You must accompany me to the principal's office."

As we walked along the hallway, she turned and looked me full in the face, staring at me, saying nothing.

"What's the matter?" I asked in a low voice. "Have I done something wrong?"

She said nothing, but gazed at me again. Her black eyes were sending me some sort of signal, but I couldn't read it. I realize now that the message she was desperately trying to communicate was *Go on your break, Mikhail Kulakov. Now. Get out of here. Leave the building.*

Suspecting nothing, I walked right into the trap. My companion left me at the office door and disappeared.

In the principal's office were not only the principal (also female) but two KGB agents, dressed in the drab, dark wool business suits of the time. Flashing his credentials, one of the agents waved a piece of paper in front of my face.

"I have here an order for your arrest," he said.

I reached out my hand. "May I see it?"

"No." He jerked it away, and delivered his next words in almost a shout. "Look! Look at the snake the Soviet power has been warming in its bosom!" Technically those words were directed at his fellow agent or the principal, but they were actually meant for me. The KGB method was to try to break the prisoner's spirit right from the start.

"Raise your arms," said the second agent. "I'm going to search your pockets."

Holding my elbows up, feeling my body pushed back and forth by prodding fingers, I felt my mind tumbling with thoughts. *These agents aren't local. They've come all the way from Ivanovo, 600 miles away. What are they going to do to me? Where will they keep me? Will there even be any kind of investigation? And what about—*

"Come with us."

"Where are you taking me?" I asked as we left the office.

"Keep moving," one of the agents snapped.

"Let me at least contact my mother. Please. May I get a message to my—"

"Keep moving."

Once outside, they quick-marched me to a new gray Moscvich sedan and drove me to the place I would later be reminded of while watching Queen Elizabeth's visit to Latvia.

I spent the first four days after my arrest in the Daugavpils prison, which was on the ground floor of the local KGB building. I can vividly remember that room. It was a small cell, about 6' x 12'. The only furniture was a foot-wide wooden bench. There was no table, no bed, no window, no running water—just a bucket that served as my toilet, and a door with a peephole covered from the other side. A single lightbulb glowed on the high ceiling.

Now that the first shock was wearing off, I found that I was not discouraged. *I've been expecting that this would happen to me someday,* I thought. *It's not like I'm being faced with something new or unusual. My father, my grandfather, and many, many other Seventh-day Adventist ministers, as well as those of other denominations, have all gone through this.*

So, spiritually and mentally I was prepared. "Dear heavenly Father," I prayed, "right now I rededicate my life to You. I place myself into Your hands."

I decided to get some sleep, but when I lay down on the bench, the lightbulb's glow bothered me. I glanced at the wall, but there was no switch. So I dragged the bench under the bulb, climbed up, and unscrewed it. Then I spread my overcoat on the bench to serve as a mattress, and lay down. But sleep was not soon to come.

Suddenly I heard guards yelling outside my door. The peephole cover clicked, there was an agitated rattling of keys, and the door jerked open. I don't know what my keepers expected to see—perhaps a suicide or an empty cell—but there I was, lying calmly on the bench in the darkness.

The guards dressed me down for turning off the light. Then, after screwing the bulb back in, they dragged the bench from my cell, which forced me to sleep on the concrete floor. Lying there in the chill draft, the sound of the guards taking other prisoners past my door, I began to learn things I never wanted to know. I was startled by the hardly restrained moan of a man in the corridor. "Hurry up! Hurry up!" the guard urged, then came a quiet reply. "Please, wait a little. I can't walk quickly," the poor man said. "You see what they have made with my back."

At that I realized that the poor fellow was being brought back to his cell after an interrogation, and must have been beaten severely.

The following day I was taken from solitary confinement and shoved into a cell with several other prisoners. Most of them were Latvian nationalists accused of various political offenses against the new Soviet regime. Once the door slammed behind me I instantly felt their probing eyes. *This guy is Russian,* they were thinking. *Is he a planted snitch?*

"Who are you?" one of them asked suspiciously.

"My name is Kulakov. I'm a teacher at the high school."

"What did you do, Kulakov, to get yourself thrown in with us?"

I paused. "I am a Christian believer," I finally said.

They glanced at each other, eyebrows raised, and I could feel the tension relaxing. *He's one of us after all,* they were thinking, *a poor guy whose ideas the party doesn't happen to agree with.*

Over the next three days I entertained them with stories from the Bible, and they listened with enjoyment.

On the third night of my imprisonment a guard with the rank of sergeant took me from my cell and brought me to a dimly lighted room—evidently the headquarters of the local KGB commander—and stood close behind me. Many bookcases lined the walls, and in the center of the room stood a huge desk piled with stacks of bulging file folders. Behind the desk sat a stout middle-aged Russian wearing a uniform with the shoulder straps of a major.

Here comes the interrogation, I thought. *I must speak very little, and be extremely careful in what I say. When in doubt, I must say nothing. I must not lie, but I must remember to protect my mother and my brothers and my fellow church members.*

The major simply stared at me for a while. At that point I had no idea what he must have been thinking, but years of being persecuted by people like him have given me insight.

Who does this kid think he is? he was probably saying to himself. *He may be bright, he may have an education, but how on earth can he dare to oppose the powerful atheistic state I am sworn to defend?*

Yet the major was human, and I have found few humans who are absolutely certain in their atheism. Deep in his heart he must have had questions that he may not have been willing or able to articulate. What he did next makes me wonder if, while viciously attacking my religious convictions, he may have been trying to eliminate his own uncertainty.

At any rate, what followed wasn't an interrogation. It was a tirade. He took a deep breath, looked me in the eye, and told me everything that was wrong with Christianity. He seemed to know that Christians avoid profane language, so he deliberately laced his speech with obscenities and blasphemy.

"You were educated in the Soviet school system, were you not?" he asked me.

I nodded.

"Then how is it possible, by any stretch of the imagination, that you could have become a Christian believer? And furthermore, how could you ever imagine that we would allow you to *work* in our educational system, to mutilate and destroy the souls of our young people?"

Since his questions seemed not so much information-seeking as rhetorical, I said nothing.

"Haven't the Nazi soldiers shown you what kind of a god you believe in? Or do you pretend not to know the words that were stamped on the belt buckles of their uniforms?"

"*Gott mit uns,*" I said.

"And translated into Russian, that is—?"

" 'God with us.' "

"Then how"—the major's voice rose triumphantly—"can you ever be so stupid as to believe in a God whose Fascist followers destroyed the lives of millions of guiltless children? If there really were a God, would He allow all those people to die?"

The major continued this tirade for a solid hour, smoking one cigarette after another and working himself into a higher and higher rage. Trying to deal a final blow to my faith, he began to tell me—using the most obscene and foul language he could muster—some disgusting anecdotes about sexual immorality among monks and priests.

Once when I thought his gaze had turned away from me, I glanced quickly around the room. Near where I was sitting was a brown leather bench with no back or armrests. On its cushion I could make out a few dark-red splotches. *Fresh blood?* I wondered.

He caught me glancing at it. By now, finally tiring, his voice had lowered to an almost conciliatory tone. "It might happen," he said, "that we'll have to put you on that bench. But not tonight. Right now we're using it for the counterrevolutionaries who are hiding in the forest with their weapons. Sergeant!"

"Yes, Comrade Major."

"Get him out of here."

Back in my cell the other men gave me sympathetic glances. They were reverently silent as I knelt down beside my portion of the plank bed and poured out my heart to the Lord in silent prayer. I prayed for Mom, and for Stephen and Victor and David. I prayed for Dad in his far-off concentration camp. I prayed for myself—but believe it or not, I had no desire to pray for freedom. How could I beg God for freedom for myself when I knew that millions of my innocent countrymen were languishing in prisons and labor camps, and in exile?

Maybe another way to explain how I felt is by telling a story I'd heard a few years earlier.

"What are you going to be when you become an adult?" someone asked a teenage boy.

"A prisoner," he said promptly.

"A *prisoner*? Why?"

"Every honest man is in prison these days," the boy replied. "My father is serving his time, and soon it will be my turn."

So how could I ask God make an exception for me, and set me free, when my father and thousands of other Christian believers were sentenced to life behind iron bars? I considered it shameful not to share the same destiny. So there in my cell I simply submitted myself to God's will and His plans for me. *Lord, all I ask is that You give me the strength to endure these hardships.*

Yet sounding through my head, crowding out my prayers, were the curses and sneers of the major. I had no personal animosity to him. I did not envy him his freedom—if what he had could even be called freedom. It made no difference to me that as my cell door clanged shut he was striding freely through the city on his way home to his family. Yet what he had said had not only greatly embarrassed and insulted me—it had also depressed me. The best way to describe my feelings is to use the words of the famous Russian poet Sergei Esenin: "I felt as if I'd stepped in a drunkard's vomit."

Into my agonized mind flashed a thought. *Would you trade places with him, Misha? Would you trade places with that KGB officer, even if you could?*

"No, Lord," I whispered fervently. "By no means. By no means. His situation is desperate. He's a spiritual wreck. But I have You, and with You I have peace in my soul. You will revive me!"

After that experience I could say with Paul, "For as the sufferings of Christ abound in us, so our consolation also abounds through Christ" (2 Corinthians 1:5, NKJV). That night in the cell I felt the presence of Jesus, and was very grateful for the comfort of His Spirit. Lowering myself onto the plank bed, I immediately plunged into a deep sleep.

Early the next morning the guard prodded me awake. "Get your things together," he said.

Since my things were my overcoat and cap, packing was easy. I put them on and followed him out into the hall. Standing in the narrow, stinking corridor were the two agents who'd arrested me.

One of them handed me a heavy bag tightly bound with string. "A parcel from your mother," he said abruptly, and the two men led me out to the same gray Moscvich car I'd arrived in. One of them rode in the back seat with me, while the other got in front with the driver.

At that early hour the streets were empty. I could see that we were heading northeast on the road toward the city of Rezekne, but where would my final destination be? Were they taking me all the way to Riga? One thing I was sure of—whether I was bound for prison or exile, I'd probably never see Daugavpils again. So from the car window my eyes swept the countryside, memorizing as much as I could of the country I'd begun to love.

Now we were on the bridge over the Daugava River. How I had loved swimming in its still waters, or sitting on its gently sloping shore watching the sunset, breathing in the fresh air with its aroma of pine trees. *Goodbye, lovely river. God knows whether I will see you again.*

Once over the bridge, our car motored steadily through the countryside. Latvia's southeastern area is called Latgalia, a tranquil area filled with small, well-groomed private farms, so different from the huge open spaces of my native Russia, where forced collective farming had ruined people's personal initiative until vast territories of land lay idle. The little Latvian farms were even more beautiful since it was springtime, the snow nearly melted, and God's fantastic world of plants awakening from winter sleep.

Yet nature's loveliness couldn't distract me long from my personal situation. *I'm probably bound for a corrective labor camp,* I mused. *And in a week I'll be 21.*

The car hit a slight bump, and the tightly bound bag on my lap shifted position. I began to think about the woman whose fingers had knotted those strings.

Two years ago Mom said goodbye to Dad as he left for his own labor camp sentence. I thought. *What courage she showed! But how does she feel now that I've been arrested? Lord, please give her comfort and courage. At least she has three other sons. Stephen's safe from arrest, anyway. Even though he's been doing lay ministry work with me, he spent five years in a field-engineer military unit on the front lines, defending our country from Hitler's armies. He's a good wage earner. He'll take care of the family.*

The car swung into Rezekne and coasted to a stop beside the freshly whitewashed railway station. Icicles formed inside my heart. I'd visited friends in this town, and I knew that all the trains from Riga to Moscow stopped at this station.

They're taking me back to Ivanovo.

This was not good news. By capturing my dad and sending him to the concentration camp, the Ivanovo city fathers, the Communist leaders, and the KGB had made their attitude toward Christian believers crystal clear. And now it was I who was being returned to face the music.

Before we got out of the car, the agent in the front seat turned around to stare at me. "Listen, Kulakov," he said grimly, "we could have handcuffed and chained you and transported you as a prisoner. But we decided to go with you by regular passenger train—if you behave yourself."

"Right," said the other. "Any attempt to run away will only worsen your situation. If you try to go underground, we'll catch you there. Both of us, plus the coach conductor, will constantly watch you, and we'll be with you even when you have to go to the toilet. But if you behave, the other passengers won't need to know that you're under arrest."

In the station we sat on a bench, one agent on either side of me, waiting for our train. I stashed my bag under the bench, and then, to see if I could learn at least something about my mom and brothers, and to calm my fears about Stephen's fate, I tried to start small talk on various subjects, but my guards kept silent.

Suddenly, without planning to, I blurted, "You haven't—arrested my brother Stephen, have you?"

"Of course not," one said.

"Why would we arrest *him?*" asked the other.

While pondering these answers, I suddenly discovered I was ravenously hungry. I'd had no meal that morning, for we'd left the Daugavpils jail before breakfast was served. I've always been thankful to God that crisis has never made me lose my appetite, because nourishment not only gives one strength but often improves one's attitude.

I reached under the bench, pulled the bag onto my lap, and started untying the string. And as the folds of the cloth separated, I saw two words written in dark purple ink: *STEPHEN KULAKOV.*

Tears welled up behind my eyelids. *So they've arrested Stephen after all,* I thought. *What will my mother do now?* I didn't trust myself to speak, but simply turned the bag to show my captors the writing.

Their eyes widened. They hadn't realized that they'd mistakenly switched the two bags Mom had prepared for her arrested sons and brought to the KGB prison the day after they were taken into custody.

The two agents suddenly became very nervous, probably wondering if in my emotional state I would try to escape. In an effort to distract my mind, one said, "Do you want to read anything on the train?"

"I want to read a Bible."

He glanced at his companion, then reached down, pulled his briefcase onto his lap, and snapped it open. "Here you are," he said, handing me my own Bible—the Bible I'd been reading during my morning devotions the day they'd arrested me and separated me from my family. I realized that when these men arrested Stephen they must have also searched our house and confiscated many of our books.

I put the Bible on my lap and opened the bag. My sweet mother had packed not only some of Stephen's clothes, but also a lot of food: dried crusts, butter, cheese, apples, flat dry shortbread, and those tasty pastries with apple filling that only she could bake. But as I lifted one to my lips, I shuddered with sorrow, thinking of the loving fingers that had touched those pastries while packing them for the sons she might never see again.

The train bound for Moscow rumbled into the station, and we boarded. The agents took coach seats, while I was forced to sleep on a narrow luggage rack over their heads. There was no bedding provided, even to the KGB. My guardians tried to sleep in shifts so that at least one could keep an eye on me, but often they both dozed off at the same time.

Lying on the rack, my Bible on my chest, I tried not to think about the Ivanovo jail. I'd been only 18 when Dad was arrested, and I'd been summoned there several times for interrogations. These experiences had always turned my stomach. The mix of tobacco smoke and obscenity in the air was so dense that, in the words of the Russian saying, "you could hang an axe on it."

What will my sentence be? I wondered. *Ten years, probably—if I make it through alive. Lord, I'm going to open my Bible now. Please show me what to expect in the years to come.*

I tipped the Book toward me. My fingers separated the pages at the midpoint, and my eyes fell on Psalm 66:10-12: "For you, O God, have tested us; you have tried us as silver is tried. You brought us into the net; you laid burdens on our backs; you let people ride over our heads; we went through fire and through water; yet you have *set us free.*" All except the last part corresponds to the New Revised Standard Version. The NRSV and other English versions translate that last phrase differently, but *set us free* is how my Russian version rendered it.

Lord, I prayed, *I accept this as a sign that I will be tested. I will have difficulties in prisons and camps, but You will finally lead me through to freedom.*

This Bible promise deeply touched me—but what touched me even more was the nearness of my Savior, and His tender care so clearly expressed in His desire to comfort me and give me peace right at that moment. Tears of gratitude filled my eyes, words of praise sang through my mind, and I fell asleep.

CHAPTER 2: I Owe So Much to Them

Before I continue with my own adventures, I believe that to truly help you appreciate God's amazing love for the Russian people—and to set the stage so that you can best understand His miracles on behalf of faithful Christians—I must take you back more than 100 years, to before the turn of the twentieth century. I'd like you to meet the man who changed the course of our family's faith—my grandfather.

"Please, can you help me?"

The Russian Orthodox priest looked cautiously at the sturdy farmer standing before him. "Help you, Stephan Victorovich? Help you how?"

"Please explain the book of Revelation to me."

A slight frown crease appeared between the priest's eyebrows. "Why?"

"Revelation is in the Bible, isn't it? And Daniel also."

"Of course. But why do you need to know about them? Maybe God has sealed them so we can't understand them."

"All Scripture," said Stephan stoutly, "is profitable for our study."

The priest shrugged his shoulders. "Then study the parts that are clear," he said, "and live by *them*. After all, you don't have a lot of time to be a scholar, do you? You're a widower. You're raising four children all by yourself. You're a successful farmer. Don't waste your precious time on the Bible's cloudy books."

The year was 1890. That year Stephan Victorovich Kulakov, my grandfather on my father's side, lost his beloved wife in death. He'd always been a religious man, but stricken by grief, he became even more interested in Christian beliefs than before.

Grandfather Stephan lived in the village of Tarasovka, in southern Russia's Rostov-on-Don region. He not only farmed but owned and operated a way station, something like the pony express stops in America's wild West. Before rail lines crisscrossed Russia, Stephan bought horses and buggies, and hired people to carry mail and passengers. Though the youngest of his four children was only 2 years old when his wife died, he never remarried but took sole responsibility for his children.

A devout Russian Orthodox believer, my grandfather began his deeper search for God with the same energy he applied to all the other areas of life. At one point he even made a pilgrimage to Kiev—on foot—in order to worship at

the famous monastery where monks lived in caves. But he came away from that visit disappointed in the way some clergymen interpreted Christianity. Though no church teaching could satisfy his interest in prophecy, he continued to hungrily devour his Bible, often reading it while on his knees in prayer.

Stephan Kulakov wasn't the only Russian concerned about the future. The end of the nineteenth century spawned tumultuous days, with Karl Marx's doctrines spreading among the small but rapidly growing urban working class. In 1905 a revolution broke out in St. Petersburg that spread 1,000 miles southward to the Black Sea.

This turmoil quickly got the czar's attention, or rather his advisors' attention. Nicholas II himself had grown up a shy and indecisive person who had never felt fully prepared to rule his country. His advisors, far more in touch with the nation than he, urged him to create some sort of parliament. So with their help he formed the Duma, which comes from the Russian word for "think."

Grandpa Stephan, well known locally as a man of integrity and religious conviction, was elected to a seat. Now, in addition to all his other responsibilities, he had to travel to the Duma sessions at St. Petersburg to think and debate and vote and try to keep his head amid the struggle of the different parties that vied for a place in Russia's future. He enjoyed this role, but still hungered for a deeper knowledge of Bible prophecy.

One day while walking the streets of the great city, he saw an interesting poster, and stopped to study it.

"This is it!" he gasped. "This is exactly what I want. Someone is giving lectures on Daniel and Revelation."

He carefully noted down the time and location, and was actually the first person to arrive at the lecture hall on the indicated day. Amazed and delighted by the speaker's clear explanations of the prophecies, he hurried forward afterward and asked for more information. The lecturer chatted for a while, then reached in his pocket, took out a cigarette case, and began to smoke.

Stephan struggled to hide his astonishment. *What is this man doing?* he thought. *How can someone read and explain the Holy Scriptures and yet use tobacco?* He himself neither smoked nor drank, considering these to be habits a spiritual person should not have.

"Tell me more about yourself," he asked the other man.

"I'm a hired translator," the man said, "for a Seventh-day Adventist publishing house in Hamburg, Germany."

"Seventh-day Adventist?" Stephan had never heard the name before.

"Yes," the man replied. "The Adventists have developed some extremely interesting explanations for Bible prophecies, and I'm using their material in my lectures."

"What you preached this evening was amazing," Stephan said fervently.

The man reached in his pocket for a card and scribbled an address on it. "Here. Write the publishers yourself. I'm sure they could provide you some books and papers in Russian."

Stephan immediately wrote to Hamburg, received some literature, and thoroughly and prayerfully compared it with the Bible. He then shared these studies with his children and relatives, not realizing the important groundwork he was laying for the decades ahead.

A few years later an Adventist missionary came to Stephan's village. Brother Koch—no one seems to have remembered his first name—had been born in Russia but had come from a strong German background. He spoke broken Russian with a thick accent, and had a hard time pronouncing some of our consonants, such as "b," which he pronounced "p." This must have produced some muffled giggles among the children, especially when he tried to say *lyubit,* the Russian word for "to love." He pronounced it *lupit,* which means "to beat."

Yet strange as it may seem, people understood him easily.

"There was something about him," older Russians who knew him would tell me later, "which spoke clearly to us in spite of the language barrier. It was his deep spirituality. His faith was built not on human wisdom or eloquence, but on the power of God. His sincerity, along with his love for us, made a lasting impression. He entered into the lives and the feelings of the people he taught."

My father knew him personally as well. "In his sermons," Dad once told me, "Brother Koch presented Jesus Christ so vividly and lovingly that preacher and time and place were all forgotten. Adults and children felt as if the cross had been erected on the soil just outside the walls of wherever Brother Koch spoke. There the Savior was taken and nailed to a tree. There His blood flowed forth for the remission of their sins."

During that remarkable visit Brother Koch presented the three angels' messages to my grandfather's entire family, and by the conclusion of his stay he had baptized 20 souls.

Grandpa Stephan not only accepted the message but offered his large, well-built house as a place of worship for the little group of believers. His newfound faith made him even more concerned about the future of his children, since Adventist schools were unheard-of. So he carefully selected state colleges for them to attend so they would be well prepared for life.

"But I want something more for them, heavenly Father," he often prayed. "I want to see my children engaged in proclaiming Your last message of mercy to our perishing world."

The Lord heard his prayer, and as the years went along both his sons, Yakov

and my father, Peter, became Adventist preachers, and both his daughters, Anna and Maria, married Adventist preachers.

But along with this devotion to the Lord's work came unavoidable tests and trials, the result of the Bolshevik influence spreading over the land.

"We are fighting a class warfare!" their fiery speakers shouted at rallies. "And we will fight this battle not only in the cities but in the rural areas! We are hereby classifying people into three groups: the *kulaks* [the rich], the middle class, and the poor. The poor are our protégés, the middle class are our friends, and the rich are our enemies." Because of this strange (to put it mildly) policy, several million enterprising landowners and businesspeople lost their property and were either killed or exiled to Siberia.

Kulak, incidentally, is the where the name Kulakov originated. Grandpa Stephan and his family were indeed persecuted—but not because of their rich-sounding name or their resources. In 1927, a decade after the revolution, the class struggle mushroomed into a religious warfare aimed at all who openly confessed their faith. Like Job in the Bible, Stephan watched in agony as the Bolsheviks seized all his property and then attacked his family. His beloved pastor son-in-law, Pavel Pilkh, husband of Stephan's eldest daughter, Anna, was arrested in 1931 and died later at the hands of his captors.

His other daughter, Maria, sent word that she and her pastor-husband, Vasili Swiridoff, had been exiled. Stephan's older son Peter (my father) was in daily danger of arrest. But to Stephan, the hardest blow of all was the news that his younger son Yakov had abruptly turned his back on the church and joined an aggressive antireligious movement known as the Militant Atheists.

"I need a place where I can go to lay my tired head," Grandpa Stephan finally said, and Anna, his newly widowed daughter, took him in. She was a teacher by profession, but once the Bolsheviks focused their anger on the faithful, all schools were closed to Christian educators. Anna had to find other employment, and worked desperately hard to earn enough money to pay rent on a miserable apartment and to buy food for herself and her little boy, Daniel.

Anna welcomed her father into her home, and did her best to make him as comfortable as possible. When I asked her what his mood was in those days, she told me, "Father's motto was the same as Paul's in 2 Corinthians 6:10: 'Sorrowful, yet always rejoicing' [NIV]. What strengthened him in his last days was the prophetic Word of God and his intimate knowledge of Jesus Christ."

Once she asked him his opinion of the advance of Communism.

"I know they're trying to build a better world that turns its back on 'decaying capitalism,' " Stephan told her. "But they're doomed to failure. As Jesus said, when one blind man leads another, both fall into the ditch. The only answer to this world's problems is the second coming of Christ. Jesus and His followers will have the last word."

Finally, in 1936, weakened by all the blows he'd suffered, Stephan Victorovich Kulakov peacefully passed away.

Twelve years earlier, in 1924, Stephan's son (and my father-to-be) Peter began a yearlong internship in Moscow—without his young family—at what today would be called the conference office. Part of the time he was a conference accountant, and part of the time he served as assistant pastor in one of the five Moscow churches so that the leaders could see what kind of pastor he might become. (Stalin's government was already limiting church activities, and there was no Adventist seminary or pastor-training school.)

Once back home on the farm in Tarasovka, Peter didn't have long to wait for his first call. Almost immediately he received a letter from the conference leadership. *Dear Brother Kulakov,* it said, *we are inviting you to be an accountant for us in the Seventh-day Adventist conference in Leningrad, and to pastor one of our churches there.*

Peter showed the letter to Stephan.

"Dad," he said, "I'm a little concerned about this call. I love the Lord, and I want to work in His vineyard. But the revolution isn't even a decade old, and the economy is still in terrible shape. Here on the farm we can at least provide ourselves the necessities. Is this the right time for me to become a pastor? How would my family and I survive in the city, where everything's so expensive?"

Stephan thought for a moment, then looked his son squarely in the eye.

"Peter," he said calmly, "I read in my Bible that the man who puts his hands on the plowshare and looks back isn't fit for the Lord's work. You have accepted the Lord's invitation to serve Him as a minister, and therefore you can trust Him for your needs."

So Peter said yes to the Leningrad call, and his father's advice stayed in his mind and gave him much encouragement in the years ahead. As Peter had suspected, moving from the placid farm to the hectic metropolis proved challenging, but he and his family were happy. His new parish was part of the famous old city that had previously been known as St. Petersburg, but had gone through a couple of recent name changes. In 1914 it had become Petrograd, and in 1924 its name was changed again to honor Vladimir Lenin, spearhead of the Russian Revolution. A walk along Leningrad's avenues was like strolling back through Russian history.

Also, his church on Vasilievsky Island contained many wonderful people, and together with these new friends the Kulakovs grew in the knowledge of

Jesus. At that time it was still possible to conduct open worship services and even rent halls for evangelistic work, so it was a young pastor's dream come true.

But it wouldn't last long, as another relative of mine soon discovered.

In Moscow my mother's brother, Alexander Demidov, was hard at work. The Demidovs had become Adventists even before the Kulakovs, and in 1925 the well-educated Alexander was invited to edit the Adventist magazine *The Voice of Truth*.

Delighted, Alexander had left his native city of Taganrog, moved to Moscow, and plunged into his new assignment—and a tangle of red tape. Since the Communists believed that all means of production should belong to the state, no church was allowed to have its own publishing house. That meant that *The Voice* had to be printed at a state-owned printing shop. However, Alexander's hard work and patient diplomatic skills paid off; the arrival of *The Voice* became as dependable as clockwork, and the magazine gained even more popularity.

But one day in 1928 everything changed. Alexander suddenly began hearing from agitated subscribers.

"My *Voice* hasn't come yet."

"Where's my *Voice of Truth?*"

"My friends don't have their copies either."

"It hasn't come from the printer's yet," Alexander would say soothingly. "Just be patient."

But a month went by, and still no *Voice*. Finally Alexander paid a visit to the printing shop. He found the manager in his office sitting behind a desk, sipping a cup of tea.

"Sit down, Comrade Demidov," the man said. "I imagine you are here because you are wondering what has happened to your church paper."

Alexander nodded.

"Well, let me tell you what has happened, Comrade Demidov. As you know, this is now a socialist state."

Alexander nodded again, a sick feeling in his stomach.

"At a recent Communist Party meeting," the manager continued, "the leaders discussed what will happen to religion in a country in which socialism has won the victory in the class struggle." A small bowl of sugar cubes sat on his desk. He picked up one of the cubes and began to play with it. "The party leaders agree that religion is doomed. It will die away all by itself."

Alexander opened his lips as though to say something, then shut them again.

"Now watch this, Comrade Demidov," said the manager. He held the sugar cube over his teacup, and let it plop into the dark liquid. "In a few minutes this sugar will melt and disappear. But now I am picking up this spoon. I am stirring the tea. And the sugar is melting faster. Do you see that?"

Alexander took a breath. "So what you're saying is—"

"What I'm saying is that the government has decided not to allow religion simply to die away by itself. It is taking steps to expedite that death." He shrugged. "In your case it means that from now on we will not print your magazine."

Alexander left the manager's office in a daze. *What will become of us, Lord?* he prayed. *What will become of us now?*

Meanwhile, in the Peter Kulakov home in Leningrad, I was just learning to take my first steps. I'd been born a year earlier, in 1927. However, before my little legs could take me very far along the Leningrad block on which we lived, my father accepted a call to move south and lead the Adventist work in the region of Byelorussia. But as soon as we arrived there, the local authorities arrested Dad and then demanded that he leave. The church leadership quickly offered him a chance to pastor in Tula, 125 miles south of Moscow, so we moved again.

Can you imagine what it must have been like for my farm-raised father to rent a one-room apartment for his family, which by then had grown to three boys? Yet this was nothing compared with what happened when I was 8 years old.

Late one night in the spring of 1935 we heard a loud rapping on our apartment door. Mother opened it, and several men, agents of the NKVD (the pre-KGB)* pushed into the room, carrying large bags. Without a word they began to search through our possessions.

What are they doing? I thought in terror as my two brothers and I huddled together in a corner. *What gives them the right to look through our belongings? And why are they tossing our letters and our religious books and magazines into their bags?*

Once the men had collected what they wanted, their leader slipped his hand into an inner coat pocket and brought out a piece of paper, which he handed to Dad.

"Peter Stephanovich Kulakov," he barked, "this is a warrant for your arrest! You must come with us immediately!"

Dad's shoulders sagged. Standing amid the books and clothes scattered about the room, he knew very well that this might be the last time he would ever see his family again. He looked at my mother, and then his head swung around to gaze at his three boys huddled in the corner. Then his shoulders straightened, and he faced his nameless nighttime visitors.

"Please allow me to pray with Maria and my children first," he said. Without waiting for permission, he knelt down with my mother and beckoned his three boys to gather around. Though only 8 at the time, I will never forget kneeling there that night.

"Heavenly Father, please bless and protect Maria and the boys," Dad prayed. "Please protect our little church. Please protect me. Lord, I entrust my family and my church into Your hands."

He then rose to his feet and faced his captors. I was too young to be able to read the expressions on their impassive countenances, so I don't know how the prayer affected them. But a strange sense of peace had descended on our family, so that when the men led my father through the doorway and possibly out of our lives forever, none of us burst into tears. We remembered that Jesus had said, "If they have persecuted me, they will also persecute you" (John 15:20). We felt no joy as we saw our father disappear, but we were sure that God's hand—God's good hand—was upon us.

Years later I read a poem by William Cowper that aptly expressed our faith and convictions:

The path of sorrow, and that path alone,
Leads to that land where sorrow is unknown.

As I look back on those years, I can't help realizing how tenderly and kindly the Lord was schooling us to fully trust in Him. He never allowed us to be tested too much, and His eyes were upon us during those trials. As each test reached its crisis, His hand was outstretched, and His voice said, "Thus far, and no farther."

With Dad in prison, my mother was left with three boys—and no income to buy basic necessities or pay rent on our little room. But things got even worse. Dad was considered a "political prisoner" of the state, and both the prisoner and his or her relatives were considered "enemies of the Soviet people." The government prohibited all private enterprise, which meant that everybody had to work for the state six days a week, with Sunday off. This was a cruel blow to my mother, a Sabbathkeeper.

But soon after Dad's arrest, Sergei Carpovich Stepanov knocked on our door. Brother Sergei was a church elder, a kindly man and, equally important for us, a photographer. Many conscientious Adventists, casting desperately about for an occupation that gave them Saturdays off, turned to photography. They still worked for the state, but were not tied to a workplace at which they'd be missed and reported on Sabbath.

Brother Sergei asked how we were doing, and comforted us as best he could. Then he turned to Mom.

"Sister Maria," he said, "I have a business proposition for you."

Mom's eyes brightened. "What do you have in mind, Brother Sergei?"

"I would like for you to develop and print my photographs for me."

Mom stared. "Me? Develop photographs? But I don't know how."

"I'll teach you. It's very simple."

"Thank you for the opportunity," Mom said fervently, still dazed. "Where is your photo laboratory located?"

His eyes twinkled. "Right here."

"Here?"

"Of course. Let's see . . ." He glanced around our tiny room. "I will bring you chemicals and equipment, and"—he pointed—"we'll turn that corner into a photo lab. I'll teach you what to do. And each time you print a batch of photos for me, I will bring money to pay you."

The photo lab was actually more of a large box, just large enough for Mother and the chemicals and not much else. We boys called it her "kennel," and day after day she spent long hours there. Brother Sergei used a large-format camera with glass negatives, and Mother's job was to go inside the kennel and make sure it was totally dark. Then she turned on a dim red bulb called a safelight, which wouldn't harm the photo paper. She would place a glass negative in a wooden frame, lay a piece of photo paper facedown on the negative, and clamp the frame tightly shut for a perfect contact. She would then turn on a white light for a certain number of seconds.

Then she would unclasp the frame, remove the photo paper, and immerse it in the liquids of three trays—first the developer, then the stop bath (which "froze" the developing process so that the pictures wouldn't get too dark), and finally the "fixer." Then the pictures were put into a big bowl full of clean water (in better equipped labs it would have been running water) to clear them of all chemicals.

One day Mom was in her kennel, working on a large and rather urgent printing job, when Brother Sergei arrived.

"I've just finished," came Mom's muffled voice. "I haven't had time to wash them thoroughly and to gloss them, though."

"That's fine," Brother Sergei said. "I'll take them with me wet."

The kennel door opened, and Mom emerged into the room, squinting in the light. In her hands was a large bowl with many photos sloshing around in the water. "Here you are," she said. Glancing down into the bowl, she suddenly gasped. "Oh, *no!* What's happening?"

We boys crowded around, staring. All the photos were turning a sickly yellow.

Brother Sergei took a deep breath. "Your fixer fluid's gotten too weak, Sister Maria," he said. "You've neutralized it with many prints that you didn't wash well enough in the stop bath. The stop bath water needs to be constantly changed."

Mom's face flamed with embarrassment. "Brother Sergei," she said in a voice that trembled with tears, "I am so terribly sorry. I know that this photographic paper cost you a lot of money. And now it is all spoiled."

We boys kept our faces pointed toward the bowl, but looked at Brother Sergei out of the corners of our eyes. *Will he be angry?* I wondered. *Will he take his equipment away and leave Mom without a job?*

I will never forget what happened next.

For a moment Brother Sergei stared at his bowl of very important photos, now all ruined. Then he turned to face my mother.

"Sister Maria," he said gently, "do not worry. The Lord continues to give me money to help the family of my beloved pastor Peter Kulakov." As he spoke, he put his hand into his pocket, drew out some currency bills, and handed them to Mom.

Around this time my mother discovered that God in His kindness had not allowed my father simply to vanish forever into the Soviet penal system.

"Your father is right here in Tula!" she told us joyfully one day. "He's in the central jail, about a mile and a half from here."

---

* The NKVD (People's Commissariat for Internal Affairs), the Soviet secret police at the time, preceded the KGB (Committee for State Security).

The World Was
CHAPTER 3: Not Worthy of Them

L et's go see him!" we boys shouted.

Mother sighed. "The prison authorities won't let us visit him and talk to him. But we can go over and stand outside, and maybe he'll see us from the window."

So the next day we all walked the mile and a half to the city jail. It was a large building with barred windows, located in an open area and surrounded by a deep ditch. The windows must have been chin-high to the prisoners, because all we could see were their heads. But suddenly one of us noticed a wildly waving hand in a second-floor window. Because of the ditch we couldn't get any closer, yet we could tell that it was our father. *And he was doing more than waving!* Lifting himself up, gripping an iron bar with one hand, Dad was making motions with the other hand and arm as though he were hugging us and holding us close to his heart.

"Dad! Dad!" Victor screamed. We boys jumped up and down, windmilling our arms in the air.

"Quiet!" Mother hissed, clapping her palm over Victor's mouth. "If the authorities know that your father has contact with his family, they'll move him to an inside room with no windows. Just wave."

Sure enough, Dad didn't attempt to call out to us, but continued to gesture lovingly to us. And we just stood there silently, telling him through body language that we loved him. This continued until Dad got so tired that he no longer could hold on to the bar. Then we turned sadly and trudged back home.

We made many trips to the edge of the ditch. Amazingly, Dad seemed to be able to sense when we were coming, because he always seemed to be first at the window to wave to us. Our mile-and-a-half journey to the jail always seemed more rapid than our return.

"Mom," I asked one day, "why can't we take the bus to the jail? It's not a lot of money."

"Maybe not," she replied. "But I'm saving every kopek I can, since it is so difficult for me to earn money alone for our family after Dad's arrest."

"But my shoes are so big and clumpy," I told her. "It's hard to walk that far in them. They fall off my feet."

"Misha," she said, using my childhood nickname, "I bought them a size bigger than you needed so you'll grow into them. Take good care of them."

So we set off for the jail again. On our way to the prison we had to cross a bridge over the river Upa. This time, when I was halfway across the bridge, I slowed down to watch the water flowing peacefully below. Not expecting my abrupt stop, one of my brothers stepped on my heel, pulling the extra-large shoe right off my foot. It rolled to the edge of the bridge and fell into the water with a splash!

We brothers looked at Mom and at each other. Everybody realized that this was nobody's fault, so we finished crossing the bridge and kept walking.

I must not let my dear father see my bare foot, I thought to myself. *He has enough trouble being in jail without having to worry about where his son's next pair of shoes will come from.* So when we reached the edge of the ditch, I tried to hide my foot behind some grass and clods of soil so he wouldn't feel bad.

Dad was kept in the Tula jail for three months. The government didn't worry much about human rights, so while there must have been some kind of investigation, there was no trial. A special committee of the Ministry of the Interior known as the Osoboe Soveshchanie summarily sentenced Dad to three years' exile in the remotest depths of Siberia's Krasnoyarsk region, 2,000 miles east of Moscow.

Fortunately, families were allowed to join the exiled person, though this probably was not as much because of the state's soft-heartedness as it was its hope that the troublemaker would have less incentive to escape, return, and start spreading decadent religious ideas again.

Once he'd gotten settled, Dad sent Mom a message. "Since there is no school for children who are Stephen's age," he wrote (Stephen was 14 and no longer in elementary school), "send him to your mother in Taganrog. You and the two younger boys join me here."

So after we'd said our tearful goodbyes to Stephen and sent him off to Grandmother, Mom and Victor and I boarded a long, slow train that took us all the way to Krasnoyarsk. But our journey still wasn't over. Dad's village was still a four-day trip mostly through the forest, but he'd been able to arrange transportation for us. A couple who worked in the collective farm had used two sleds to carry farm equipment to Krasnoyarsk for repair, and Dad asked them if they would mind bringing us back with them.

It was winter and the temperature was far below zero, so Mom bought a huge fur coat to keep us warm. She even smeared goose fat on our foreheads and noses to keep us from getting frostbite. There were no hotels or even inns along that bitter journey, but in his message to Mom, Dad had mentioned that there were several private homes we could stay in at night. We found the Siberian people very hospitable. Since most were exiles themselves, they had deep compassion on the new arrivals.

In wintertime all the homeowners had the custom of placing a piece of bread in a small opening in one of the logs of the porch. Any passerby who was hungry, even if not staying the night, could have something to eat.

Toward the end of the fourth day, as the sun was going down, we noticed a huge mountain up ahead. Smoke was rising from the chimneys of a few small houses clustering at its base.

The farmer pointed with his whip. "There it is," he said. "That's the place you've taken this long journey for! And look—I think I see somebody coming!"

Sure enough, in the distance I saw Dad, wearing a black fur coat and a huge cap with ear-flaps, bounding through the snow to greet us. We sprang from the sled and darted forward past the horses. Dad's face was a deep red, partly from excitement and partly from laboring through the snow. He crushed Victor and me in a warm embrace. His mustache touched my cheek, and I was startled to feel that it was filled with tiny icicles.

In my mouth I felt the salty taste of Dad's tears, which told me more than any words how much he'd missed me.

Our new home was a log cabin in the village of Krasni Klyutch. The cabin was small, but the logs it was made of were huge—giant trunks of pine trees. And the bone-cracking cold we felt on our four-day sled trip was quickly thawed out by the steady fire in the stove. Since a huge forest surrounded the village, Dad was able to get all the wood we needed to heat the house.

However, as the song says, the weather outside was frightful. Huge drifts of snow rose to the roof edges, and the flakes fell so often that Dad had to dig a path from the front door almost every day. But during the long winter evenings we were safe and cozy. Mom would light the kerosene lamp and set it on the table, and we would all gather around and spend long hours reading our Bibles and memorizing passages my parents thought important for us.

I'm so grateful to Mom and Dad for showing us children, through the example of their lives, how Bible knowledge is practical. Whenever I repeat "The Lord is my shepherd" or "Thy word is a lamp unto my feet," I think of the orange flame of that kerosene lantern and the snow falling softly on the roof.

Dad, of course, was the one who had to battle the snow and go to work, because every exile had to have a job. All the villagers were members of a *kolkhoz* (a collective farm), owned not by one person but by the state. Dad applied there for a job.

"What are your skills?" the manager asked.

"Any kind of farm work," Dad replied. "I grew up on a farm. But I can also do accounting."

The manager glanced up alertly. "Accounting?"

"Right."

"You're hired!" The man gestured toward several ancient ledgers. "Our finances are in utter disarray. See if you can get those books into shape so we can figure out where all the money's going."

As Dad paged through the ledgers, he thought, *The problem with these accounts is that no one has cared enough to spend some thoughtful time with them. That's what's wrong with the Communist system—if everyone owns everything equally, nobody's accountable.* Over the next few weeks he put in place the financial systems that he and his father had used back on their own farm. The manager was delighted.

Soon, however, the regional Communist authorities heard about his work.

"Who is your new accountant, comrade?" they asked the manager.

"His name is Peter Kulakov."

"Where did you find him?"

The manager shrugged. "I think he's from the west, near Moscow. He's doing a great job."

"The quality of his work isn't the point," the authorities told him. "Is he an exile?"

The manager sighed. "I think he might be. But—"

"Don't you realize, comrade, that every exile is an enemy of the state?"

"Yes, of course. But—"

"And don't you know that enemies of the state should not occupy responsible positions that might give them access to important information?"

This time the manager merely looked at the floor and nodded.

"You are hereby directed to remove the exile Kulakov from his accounting responsibilities."

So Dad had to close those ledgers and walk all over the farm and the village doing manual labor. When my usually very patient mother learned of his dismissal, she became upset.

"The authorities are insane," she said. "You've just brought their finances under control, and how do they reward you? They send you out to repair fences!"

But Dad was philosophical.

"We must remember the real reason we are here, Maria," he reminded her. "This is a blessing in disguise, since I am now in an excellent position to meet new people and share my beliefs. You wouldn't believe how many people are hungering and thirsting for the Word of God."

As his exile dragged along, however, Dad was getting more and more restless. And finally, when his three-year banishment sentence expired in May of 1938, he'd had enough.

"Let's go," he said. "Immediately! Start packing. We're not staying here one day longer than we have to."

Mom looked at him, puzzled. "But Peter, we've got to stay at least another week."

"Why?"

"Misha's elementary school final exams. He needs to take them so he'll be eligible for high school."

Dad snorted. "Forget about his exams. He can take them when we get to Samara."

"Just one week? Please?"

"Don't you understand, Maria? It's like a warden coming to let a prisoner out of jail, and the prisoner saying, 'No, I'm staying one more week.' We're leaving *tomorrow*." Like a wild bird whose cage was suddenly opened, Dad's yearning for freedom was too great. "With unfettered foot and a wind's-will wing," he was willing to fly from there as soon—and as far—as he could. Our destination was the big industrial city of Samara, 500 miles east of Moscow.

I was 11, and for the past three years I'd attended a log schoolhouse with a couple dozen other students. And now, rather than sitting with my friends and taking my exams administered by teachers I knew, I had to take these exams from unfamiliar teachers in a brand-new three-story building with several hundred students I'd never met before.

Traumatized and humiliated, I failed my Russian grammar and spelling exams, and made too many mistakes in writing the dictation. The next day as I was walking in the school hall, the school principal, who was a woman, stopped me.

"Are you the new student who came to us yesterday?"

"Yes, I am," I answered cautiously.

"Get your book bag and leave this school."

I stared at her.

"Go. Quickly!" she snapped. "You've written the dictation worse than any other student! You are impossible to educate!"

When I arrived at home, my face still wet with tears, Dad was shocked. "I'll go there tomorrow," he told me, "and I'll see what I can do. This is just not fair."

Of course it's not fair, Dad, I thought, but I didn't say it. *Why couldn't you have let us stay just one more week in Krasni Klyutch? I would have passed those tests with flying colors.*

Because of my dad's exceptional diplomatic skills and God's overruling hand, the school administration changed its mind. I was given another chance to take the exams, and this time, without all the bewildering pressure, I passed them.

Even though it was glorious to be a returned exile, Dad knew that, in any part of a country with an atheist government he'd never be able to be a full-time Christian missionary. For one thing, he—like everybody else in the Soviet Union—had to work for the state. For another, there was no church organization that could support him financially. So he followed the example of other Adventists and became a photographer.

"But I'm not discouraged," he told us, and then quoted one of his favorite mottoes: "If you can't be free, be as free as you can." Everywhere he went with his camera, he cautiously took the spiritual temperature of the people he talked with, and began secretly studying the Bible with those who were interested in God's truth.

Even though we didn't have a lot of money, my parents had managed to save a few rubles while in exile, so when we got to Samara we didn't have to get an apartment but were able to buy a dwelling. "Dwelling" is a good word for it. We boys called it "our house," but it was actually more of a half cave. It had been made by cutting into the side of a steep hill, so that the back wall and the two side walls were made of dirt. The roof was just a continuation of the hill, so if we ever wanted to get up on our roof, we climbed the hill and ran down on top of the house!

Our cave house didn't have electricity or a sewer system. Often Mom would send my brother Victor and me to a store, where we stood in line for long hours waiting for kerosene, which we used to cook our meals and light the house in the evening. Water for drinking and other household needs was provided by the "Misha Kulakov Running Water System." At 11, I was the older of the boys, and my job was to carry two huge buckets on a shoulder yoke a few blocks to a street faucet. After filling the buckets, I would attach each to one end of the yoke, fit my shoulders under it, and lift. Naturally I wanted to fill the buckets really full (so I wouldn't have to make as many trips), so once the heavy yoke was on my shoulders, I would drape an arm over each end to steady it. One day as I staggered through our neighborhood, I heard a neighbor say, "See that kid? He looks like a crucifix."

Into those hard times came a great joy—a child was born into our family. My new baby brother, David, became a living toy for Victor and me. Since there was no daughter in the house, I became David's chief nurse. I would sit

39

at his cradle and watch him for hours, admiring his delicate skin and his sweet breath, marveling at his helplessness, his many needs and demands. What a wonder it was to learn first hand the complexity and fragility of human life.

Not long before David's birth my dad had invited his widowed sister Anna Pilkh and her son, Daniel, to join us in Samara. When they arrived, Mom and Dad somehow found room for them in our humble dwelling. Anna, a diligent and hardworking woman, had acquired some medical knowledge, and was able to get a job as a nurse at Samara's main train station.

Anna was no stranger to persecution. Her husband, Pavel, a native Austrian, was already an ordained Adventist minister when he was drafted into the Austrian army in World War I.

"I'm a noncombatant," he had protested to the officers in his unit. "God commands me not to kill my fellow human beings."

This made his fellow soldiers so angry that as the Russian army advanced toward them, they tied Pavel with ropes and left him in a trench to the mercy of the enemy. He was captured, and once he'd arrived in Russia he decided to stay there.

He immediately went to work in the Trans-Caucasus region and helped found the Tbilisi church in Georgia; later he worked in the North Caucasus region. As I've traveled over Russia I've met many elderly church members he'd ministered to.

"He was a very kind and selfless person," they told me. "We can still remember him walking barefoot from village to village. Shoes were expensive and very scarce, so he traveled barefoot, with the shoes tied around his neck by the laces. Just before he got to town he would put them on."

As happened with most Adventist members and pastors, Uncle Pavel was arrested in the 1930s. He began serving his sentence in hard labor camp, doing work on the construction of the Volga-Don Canal. For a long time Anna didn't know where he'd been taken. Finally, after receiving his first message, which told her where he was, she traveled to that camp, which was quite an ordeal in itself.

Amazingly, her pleas to the administration and the guards were answered. "You may talk with him for no longer than five minutes and only in our presence," the guards told her.

Five minutes only? she thought. *And with guards around?*

Finally a door opened, and a frighteningly emaciated man stood before her. Anna stared at him. *Who is this?* she was asking herself. *This can't be my Pavel!*

But then she looked into his eyes—and there she saw the familiar look of love. The hard work and lack of food had not quenched his love for her, and that love was the only thing she could recognize.

"Annchen, Annchen," he repeated over and over as they embraced.

"You look so hungry," she sobbed. "You're sick. You need rest."

"The Lord is good," he whispered in her ear. "Even in this place the Lord is with me. He needs me to help those who are dying without any hope."

"The time is over!" one of the guard snapped, grasping Pavel's hand and pulling the two apart, and ushering a weeping Anna outside. She would never see her husband again.

Shortly after the visit Aunt Anna received his last letter, which she treasured the rest of her life. She showed it to me, written on plain, worn paper. I'll never forget those lines:

Dearest Annchen,

You know how much I love you and our dear son Daniel. Let us keep our courage. The Lord will come soon, and though I might die here, we shall be together forever. Nothing can separate us from His love. But for now I have a work to do here.

We shall see each other again. Let us be patient.

Your loving husband, Pavel.

For decades my wife and I, along with the rest of the family, assumed that Pavel had died from a combination of starvation, illness, and camp brutality. But in the late autumn of 2007, when this book was in its very final stages, I received some even more tragic information from Pavel's grandson, Mikhail Pilkh.

On the outskirts of Moscow during the Soviet era was an area called Butovo, which had always been surrounded by a great deal of secrecy. It was only after the collapse of the Soviet Union that we learned its full name: the Butovsky poligon (the Butovo shooting range). Within a secret police compound commanded by the NKVD, more than 20,000 people from all walks of life were executed and buried in mass grave pits. According to an online New York *Times* article by Sophia Kishkovsky (June 8, 2007), the victims included everyone from "peasants and factory workers to czarist generals, Russian Orthodox hierarchs, German Communists, Latvian writers, invalids, and even Moscow's Chinese launderers, dozens of whom were executed as enemies of the people."

And at least one Seventh-day Adventist.

Human rights activists discovered some lists of names of those who were shot there and uploaded them to the Internet. The executioners kept gruesomely efficient records. As Mikhail Pilkh searched through those names, he found this line:

Pilkh/Pavel-Ivanovich/1895/Austria/03.09.37

41

Pavel Pilkh would have been 42 years old when he was shot in 1937.

In those trying times God lovingly provided us with priceless sources of encouragement. In our worship times our family, together with Aunt Anna and her son Daniel, drew courage not only from the Word of God but also from the wonderful Russian Adventist hymnal *Psalms of Zion*. This book had been printed and bound with top-quality materials in the state printing shop in 1927, barely a year before the government banned all church printing, a ban that would last 70 years.

The *Psalms of Zion* songs were excellent. Some were translated from English and German, but many were written by deeply spiritual Russian servants of God, most of whose music expressed their personal knowledge of God's love and care as they endured persecutions by the czarist government.

Among the best were the hymns written or translated by Yan Wilson. It's no exaggeration to say that as I write these words, 80 years since that hymnal's publication, not a single church service is held in the entire huge territory of Russia without singing at least one of the songs written or translated by that man.

So in our Samara home we cradled that precious hymnal and sang:

In the caring arms of Christ
I fearlessly look into the future
As I wrestle with my dangerous enemy
Jesus is my stronghold.

That's "Safe in the Arms of Jesus" the way Yan Wilson rendered it into Russian. (Rather than simply use the usual English version of song, I've chosen to translate it back into English from Russian so that you can get a sense of the actual meaning of the phrases that encouraged us during those dark times.)

As I sang there in that Samara dwelling, my eyes traveled to the corner of the hymnal page to the initials Я. В. The backward "R" sounds like "yah" in Russian, and the B sounds like V. Yan Wilson (we pronounce it Vilson), the Adventist leader behind those modest initials, was a hero to me and all other Russian Adventists.

Though I didn't know it until much later, at the same time that Dad was in the Tula jail, the 54-year-old Yan Wilson and his wife had been captured by the secret police, and were enduring their own exile in a labor camp several hundred miles northeast of Moscow. Let me pause in my own story and briefly tell you his.

If Yan Wilson's last name sounds English, it's because it probably is. We don't know where he was born, but nearly two centuries ago, while traveling either from America or Great Britain, his ancestors were shipwrecked near a European shore, and settled in central Europe before finally moving to Latvia.

In the mid-1800s Yan's father moved his family further eastward to St. Petersburg, Russia, where the eminent Count Shuvalov hired him as a forestry officer. Yan, one of nine children, was born in 1883.

Nobody really knows when Yan Yanovich Wilson became an Adventist, but by age 26 he was already in the leadership of the Russian Adventist organization. Life wasn't easy under czarist rule, but it got definitely dangerous after 1917, when the atheistic Bolsheviks toppled the government. They began to hunt down and destroy intellectuals and thinkers of all kinds, including Christians. Yet Yan continued to elude the authorities, and in the early 1920s we find him secretly training Adventist young adults for the ministry.

"You must *know* the Word of God," he told a group of 30 young people who had gathered in the home of a wealthy mill owner named Burmistrov. "Not just know *about* it—you must *know* it. You cannot be fruitful ministers unless your faith is deeply grounded."

He gripped his Bible in his fist and raised it high. "I challenge you not simply to learn verses to support Bible doctrines. *I challenge you to know what is in every chapter of this book.*"

By now his students' jaws were hanging open. "You want us to memorize the whole Bible?" they gasped.

He shrugged. "The more you can learn by heart, the better," he said. "But I at least want you to be able to give a summary of any chapter I ask you about. This is not an option. I *require* this of you. Here," he said, handing someone his Bible. "Test me. Tell me book and chapter, and I'll tell you what that chapter contains."

The astonished students discovered that Pastor Wilson could not only summarize each chapter, but could quote much of it by heart! Their eyes huge, they got to work. Day by day their teacher quizzed them, and day by day their Bible knowledge grew. Later I would meet several of these students who had gone on to become skilled workers for Christ, leaders whose grounding in Scripture was so strong that they were able both to resist the seductive ideologies of Soviet propaganda, and encourage others to do the same.

Many years later, after Communism's fall, I met Yan Wilson's daughter Wanda, who related to me the heartbreaking story of his final capture.

She told me that in 1937 her father was exiled from Moscow to the provincial city of Lipetsk. Like my own father, Wilson didn't allow this to deter him from sharing his faith, and he began conducting worship services in a small house. However, among the worshippers was a planted informant, who reported him to the NKVD.

"I came home from work one evening," she told me, "and found both my parents gone. The neighbors told me that the police had spent the entire day searching our house."

After a sleepless night Wanda hurried to NKVD headquarters to find out what had happened. She was shown into the office of her parents' interrogator, and during their conversation she discovered that his wife had once been a classmate of hers. This broke the ice.

"I want to see my parents," she said.

He sighed. "I can't let you do that. It's against regulations."

"For a few minutes?" she begged.

The interrogator glanced uneasily around him and lowered his voice. "Let me be very frank," he said. "Even though I'm in the position I am, I myself am living in constant fear. However," he said in a tiny whisper, "I have a plan. But you must help."

Wanda leaned forward. "I will do whatever I can."

"Your parents are in separate cells," he said. "But once every week at a certain time, they will both be brought to my interrogation room. If you are here at that time, I think I can arrange for you to meet with them."

"Every week?" she asked eagerly.

"Possibly," he said. "But for just a few minutes."

In her brief conversations with her mother and father over the next several weeks Wanda learned that, as was common with other religious leaders who'd been arrested, they'd been charged with "anti-Soviet agitation."

"This is simply not true," Wanda insisted to the interrogator in a meeting with him. "My parents are not working against the interests of the state."

"I believe you," he said.

"Then can you help them?"

He shook his head sadly. "There is nothing I can do."

The Wilsons were interrogated for three months. During this time Wanda was able to visit with them briefly every week, with the help not only of the interrogator but of one of the prison guards, the son of a kindly neighbor. But then came the horrifying news that her mother and father were to be sent to labor camps in the Soviet Union's polar region.

Wanda heard this barely in time. She hastily packed a basket of food and hurried to the prison. From a distance she watched as her parents and other political prisoners, along with hardened thieves, murderers, and other criminals, were marched by guards directly from the prison to the rail station and herded along the platform toward a line of cattle cars.

Wanda gripped the basket of food and ran toward the guards. "Please," she gasped. "Please let me give this to my mother and father!" One of the guards pushed her so hard that she staggered back.

By this time the Wilsons were inside the cattle car, and in desperation their daughter ran back and forth along the platform looking for a window or unlocked door. The train began to move, and picked up speed. Distracted by grief, and still holding the basket, Wanda began running behind the train. Suddenly she tripped on a railroad tie and fell flat on her face. Her basket somersaulted ahead of her—homemade rolls, boiled eggs, and apples scattering everywhere. She lay where she'd fallen, sobbing and pressing her face to the earth.

She later learned that once her parents arrived at a transit camp, they were separated and never saw each other again. Her mother, an experienced nurse, was allowed to work in the camp hospital. But her father couldn't survive the harsh conditions in the labor barracks, where hungry prisoners sometimes fought to the death for a piece of bread. As far as Wanda can tell, Yan Wilson—Adventist leader and hymn writer—died a martyr's death in 1939 from disease and exhaustion.

In the late twenties and thirties millions of Soviet people died of hunger, disease, and persecution. Such a fate touched my family as well. Two girls were born to my family before I was born, but both died early, one after the other, because of the epidemics and poor living conditions made worse by World War I and then by the Russian Revolution. I'm very grateful to my parents for giving me three brothers, because without them I would have been deprived of many lasting joys and helpful experiences. But the lack of a sister made me awkward and shy around girls.

And our extreme poverty made it even worse.

"Mom and Dad," I said one day late that autumn, "I really need a warm coat for the winter."

"I'll get you one tomorrow," Dad said. "We don't have a lot of money, but I'll do what I can."

The next day he came home with a coat—a checkered one with a white rabbit-fur collar.

I gasped. "Dad, this is a *girl's* coat!"

"It's all I could afford," he said. "You'll have to wear it. We don't want you getting sick."

So I had to wear it. There was no other choice. You can imagine how the other schoolchildren treated me. They mocked me mercilessly.

Mom knew how I felt. Once when the two of us were alone in the house, she came up to me and gave me a hug. "Misha," she said, "I know how you feel about that coat. I am so very sorry. But don't you see that right now your loving father and I can't do anything to change the situation? We simply have no money to buy another coat for you. Please be patient. Maybe next winter we can get you something more suitable."

I sniffed a couple of times, trying to keep from weeping. She waited for a moment, then said, "We're having hard times because we are following Jesus Christ, Misha. But one day in His kingdom He'll give us beautiful robes of righteousness to wear."

And then she began to quote, by heart, from Hebrews 11:

"Some faced jeers and flogging, while still others were chained and put in prison. They were stoned; they were sawed in two; they were put to death by the sword. They went about in sheepskins and goatskins, destitute, persecuted and mistreated—the world was not worthy of them. They wandered in deserts and mountains, and in caves and holes in the ground. These were all commended for their faith" (verses 36-39, NIV).

CHAPTER 4: Blessed Are the Persecuted

To my great relief, the Winter of the Girl's Checkered Coat finally passed, and within a year we'd moved from Samara to the city of Maikop, and from there to Ivanovo, 175 miles northeast of Moscow.

Two weeks after we arrived World War II began its ominous thunder beyond the Western horizon. And though the Nazis almost immediately broke their nonaggression pact with Stalin and poured across our border, despite the loss of 20 million soldiers Russia stood its ground. But it would be 1945 before Hitler would be totally defeated.

From 1942 to 1947 I studied at the local art school while helping my father in his missionary work. He organized several small groups of believers in Ivanovo and the surrounding towns, and we conducted clandestine worship services in our home. In August of 1945, late at night, far away from the city lights, my father secretly baptized eight people, including me. I was 18 years old.

Once in a while I would take a weekend off and travel to Moscow and attend church there. It was then that I became friends with Pastor G. A. Grigoryev. Shortly after my baptism I made another visit to him.

"Mikhail," he whispered to me that Sabbath after the service was over. "I need to speak with you."

"Sure," I said.

"In private."

Once we were alone, he said, "You must be more careful."

I gave him a puzzled look. "More careful? What do you mean?"

"I saw you talking with Brother Ivan."

"I did meet someone named Ivan, yes."

Pastor Grigoryev's voice became very serious. "I have my eye on him. I noticed that as soon as he saw you, he waited very patiently until he had a chance to talk with you."

My eyes widened. "So you think he's—"

"An informer? I do." He glanced around and lowered his voice. "He always takes notes on any new members or visitors. So be careful back in Ivanovo. You just never know. Some of the people the KGB sends us can really make you believe they love the Lord."

Returning home, I found my parents chatting with an elderly church member I'll call Mr. Klanov, who'd been baptized with me. He'd told us how in the 1930s he'd been imprisoned and had lost his family. He'd almost starved to death while in a labor camp, but—according to him—he'd miraculously obtained his freedom. I told Klanov and my parents everything Pastor Grigoryev had told me about his suspicions of Ivan.

Soon after that conversation my father was arrested. Several weeks later I was summoned for interrogation at Ivanovo's KGB offices.

"Is it true," demanded my interrogator, "that while in Moscow, Pastor Grigoryev spoke to you about a man named Ivan?"

My skin prickled. I thought to myself, *Not only is Ivan an informer, but so is the saintly Klanov! What danger have I done with my babbling tongue?*

And then, in those next few milliseconds, a struggle began in my heart. Mom and Dad had trained me to be honest and polite, and to respect authority. On the other hand, I didn't want to say anything that might put Pastor Grigoryev in danger. The interrogator's question had caught me off balance.

What shall I say? I asked myself.

"Kulakov," the interrogator growled, "answer the question!"

I couldn't simply refuse to answer. Years later I would learn that in America and other civilized countries of the world, people who are accused have the right to refuse to incriminate themselves. There was no such legal provision under the Soviet system. I must give some kind of answer.

I wasn't concerned about punishment. All my emotions and thoughts were concentrated on finding the answer to one question: *How can I behave and speak so trustworthily so as to protect my dear friend Pastor Grigoryev and still keep a clean conscience?* I knew Jesus' promise that the Holy Spirit would teach us what to say in moments of crisis like this. But at that time I had also to recognize how careless I had been in not learning the true meaning of another of Jesus' statements: "I send you out as sheep in the midst of wolves. Therefore be wise as serpents and harmless as doves. But beware of men" (Matthew 10:16, 17, NKJV).

So I lied.

"I do not remember," I said, and immediately felt a hot blush of shame mount my cheeks. The interrogator saw the blush, pounced on my denial, and asked me the question again and again over the next several hours, threatening and intimidating me. Each time I gave the same answer.

Eventually I was let go, and went home ashamed of myself, hating myself. I begged the Lord for forgiveness and for Pastor Grigoryev's safety. By God's grace both were granted to me, though this wasn't the end of the story. Two years later this question was asked me again. I will tell you what happened in a later chapter.

Fortunately, as I say, Pastor Grigoryev was not arrested, but my father was again in captivity. He'd been charged with violating Article 58 of the Soviet Criminal Code, committing "anti-Soviet agitation." He was accused of conducting illegal meetings and—I quote directly from his charging papers—"agitating people against the Soviet government, and encouraging members of sectarian groups in Ivanovo and neighboring cities to stop work in Soviet enterprises on Sabbath days. Besides this, he organized the collections of monies for giving material help to those who were already sentenced for their contrarevolutionary activities."

Dad remained in the local prison for the next year and a half, undergoing continuous interrogation. In spite of the authoritarian arbitrariness of the justice system, and no matter how much "evidence" they invented, the Ivanovo courts kept failing to sustain the KGB's accusations against him.

And during that time the KGB continued interrogating me—and trying to recruit me to be an informer.

"How many visitors do you have at your secret anti-Soviet assembly?" the interrogator would ask. Our questioners never called our meetings "worship services," because this would be an admission that the government was persecuting us because of our religion, which they denied. So they relabeled our church services to make us sound subversive.

By this time I was accustomed to such challenges, and better able to exercise "serpent wisdom" and "dove harmlessness."

"Well," I answered politely but evasively, "we do not have any lists of our guests, or those who express their desire to come to our place to pray to God together with us."

On and on the sessions lasted, often until the wee hours of the morning. Finally the interrogator asked me, "Would you like to see your father?"

I said nothing.

He shrugged. "Well, we're going to give you an opportunity to *hear* him, at least."

It was Colonel Victorov, the Ivanovo region's KGB chief, who orchestrated the performance. He had a guard position me in a reception area beside the open door of his office so that I could be near the office but not see inside. Then other guards brought Dad into the colonel's office through another door. Dad had no suspicion that I was there.

"So, how are you feeling, Peter Stephanovich?" the colonel asked.

"As a prisoner here I have certain inconveniences," I heard my precious father's voice reply. "But I have not been abandoned by my God in this place, so I do not grumble."

The conversation continued for a while, and then my father said, "May I be allowed to have a Bible?"

"Of course not," the colonel snarled. Shortly after that I heard the sound of shuffling footsteps, and a door closed. The colonel then appeared at the door I was sitting beside. "Come in."

I entered the office, and any faint hope I may have had of Dad's still being there vanished. They'd taken him away without even giving us a chance to see each other.

"So," said the colonel. "What do you think? Do you understand now that life in prison isn't a bowl of cherries for your father?"

I said nothing.

"Listen to me very carefully, young man," the colonel growled. "If your father had come to us on his own, by the front door, he could leave the same way. But since he didn't—since he had to be brought here through the *back* door . . ." He let the sentence trail away. Then he said, "I'm sure you understand what I mean."

Of course I understood. The colonel was telling me that if Dad would have become an informer, he would have been released. And now the colonel was making the same offer to me.

I sat for a moment in silence. But I was thinking, not of the colonel's words, but of my dear mother. Every night that I was interrogated she spent in prayer. When I returned home, I would find her on her knees, beseeching the God of heaven. Maybe that's why at that point I lifted my eyes to the colonel's.

"You may just as well keep me here," I told him flatly. "I can never do what my conscience does not allow me to do."

But they let me go. It was early morning by now, but as I approached the house I could see my mother through the window, on her knees in prayer. When I opened the door, she looked up at me and said something that remains in my memory to this day.

"Misha," she said, "now I understand the words that Simeon spoke to Mary in the temple: 'Yea, a sword shall pierce through thine own soul also' [Luke 2:35]."

Court trials such as my father's were held in "closed session." It's possible that some of my readers who may not be familiar with that culture will imagine that these were secret courts. This wasn't the case. The Soviet authorities rarely feared publicity in these matters. The truth was that it was the average citizen who was afraid—afraid to attend court trials, or even visit police stations or KGB offices. Who knew what could happen to them if they went near those places?

However, the authorities did avoid publicity when it was in their interest. So for political offenders they conducted "closed" courts, which meant that the soundproof doors of the trial chambers were shut. They were fully confident that no curious person would dare to loiter in the hall, and it was certain that the subservient newspaper press would never try to discover any information unfavorable to those in power.

In Dad's case, neither Mom nor any other relative of this "enemy of the Soviet people" was informed of the trial date. Thank God, one or two of the witnesses for the prosecution were actually honest people who sincerely sympathized with us. Months went by, and finally in the autumn of 1946 one of these witnesses bravely slipped Mom some information.

"Your husband is coming up for trial again," he said. "It's probably going to be his last."

Mom was alarmed. "His last?"

"What I mean is that he'll be sentenced this time," the friend replied. "Probably to a labor camp."

"When will the trial be held?"

The witness told her the date, and then said, "You won't be allowed into the trial room. But if you stand outside the building, you'll see them escorting him in and out."

So on the first day of the trial, Mom and my two brothers and I took up our positions just outside the courthouse door near where a police guard stood. Around a street corner came a black raven, an unmarked police car.

"Get back! Move away!" the police suddenly shouted at us.

We retreated, and from a great distance we saw Dad emerge from the car.

"He's so *pale*," my mother whispered. A year and a half in a dark cell had robbed Dad's face of any color. "Look!" she cried. "He sees us!"

A loving smile had spread across Dad's face. His eyes sparkled with joy, and our smiles sparkled back at him. Once he and his escorts had disappeared into the courthouse, we hurried inside, but by then the courtroom doors were tightly closed.

What I'm about to describe might sound surprising, but let me explain. Those who have absolute power, power that isn't shared in any way by others, employ many formalities. For instance, this courthouse's main lobby had soundproof doors. But this was merely a formality, because nobody would dare approach one of those doors and press his ear against it.

What's more, the authorities were so confident of the terror they inspired in the public that once the front courtroom doors were locked, they didn't worry about the side doors. In my restless wanderings after Dad had entered the courtroom I'd glanced down a dark hallway and had seen some people entering what I thought must have been a side door into the courtroom. A bit later I drifted casually down to where two large bookcases stood against the wall. There, between the cases, was the door—and a second glance showed me that it wasn't tightly closed.

This carelessness could have happened, as I've mentioned, because of the authorities' confidence in how well they had cowed the average citizen. Or the door crack could have come from the building's poor condition, for as a result of the recent punishing war, few public buildings received proper maintenance. Or maybe God in His mercy prevented the guards from closing it completely so that I could be given the chance to be inspired by my father's behavior at his trial.

Whatever the reason, I quickly began a cat-and-mouse game. I would wander down the hall, slip between the bookcases (out of sight of anyone who might see), and collect as many details as I could. Then I'd casually wander back and whisper what I'd heard to Mom and my brothers.

Thanks again to the providence of God, the door crack was at the correct viewing-angle to allow me to actually see my father sitting next to his court-appointed female lawyer, a woman with the last name of Kulikova. My readers may wonder why the Soviet state would grant the privilege of a defense attorney to someone they'd already preconvicted. Here's why. As soon as World War II ended, the cold war between the superpowers began, and Western governments—including leaders such as Winston Churchill—began to publicize the Soviet government's repressive activities and call them to account. We would even see such headlines in the Soviet press as "Churchill Rattles the Sabers."

This pressure, especially from the United States, began to have some effect. The Soviet government took steps to at least create the appearance of respecting human rights. So the courts provided the accused with an advocate, though this was another of the "formalities."

But as I listened, I was startled to discover that Attorney Kulikova was actually trying to defend Dad. She seemed to respect him deeply and to be visibly moved by what he was saying. I later learned that in private she told my father to speak freely.

"The prosecutor will tell you to stop talking about religion and your faith," she said, "but go ahead and speak about it."

"Are you sure?" Dad had asked.

She nodded. "Tell us these things. Please. We do not know anything about God or the Bible. I myself would appreciate it, and I know that some of the people on the jury would too."

So through that door crack I watched as my father presented the message of salvation during his trial, as the apostle Paul had done so long ago during his. When the prosecutor asked a question, Dad would do his best to answer it in a way that showed God's great love, the gospel's beauty, and the Bible's trustworthiness.

"Stop! *Stop!*" the judge would shout, covering his ears. "Prisoner, I told you to answer the question directly. Cease this religious propaganda. You are an enemy of the Soviet state! And as for the churches you have organized, it's a shame to see such ugly sores growing on the state's healthy body!"

Yet thanks to Attorney Kulikova's advice, God's message was resonating in the ears of many as the days went by. Once, during a break in a court session, a small elderly woman emerged through the soundproof doors and approached us.

"Are you Peter Stepanovich Kulakov's family?" she asked.

Mom nodded. "I am his wife, and these"—she gestured toward my brothers and me— "are his children."

The woman gave us what I can only call a loving smile.

"Oh, I have learned *so much* at this trial!" she said fervently. "I've been sitting in that courtroom day after day, and I've been thinking, *How can I express my gratitude to this courageous family?* So when I heard during the interrogations that your husband's father was a member of the first Russian Duma, it dawned upon me to give you something special."

As she said this, she opened her purse and handed to Mom a small, old book.

"This book contains the pictures of all members of the Duma. And here," she said, turning to a page she'd marked, "is your father-in-law." Needless to say, this book has become one of our family's most precious relics.

Yet as I listened through the door crack, I couldn't help privately fuming as I watched this travesty of a trial. *Dad's being falsely accused,* I thought to myself. *As a Christian, I believe of course that God allows governments to exist, and that it's not our duty to oppose them. And evidently the Holy Spirit has been helping Dad communicate this message to the jury, because this has been his third trial on these same charges. But this is getting ridiculous.*

But this time the prosecutor wasn't going to let Dad escape. After Attorney Kulikova had delivered a thoughtful and very touching speech in Dad's defense, the prosecutor pulled out all the stops. After heaping scorn upon the defense's arguments, he became personal.

"It is clear to me," he bellowed, "and it must be clear to every thinking person here, that the advocate Kulikova has fallen in love with the accused. After all, he's a good-looking man. That's why she's been trying to pull the wool over our eyes to conceal his very obvious guilt!"

So he prevailed, and behind the closed doors of provincial court Dad was sentenced to 10 years' corrective labor, which would begin in a camp in Komi, near the Arctic Circle, and later continue in Khazakhstan.

Ten years? I thought, my heart nearly stopping as I heard those dreaded words. *Oh, Lord, please, please grant me an opportunity to see my father before he's taken away. I want to encourage him, to thank him for all he has done for us, and to assure him that his children value his example and will always follow Christ whatever the journey's difficulties.*

I raced down the hall and around the corner to where my family sat. The door opened, and the judge and the prosecutor appeared. Mustering up my courage, I introduced myself.

"I am the son of Peter Kulakov," I said. "Has my father received his sentence?"

The judge nodded. "Ten years in a labor camp," he said.

"May I be allowed to have a short visit with him? I understand that camp prisoners are totally isolated, and no visitors are allowed."

The judge shook his head.

"He may die there," I said desperately, "and I may never see him again!"

"It's not my job to organize meetings with convicts," the judge said shortly, and walked on.

Out of the corner of my eye I'd been watching to see where Dad had gone, and to my delight I discovered that he hadn't yet been taken to the KGB offices—where I would never have a chance to see him. He was still in the court building while his papers were being prepared. *It's now or never,* I told myself, and I found a quiet corner and opened my heart to the Lord in a short but urgent prayer. Almost immediately I heard an inner voice say, "Your request will be granted."

Dad's probably somewhere in the basement chambers, I decided, and when no one was looking I descended the steps. There in the hallway outside a cell door I found a young soldier standing guard.

"My father has just been sentenced to 10 years in a labor camp," I whispered to him. "Could I have five minutes with him? Five minutes only?"

We looked into each other's eyes. The soldier probably wasn't much older than I was.

"Please," I begged. "Just five minutes."

Glancing around to see that no one was watching, he turned the key in the lock and opened the door.

"Misha, *Misha!*" Immediately I found myself in the strong embrace of my father. For a few seconds we babbled together, he telling of his love for me, and I telling him how grateful we children were for his steadfastness. Finally he shushed me.

"Mikhail," he finally said. "I know that soon they will arrest you, too. During my interrogations and my three court trials they've been gathering material against you as well."

He felt my body stiffen, and hugged me harder.

"Don't be afraid of this, son!" he told me. "This is the path Jesus has trod before us. He has prepared the way for you and me. The Lord will be with you, and He will give you all the encouragement you will need. He will support you."

One of his hands ruffled the dark curly hair on my head. "They'll cut your hair. But don't worry. It will grow back again. Mikhail, remember that all the faithful followers of Jesus have gone down this path. Your father has traveled it more than once. So don't be discouraged. The Lord will strengthen you."

Then his voice took on an even more serious tone. "Do you know who reported us?"

"Was it Klanov?" I whispered.

He nodded, and told me that it had indeed been Klanov, and another new believer, whom I will call Ptakhina.

I was startled. "Surely not Sister Ptakhina. She's a wonderful Christian woman."

"Don't call her 'sister,' " he said grimly. "Ptakhina is no sister to us. Do not ever let Klanov or Ptakhina enter our house again. If you do, they'll report on your activities."

There in that cell with my father, the precious seconds ticking away, my mind wrestled with his counsel. My thoughts flashed back over the past few months. During that time I'd been serving as lay pastor for the believers in Gorky (its original name of Nizhny Novgorod was restored in 1990), 100 miles from where we lived in Ivanovo.

In that little group was a truly faithful Christian woman, a spiritual mother of the church, named Anna Bukhalina. Though disabled, and single all her life, Anna had a bright and encouraging personality. In 1933 she'd been arrested and had spent several years in prison for her religious activities. She told me of a conversation she had had with other women in her cell. "Why are you here?" was the topic of discussion, and for most of them the answer was that they'd hidden their gold and jewelry when the government demanded they turn those items in.

"Anna Bukhalina, why are *you* here?" someone asked.

"I too kept my gold," she replied.

"You too? How much jewelry did you have?"

Anna's eyes twinkled. "I'm talking about the gold of my faith in Jesus."

As she told me of her incarceration, she said something that would later cause me to wrestle with Dad's words in his cell.

"Mikhail," Anna had suggested, "let me turn your attention to the teachings of Christ concerning loving our enemies. I choose to pray for them, because I love them. I wish to wash their feet, as Jesus washed the dirty feet of Judas. If Jesus loved Judas, why shouldn't we show our love to our enemies?"

"But Sister Anna," I said, "if they join our church and then report on us, we might go to prison."

"Most of these people are unhappy, Mikhail," she replied gently. "And they're frightened. They betray us because they're desperately trying to preserve their own lives and freedom. But doing this makes them miserable. We must show them our love. After all, if they attend our meetings and discover that we are a peaceful people who pray for the well-being of the government, isn't that a good thing for them to report? Isn't that a witness to the authorities?"

Anna's powerful wisdom had moved me so deeply that in the final moments in my father's cell I raised my head to him. "I will remember what you told me about Klanov and Ptakhina," I said, "but Jesus didn't ever close the door to Judas."

He nodded thoughtfully. "You're right, of course," he said, "but be careful. *Be careful.*"

At this point our reunion was suddenly interrupted.

"What's happening here?" a loud voice shouted. The commander of the guards burst into the cell. "Soldier, what have you done!"

I was ordered to leave immediately, and I left not only with great grief at parting with my father but also with a heavy load of guilt for what might happen to the young soldier who was so kind to me.

Dad's urgent warnings led me to keep a closer eye on Klanov and Ptakhina. As I watched them, knowing what I knew, I began to understand what Anna had said: informers were more to be pitied than censured.

CHAPTER 5

I Have Overcome the World

Dear Reader: I now return to the events I was describing at the end of Chapter I, when with my two arresting KGB agents guarding me I was traveling aboard a train bound from Rezekne, Latvia, eastward toward Ivanovo.

Once our train had arrived in Ivanovo, the two agents put me into a car that was waiting for us at the station, and brought me to the regional KGB office. One stayed with me in a waiting room while the other went to report our arrival. Finally I was ushered into the presence of a KGB captain named Kurochkin, one of the chief interrogators. I knew Kurochkin well, because when Dad was arrested two years earlier, Kurochkin had personally conducted searches at our house and had summoned me several times for interrogation.

Now when he caught sight of me, his face twisted into a sarcastic smile. *Ahhh,* his expression said, *I am really going to enjoy this.*

"Well," he said. "At last. You're here." He glanced at the bag I was carrying. "Where's your *svetilnik?* Hand it over."

I reached into the bag, took out my Bible, and handed it to him. *He's already been informed that I'd been given my Bible,* I thought, *and now he's just proving to me that he knows the Christian code word for it.* (The psalmist says that God's Word is a "light" unto our feet, and in Russian *svetilnik* means "lamp.")

Kurochkin then picked up his phone receiver and said a few words into it, and, when a guard appeared, gave him a piece of paper that evidently contained directions about me. After glancing at the paper, the guard led me through long passageways into the KGB prison, which—as far as I know—still stands today.

We went down one long flight of stairs after another until we came to a room without windows. A lightbulb, hanging from the ceiling by a long wire, lit the room so dimly that I didn't immediately see a uniformed man sitting at a table. By his gloomy expression I deduced that he was the chief warder. After giving his own scrutiny to the paper, he muttered something that I couldn't hear to the guard. Then he looked me up and down with apathetic eyes.

"Remove your clothing," he said.

I was completely searched, as were all my clothing and the bag my mother had given me. The guard snipped off all metal snap-buttons and clasps (so I couldn't sharpen them into weapons), and took away my belt (so I wouldn't hang myself) and my watch (because the KGB's whole point was to disorient their prisoners and cause them to lose track of time). Then I was led out of the room and further down the dark corridor to an iron door with a bar across it secured by a lock. A soldier on duty there unlocked the door with a chilling metallic jangle. Once I walked through, the door clanged shut.

I looked around. *This isn't a cell,* I decided glumly. *This is a box!*

The small room was absolutely empty except for a black tin toilet bucket in a corner. *This is it,* I thought. *I'm in* odinochka—*solitary confinement.* There were no windows. The only illumination came from one lightbulb in the ceiling. The walls smelled damp. The one positive thing about my box was that its floor was made not of concrete as in the Daugavpils prison, but of wood, painted so long ago that the color was scuffed and worn away. *A small blessing but a blessing nonetheless,* I mused, *because the floor is all I have to sleep on, right down there beside the toilet bucket.*

I turned and studied the entrance I'd just come through. A rectangular hole had been cut in the exact center of the door, and pressed against the other side of the hole was a metallic cover that could be opened only by someone outside. Prisoners contemptuously called this the *kormushka* (feeding trough). As the jailer opened the cover toward him, it swung down to a horizontal position, and he would place a bowl on it filled with something resembling food, which I retrieved by reaching through the opening. The *kormushka* had another purpose, too. The jailer kept an eye on me through the *volchok,* a little peephole higher in the door, and if he decided he needed to threaten me about something, he would flip open the *kormushka* and bellow through it.

Since I had no clock, no wristwatch, not even windows to see how dark the sky was getting, I had to depend on my body rhythms to tell me when to go to sleep. When I decided it was night, I lay on my back on the wooden floor, tucked my sack under my head for a pillow, closed my eyes, and shivered in the cold, trying to ignore the lightbulb's blood-pink glow through my eyelids. This went on for several nights.

Each morning I would discover to my surprise that somehow I had fallen asleep after all. Often I would be awakened by the clicking of the *kormushka* door as a guard provided my breakfast. My muscles still aching from the cold and the wooden floorboards, I would roll over, sit up, and examine what was in the bowl—watery porridge or gruel, or something that seemed like silage. In the afternoon I was given some soup with a slice of bread, and in the evening a bowl of hot water, a teaspoon of sugar, and another slice of bread. It wasn't possible to starve to death on that diet, but the feeling of hunger never left me. I'll never forget that feeling. Even nowadays I can't bear to see food wasted.

To stay in solitary confinement for a long time without books, or radio, without even a piece of paper or pencil, without the chance to talk with another human being—and with absolutely nothing to do—is a torture not everybody can endure. I had no idea how long I would be held there, so I tried to discipline my thoughts. I created a mental curriculum of what I would think about, and in what order. I repeated Bible passages I'd memorized, and reflected thoughtfully on them. I thought about the people in my life, and prayed for them. Having no way to keep track of minutes and hours disoriented me, and I wasn't always able to keep to my plan, but I tried.

Many times I thought of my family, wondering how my mother and Victor and David were faring. Much later I would learn that our faithful heavenly Father had arranged for their welfare. One of the men baptized with me in August of 1945 was a specialist with rare skills in sheet metal work. Shortly after Dad was arrested, this man came to visit my mother and brothers and me.

"What I do for a living is a perfect job for an Adventist," he told us. "People in my profession work for the state like everyone else, but we can basically keep our own hours." He glanced at 16-year-old Victor. "Would you like to come with me to the factory where I work? You could be my apprentice."

Victor instantly agreed, and by the time we moved to Daugavpils two years later, he was astonishingly skilled. In Daugavpils he continued to develop his abilities, and after Stephen and I were arrested he got a job that provided a steady income for at least the essentials. As I said before, however, I could not know in prison that Victor was now employed, so I continued to pray for God to preserve them.

Though I couldn't measure minutes and hours in my cell, I could keep track of the days, mainly by counting breakfasts, lunches, and suppers delivered through the *kormushka*. And finally, after several lonely days, a guard arrived and led me out into the hall. *At last,* I thought, *a change of scenery! I wonder where I'll be taken next.*

Far down the long corridor I was ordered to stop by the door of another cell. *Now I understand,* I thought. *First of all they put you in the* odinochka *to get your attention, and then they relocate you to a "normal" cell. And you'll have already gotten a taste of where they could put you again if you misbehave.*

As the door swung open to my new cell, my heart began to beat rapidly. Inside was a live human being! Though we'd never even seen each other before, the other prisoner and I spontaneously embraced again and again. And when the guard clanged the door shut and locked it, we sat down on our cots and burst into conversation.

"My name is Mikhail Kulakov," I said.

"I am Ivan Fyodorov." He looked to be about 60, with close-cropped gray hair, the same as all the other prisoners. "I am so glad to see you! Have you just come from the *odinochka?* So have I! It was terrible being alone! How I suffered!" And for several minutes he described in detail all he'd gone through.

As he talked, I glanced around the room. He noticed my gaze, and smiled broadly.

"The beds!" he said. "Look at our iron cots! Real beds!"

There were three cots in the room, bolted to the floor and arranged corner to corner in a horseshoe pattern. Each was only about two feet wide and barely six feet long, and had no springs, just a crisscross pattern of thin metallic strips welded to the frame, over which was thrown a thin quilted mattress.

"Those cots look stiff," I said.

He nodded. "But better than the floor, yes?"

"Yes," I said earnestly. "And there's bedding, too."

Since Ivan had come first to the cell, he'd already shrewdly chosen his cot—far enough from the window so that he wouldn't catch cold, and also as far as possible from the *parasha,* the toilet bucket. I placed my sack on the cot opposite to his, but it really wouldn't have mattered where we slept. The acrid stench of the bucket was always present. The cell was painted a sober gray, and measured 11' x 7'. With three six-foot cots, that didn't leave a lot of extra space to try to get some exercise.

But at least there was a window! True, it was criss-crossed by thick bars, and covered on the outside with a wooden screen that the prisoners called a "muzzle." But at the top, just above the screen, we could see a strip of sky, which let a little illumination enter the cell during daylight hours. In the evening, just as night fell, I would go to the window and look up at the stars.

Thank You, God, for this piece of the sky, I prayed. *It helps me feel a connection with my Creator and Savior.*

Suddenly the *kormushka* clanked open. "Bedtime!" roared a guard.

I took a close look at the bedding. "This pillowcase is gray," I said to Ivan. "I wonder if that was its original color." He grunted and shrugged. Before I lay my head on it I covered it with my jacket. Then I reached for the blanket to wrap it around me, but it smelled so strongly of someone else's sweat that I shuddered and shoved it away.

Looking back on that prison experience, I now realize that some government agency in the postwar Soviet world must have passed at least minimal regulations about the proper care of detainees, which to some extent lightened the life of millions of prisoners in prisons and concentration camps. We prisoners weren't told about these reforms, of course. But we could sense these guidelines, even though the prison commanders followed them grudgingly.

Our meals, for example, though not excessively nutritious, at least came regularly. Once a day, usually in the morning, we were led out to a toilet. Every tenth day we got the opportunity to wash ourselves, though we each were given not more than five to seven minutes for doing this. Another 10-day cycle provided us with a change of literature. We were lent books by Russian or foreign authors who presumably had been approved by the Communist regime. Some of the books were interesting, and some weren't.

For 15 minutes a day we were led out to a courtyard with high brick walls topped with watchtowers. We had to walk silently, in single file, our hands behind our backs. If I tipped my head back to gaze at the sky, a sentry shouted, "Look downward!"

The ground was footworn and grassless. *My father must have walked here,* I suddenly thought, *just like me, head down, hands behind his back.* As I drew near one of the courtyard walls I could hear someone pacing with a light, even stride just beyond it, evidently in another narrow courtyard like this one. *I wonder if that's Stephen,* I thought, a lump in my throat. *That's his walk.*

Aside from the toilet trip and those precious 15 minutes of fresh air and exercise, Ivan and I languished in our cells. I discovered that I wasn't as lucky with my cellmate as I thought I'd been. Once he'd told me all about his sufferings in solitary confinement, his conversational flow pretty much dried up. He seemed to have no interest in meaningful discussion. The only thing I remember in detail is his story about the night of his arrest.

"When I retired," he told me, tears in his voice, "I bought a cow. Her name was Burenka. She loved me very, very much. She was my pet. Then one night the KGB came for me in the black raven. As they led me out of my house, my dear Burenka stuck her head out of her stall and mooed with sorrow. I could still hear her from inside the car as we drove away. *Mooooo . . . moooo.*"

I spent nearly a month alone with Ivan, and the first time I heard that story it was beautiful, even touching. The tenth time I heard it, it had lost most of its charm. By the twentieth time its fascination had totally departed.

When I tried to speak to him about God, I found that he had absolutely no interest in the subject.

"So you don't believe in the existence of God?" I asked him.

He shrugged. "I don't deny that He may exist," he said in a bored voice. He told me that the only things he connected with God were certain rituals or celebrations during which he and everybody else got very drunk. He refused to think of God as the person with whom it is possible—and necessary—to live in everlasting fellowship.

"That means nothing to me," he told me flatly. "It is useless to me."

For a while I blamed myself for being unable to arouse his interest in eternal things. As he sat on his bed I told him stories from the Bible in as interesting a manner as I could. But even as I talked, his head would start to droop. Soon his chin landed on his chest, and he would fall into a doze.

Dozing in the daytime, however, was against prison rules. The jail guard turned out to be the ally of the God of heaven. Peering through the peephole, he spotted the somnolent Ivan. *Clank* went the *kormushka,* and the guard's roar filled the room.

"No sleeping during the day, prisoner! You do that one more time, and you'll get thrown into the *kartser!*" The *kartser* was a narrow box used to punish someone who'd broken prison rules. If you'd been put in the *kartser* you had no heat, no regular meals, and no bathroom privileges. Only the prison's chief warden could authorize a prisoner to be taken there.

Hearing the dreaded word, Ivan twitched, snorted a couple of times, and jerked his head upright with a terrified stare. As I talked, he may have listened to what I said, but he never took part in spiritual conversations. They were, in the words of a Russian proverb, "fodder not into the horse." I remembered Jesus' comments in Matthew 11:15: "He who has ears to hear, let him hear!" (NKJV). Tragically, Ivan seemed spiritually deaf.

Sitting there in my bunk, 21 years old, gazing at this man three times my age, I thought sadly, *What a tremendous responsibility we have, we who call ourselves Christians. Here in Russia, it's the Christians who are partly the reason that many of our fellow countrymen are alcoholics, that the crime rate is rising, and that most of our children are growing up without a knowledge of anything holy or eternal. If each Christian had worked and prayed earnestly for the salvation of his friends and neighbors, how much happier—and liberated—our land would be! Ivan Fyodorov and other nonbelievers will never taste the joy of life's fullness until they come to know the Savior and receive Him into their hearts.*

The days dragged along. One of the curses of confinement, especially with someone who doesn't share your interests, is how frankly bored you get. During the first few days I studied all Ivan's peculiarities, all his gestures, all his habits and ways of behaving. Then just when I thought I was doomed to stare at his gray head forever, a new prisoner was brought to our cell.

Averbakh (I don't remember his first name) was a middle-aged Jew with a pleasant, handsome face. As he told us about his own adventures, I found my jaw sagging at the inexplicable workings of Soviet authority.

"You two are new prisoners, right?" he asked us, looking us up and down.

We nodded.

"I've already spent eight years in concentration camps," he said. "Then they let me go free for a couple of years. But then they arrested me and tried me on new charges."

He paused, and his face twisted into a bitter smile. "And what makes it all so crazy is that I was as faithful a Communist as you'll find anywhere. I bought into the party line. I believed it. I *lived* it. Then one day the NKVD came for me, and brought me to trial, and told me the charges. They were false! I did nothing they accused me of! Nothing!"

"You got caught in a purge," I suggested.

He heaved a deep sigh. "I got caught in a purge."

Years later I would read the works of Alexander Solzhenitsyn, the Russian intellectual and philosopher, who had also spent many years in the camps. Solzhenitsyn carefully studied Joseph Stalin's purges, especially the terrible years of 1937 and 1938. Here's the conclusion he came to:

"The composition of the hordes who were arrested in that powerful wave and lugged off, half-dead, to the Archipelago was of such fantastic diversity that anyone who wants to deduce the rationale for it scientifically will rack his brain a long time for the answer. (To the contemporaries of the purge it was still more incomprehensible.)

"The real law underlying the arrests of those years was *the assignment of quotas,* the norms set, the planned allocations. Every city, every district, every military unit was assigned a specific quota of arrests to be carried out by a stipulated time. From then on everything else depended on the ingenuity of the Security operations personnel."[1]

Later in my own camp experience I became acquainted with several political prisoners. In a soft whisper one of them told me the following tragic-comic story, which I will tell in the words of Solzhenitsyn, who later recorded it in *Gulag:*

"Here is one vignette from those years as it actually occurred. A district Party conference was underway in Moscow Province. It was presided over by a new secretary of the District Party Committee, replacing one recently *arrested.* At the conclusion of the conference, a tribute to Comrade Stalin was called for. Of course, everyone stood up (just as everyone had leaped to his feet during the conference at every mention of his name). The small hall echoed with 'stormy applause, rising to an ovation.' For three minutes, four minutes, five minutes, the 'stormy applause, rising to an ovation' continued. But palms were getting sore and raised arms were already aching. And the older people were panting from exhaustion. It was becoming insufferably silly even to those who really adored Stalin. However, who would dare be the *first* to stop? The secretary of the District Party Committee could have done it. He was standing on the platform, and it was he who had just called for the ovation. But he was a newcomer. He had taken the place of a man who'd been arrested. He was afraid! After all, NKVD men were standing in the hall applauding and watching to see *who* quit first! And in that obscure, small hall, unknown to the Leader, the applause went on—six, seven, eight minutes! They were done for! Their goose was cooked! They couldn't stop now till they collapsed with heart attacks! At the rear of the hall, which was less crowded, they could of course cheat a bit, clap less frequently, less vigorously, not so eagerly—but up there with the presidium where everyone could see them? The director of the local paper factory, an independent and strong minded man, stood with the presidium. Aware of all the falsity and all the impossibility of the situation, he still kept on applauding! Nine minutes! Ten! In anguish he watched the secretary of the District Party Committee, but the latter dared not stop. Insanity! To the last man! With make-believe enthusiasm on their faces, looking at each other with faint hope, the district leaders were just going to go on and on applauding till they fell where they stood, till they were carried out of the hall on stretchers! And even then those who were left would not falter. . . .   Then, after eleven minutes, the director of the paper factory assumed a businesslike expression and sat down in his seat. And, oh, a miracle took place! Where had the universal, uninhibited, indescribable enthusiasm gone? To a man, everyone else stopped dead and sat down. They had been saved! The squirrel had been smart enough to jump off his revolving wheel.

"That, however, was how they discovered who the independent people were. And that was how they went about eliminating them. That same night the factory director was arrested. They easily pasted 10 years on him on the pretext of something quite different. But after he had signed Form 206, the final document of the interrogation, his interrogator reminded him:

" 'Don't ever be the first to stop applauding!'

"(And just what are we supposed to do? How are we supposed to stop?)

"Now that's what Darwin's natural selection is. And that's also how to grind people down with stupidity."[2]

During my incarceration at Ivanovo's KGB prison I noticed that prisoners didn't spend a lot of time in the same cell. Only God and the KGB knew why this constant shifting occurred, but this rotation at least gave me a change of scenery and a chance to meet new people.

So one day I had to part with Ivan and Averbakh, and was led to my new cell, which was already occupied by two men. I sat down on the cot reserved for me and studied my cellmates.

"My name is Mikhail Kulakov," I said to the younger of the two.

"My name is Alexey," he said. He seemed to be about 25, not much older than I. But his thin body, his pale, hollow cheeks, and his somber expression told me that he was an old inmate at this "state house."

The other man seemed not to notice me. He was a short man of about 30, with black, messy hair that hadn't yet been given the usual close-cropped prison haircut. "My name is Mikhail Kulakov," I said to him.

He muttered something inarticulate, his face a map of displeasure and despair. Seated on his bed, he had pressed his back squarely against the cell's brick wall, as though he were trying to topple it. Alexey and I both tried to get him to talk, but he barely paid us any attention. He just sat there muttering to himself, once in a while hitting his head on the wall behind him. Gradually, from the troubled fragments of speech that came from his lips, we were able to piece together the following story.

This man had been no radical or rabble-rouser, but a devoted Communist. During World War II he'd risen to the rank of lieutenant colonel, and had been badly wounded and captured by the enemy. Somehow he'd managed to escape and return to the Soviet side, where he got medical treatment.

He was restless to get back to the front lines, but party leaders had requested that he be relieved of his duties so that they could appoint him as administrator of (if I understood his anguished mutterings correctly) the Gavrilovo-Possadsky region. After he'd spent some time in this important role, the KGB had suddenly arrested him, without warning and without any reason he could think of.

"What kind of justice is *that?*" he would snarl to himself in our cell. "What was my crime? Was it being taken prisoner of war? Was it because I bled profusely from my wounds? Was it that I managed to escape the Nazis? Was it because I wanted to return to the front and fight again? What was it? *Why am I here?*"

He stared around at the walls of the cell. Then he snapped, "This isn't a state institution. This is a private gang!"

Clang! The *kormushka* opened, and a jailer shoved through some bowls of skilly, a sloppy mixture of oatmeal flavored with meat. Alexey and I took a bowl apiece, and I held out the third to the lieutenant colonel.

"No!" he shouted, waving it away. "I am declaring a hunger strike! I demand a meeting with the public prosecutor!" He continued to shout this at the top of his voice, and a half hour later he was taken from the cell—either to be force-fed or to be confined in the punishment cell, I never learned which. We never saw him again.

This day turned out to be one of the gloomiest in my entire life, and not only because of the unjustly-treated officer. Every once in a while, while he was still in our cell, I tried to take my mind off his mutterings by reading a little book someone had left there. For my already-depressed spirit, that book was the straw that broke the camel's back.

Its title was *Anton, Poor Wretch,* and it was written by noted author Dmitry Grigorovitch. It was a very well written—*too* well written—story about a poor Russian peasant during the days of Russian serfdom. Grigorovitch wrote it, no doubt, as a cautionary tale to be read by farmers at the end of a day in the fields, or businessmen relaxing before supper.

I do not, however, recommend that *Anton, Poor Wretch* be read in a cell while trying to distract one's mind from an aggrieved lieutenant colonel. I would stare dolefully at my cellmate banging his head against the brick wall behind him, and then I would open *Anton* and read of the peasant's agonies, and sadly close the book and listen once more to the officer's heartbreaking mutterings. And when he was finally marched out of the cell toward whatever oblivion awaited him, I found myself in the depths of the first, and only, really severe depression of my life.

I frankly do not know where that spirit of despondency would have taken me if a Bible verse I'd learned in childhood hadn't suddenly sounded in my mind: "Is anyone among you suffering? Let him pray" (James 5:13, NKJV). Tears welling up in my eyes, I bowed my head and poured out in a whisper all my troubles to the Lord. As I prayed, another verse—one that my parents loved—came to me: "In the world you will have tribulation; but be of good cheer, I have overcome the world" (John 16:33, NKJV). With those words the heavenly rays of divine light penetrated the walls of my gloomy prison cell and brought encouragement to my soul.

---

[1] Aleksandr I. Solzhenitsyn, *The Gulag Archipelago* (New York: Harper & Row, 1973), p. 71.

[2] *Ibid.,* pp. 69, 70.

CHAPTER 6: **Identifying Our "Crime"**

My investigation lasted six months. "Six months" is easy to say now, but then I had absolutely no way of knowing how long I'd be there.

Cell dwelling was hard, but the most disgusting and excruciating experiences of all were the interrogations. They were always held in dark, drab rooms filled with tobacco smoke. A freestanding cabinet stood against one wall, its two wooden doors separating it into two parts. An interrogator sat behind a desk, and I, the prisoner, sat on a chair facing him. My interrogators' faces were always unfriendly, their language always abusive, and their questions always crafted to confuse me and trap me in my words. I felt constantly under tension.

The authorities often used sleeplessness to try to break the prisoners' will and befog their reason. I could be interrogated at any time during any 24-hour period, as they worked around the clock trying to make me sign self-incriminating documents or to trick me into letting slip evidence against my friends and other Christian believers. Often I was so tired that I did not know the time or even the day of the week.

After each session I was marched back to my cell, exchanging the tobacco stench for the stench of old urine in the toilet bucket, but the persecution continued even in the cell. Daytime sleeping, of course, was forbidden. But I was not permitted to lie down on my cot or even lean up against a wall. Though my body was desperate for sleep, a guard always seemed to be looking through the cell door's peephole, and if I started to nod off, he would roar, "*Wake up!*" Simply trying to stay awake drained my energy even more.

At last the prison's 10:00 p.m. bedtime would arrive, announced by the guard's rap on the door and brusque command "Time to sleep!" I would topple onto my cot into immediate unconsciousness, only to be awakened soon afterward and hustled off to yet another interrogation, which might last for several hours. Then I would "crash" on my cot again, only to be shouted awake early in the morning.

But though I endured mental torture, I was not physically struck or beaten. My interrogator would tower over me, threaten me, almost convince me that a severe thrashing awaited me, but it never happened. What influence God used to bind that man's hands, I can only guess. Perhaps John Ruskin was right when he said, "Multitudes think they like to do evil; yet no man ever really enjoyed doing evil since God made the world."

Decades later, after the Communists lost power, I joined many other so-called political prisoners in requesting from the KGB archives some of the materials used in my case. The following is an extract from those files, which I've translated into English:

Confirmed by:
Col. Victorov,
Bureau Chief of MGB,
Ivanovo Region
(signature and seal)
March 11, 1948

Arrest sanctioned by:
Public Prosecutor,
Chief Justice of the
Ivanovo Region,
Ushkanov
(signature and seal) March 13, 1948

ARREST DECREE
IVANOVO, MARCH 11, 1948

I, Capt. Kurochkin, vice deputy of the Head Administrator of Department "O" of KGB [formerly MGB], Ivanovo Region, upon review of the matter relative to criminal activity of—KULAKOV, Mikhail Petrovich, born in Leningrad in 1927 into a family of a sectarian preacher, prosecuted for anti-Soviet activities, nonpartisan, Russian, citizen of the U.S.S.R., temporarily residing in the city of Daugavpils, Latvian S.S.R.

FINDING

Kulakov, predisposed to hostile attitude to VKPB [the Communist Party] and the Soviet Government, a member of an anti-Soviet sectarian group of Adventists, over a period of some years, in his apartment as well as in apartments of other participants of that group, organized illegal assemblages, preached sermons with anti-Soviet content, motivated members of the group to refuse work at Soviet enterprises on Saturdays, as well as refuse military service in the Soviet Army, and distributed various counter-revolutionary, provocative fabrications. In this setting he conducted anti-Soviet propaganda, recruited youth to join the SDA movement, and manipulated them into anti-Soviet directions. Besides this, he organized collections of funds to financially assist those sectarians who were convicted of counterrevolutionary activities . . .

These accusations brought against me were typical expressions of intolerance and hatred toward any ideology foreign to the government, and I heard them repeated again and again during my six months at the Ivanovo prison. From the "evidence" they presented I was able to deduce that my brother Stephen was indeed being held in this same prison, though from the day of our arrests we never saw each other. But we were both charged with the same crimes of "group anti-Soviet agitation." Our conversations during our home church meetings with anyone who had taken an interest in religion were considered serious offenses against the Soviet state.

One day my interrogator brought up a familiar name.

"You are acquainted with a woman named Ptakhina," he stated.

I said nothing.

"Not only did you draw her into your anti-Soviet conspiracies, but you added to your guilt by joining your brother in trying to influence her son to accept your ideas."

Now I understand something I've always wondered about, I thought silently. *Dad warned me about this woman during our few minutes in his basement cell. But this clears up another mystery.*

In 1946 Stephen had returned home from the army, where he'd experienced a powerful spiritual conversion. He was filled with zeal to share with others his joy in the Lord.

"Stephen," I had said as I repeated Dad's warnings about Ptakhina, "we've got to be careful."

"Are you sure Dad knew what he was talking about?" he asked incredulously. "The way I look at it, she's a godly former Baptist lady who's spent a lot of time in prison and gone through many difficulties."

So when Ptakhina asked to talk with us one day, Stephen was all ears.

"I am worried about my son," she told us. "He is godless. He has no time for Christianity. You young men are his age. Maybe he will listen to you. Please, come and tell him about our God."

"Of course we'll come," Stephen said promptly.

But once he and I were alone, I repeated Dad's warnings. "She's KGB," I insisted. "She's part of the reason Dad's in a labor camp."

"We must go witness to him," Stephen said firmly, "and let God take care of the consequences. You might as well come along, because if you don't, I'm going by myself."

So I went with him. Sure enough, Ptakhina's son was indeed a cynic, who not only laughed at everything holy but continued to smoke cigarettes during our conversation, deliberately filling the room with the fumes. My brother debated with him, pressing home every valid argument proving the truth of the Christian faith and the existence of God. The young atheist laughed louder, pausing occasionally to engage in heated rebuttal.

During the discussion I happened to glance at Ptakhina. *What's the matter with her?* I asked myself. *She seems really nervous. I've never seen her like this. I know she's concerned about her son's salvation, but she's shaking all over—her head, her hands, her feet.* She caught me staring at her, and tried to conceal her agitation.

And now I knew why. Obviously the authorities had forced her not only to inform on us but also to invite us to talk with her son, thus providing the government even more evidence of our "subversive" activities. Like thousands of others, she'd allowed herself to become an instrument of the KGB.

Another witness brought before me was in an even sadder position.

In the months before Mom, my brothers, and I left for Latvia a young girl named Sonya, along with her older sister, Elizabeth (my classmate at the art school), had begun attending our home worship services. Sonya made no secret of the fact that she had fallen deeply in love with me. Remembering my mother's counsel, I behaved carefully and formally to this young woman, while studying her carefully.

She's obsessed with me, I decided, *but she has no real interest in becoming a Christian. And even if she did, she'd never be able to endure life as a pastor's wife, especially under Soviet oppression.*

"Sonya," I finally told her, "you know that most likely I will wind up in prison. It would be terribly hard for you to live with that constant threat." And even after I left for Latvia, I wrote letters to her trying to turn her attention toward the Savior.

Now, as it turned out, my interrogator knew all about Sonya.

"This young woman testifies," he said, his eyes on a paper on his desk, "that you would not permit her to become a member of Komsomol [the Communist youth organization]. Do you agree with this?"

"No," I said.

He turned the paper and beckoned me to look at it. "It's right here in the transcript of her interrogation. See? And that's her signature at the bottom. Do you refute her statement? Don't you see her words?"

"I see the words, but they cannot be hers."

"Why not?"

"Sonya and I never had any conversations about the Komsomol."

"Whose words are these then, do you suppose?"

"They must be the words of her interrogator," I said.

"Oh!" He grabbed for his pen. "You are slandering our Soviet system of interrogation?" He scribbled an emphatic sentence or two about this on his interrogation pad.

Poor frightened Sonya, I thought. *Her interrogators must have terrified her so completely that she signed every false accusation they put before her.*

I discovered how true this was when they actually brought her in to face me. There, in the presence of the prosecutor and the interrogator, she had to listen as every one of her statements was read to her.

"Is this true?" the prosecutor asked after each one.

After each question, before she gave an answer, Sonya looked at me with eyes full of love, wishing to get some sign from me. Catching my puzzled expression or shrugged shoulders, she denied every one of the accusations.

The prosecutor realized that he was losing the case, so he and his team quickly changed their tactics. "So!" he growled. "It now appears that you have given us false testimony!"

She stared at him, agony in her eyes.

His voice hardened. "How about it, witness? Would you like to trade places with the accused?"

Scared, Sonya lowered her head. Avoiding my eyes, she said, "It's true."

"What is true?"

"What I said about how he didn't want me to join the Komsomol."

"Sonya," I said, "when did I ever tell you anything about the Komsomol?"

She looked at the prosecutor. "Well," she mumbled, "he never actually said this to me, but it was in one of his letters."

"How could I have written that in a letter?" I said. "All my letters were censored."

Suddenly the cross-examination was terminated. As I was being escorted from the room, I looked at Sonya, and tried to show her by my expression that I understood her difficult situation and held nothing against her. Since that day we have had no contact of any kind with each other.

As I look back on my trial, my severest mental torture had to do with how best to protect the pastor and church leader Grigoryev. In chapter 4 I mentioned that when I visited his Moscow church he warned me against Ivan the informer and how, when I returned home, I innocently repeated his warnings while the elderly Klanov (who turned out to be a spy) was present. Later, while interrogated during my father's investigation, I lied and said I didn't remember my conversation with Grigoryev.

And now, at my own trial, the prosecutor pounced on this topic.

"Did Pastor Grigoryev give you a warning about the man named Ivan, and did he warn you against informants in general?"

My choices were simple, but each was deadly.

I had always been trained to tell the truth, and if I testified that Pastor Grigoryev had indeed warned me about the secret agents, I would jeopardize the freedom of our beloved leader of the Adventist Church in the Soviet Union. If I told them that he had not made such statements, I would be lying, and my God-fearing parents had not raised me to be a liar. And in the Soviet legal system there was absolutely no option to refuse to answer. You answered yes, or you answered no, and that was that.

But refusing to answer was the course I decided I must take. I remained silent. *Lord, please deliver me from this dreadful trap,* I prayed. *What should I do? I know that Rahab lied to preserve the lives of the Israelite spies. But I don't want to lie.*

Naturally my silence did not sit well with the prosecution team, and cost me several sleepless nights of interrogation. In my soul I blamed myself for not being cautious to avoid my earlier lie. I even blamed other, wiser people in my life, those who had discovered how to be wisely cautious but had not taught me their principles.

It was at that point that I began to see new light in John's testimony about Jesus: "Many people saw the miraculous signs he was doing and believed in his name. But Jesus would not entrust himself to them, for he knew all men" (John 2:23, 24, NIV). The need of prudence, coupled with genuineness and truthfulness—the virtues presented by Jesus in the images of serpents and doves—became clear to me (see Matthew 10:16).

And then I decided to take a step beyond silence. After a deep struggle in my soul, and much time spent in prayer and reflection (and contrary to all my habits and inclinations), I put my refusal into speech.

"I will not answer this question," I told the interrogator.

I won't describe all the obscenities and threats that landed on my head when I said that. To tell these things would render this book unpublishable. Suffice it to say that I have brought to the Lord my request for forgiveness for my imprudence and wavering, and I pray that my bitter experience may serve as a warning to my brothers and sisters in Christ.

Those years were a sad and terrible time for people of conscience. Though international pressure had forced the open Soviet courts to begin recognizing certain human rights, prisoners like me were tried secretly, before the Special Board (the Russian acronym was OSO), a three-man committee of the People's Commissariat of Internal Affairs. Fortunately, these boards were abolished after Stalin's death in 1953. The open courts wouldn't have been convinced by the flimsy evidence by which I was convicted.

I learned of my sentence when they escorted me to the office of the chief warden. He nodded to a man in civilian clothing sitting next to him, who was evidently a representative of the OSO.

"What is your name?" the OSO agent asked in a callous, emotionless voice.

"Mikhail Petrovich Kulakov."

"By the decision of the Special Board, according to Article 58, parts 10 and 11, of the Criminal Code of the U.S.S.R., you are sentenced to five years in corrective hard-labor camps." He pushed a pen and a declaration-of-sentence form across the table toward me.

Immediately after I'd signed the paper, a startling thing happened. The chief warden gave a sympathetic sigh.

I glanced at him warily.

"Misha, Misha," he said, and there was emotion in his voice. "Young man, during your six months here you have behaved in such an exemplary way that you did not violate even one prison rule!"

Suddenly he found himself at the receiving end of a puzzled and ominous stare from the representative of the OSO. Perplexed, the warden quickly backtracked, and choked the sympathy out of his voice. "But alas," he continued firmly, "your God has betrayed you. During your years of wandering in the labor camps you will curse your father for making you a Christian."

With these words he called the guard and sent me back to my cell.

There sitting on my iron cot and recalling all that had happened during the past few minutes I could not help thinking about the rather strange behavior of the warden. *He's certainly had a year and a half to observe my dad's prayerful prison lifestyle,* I thought, *and he's seen how Stephen and I have behaved. I'm sure he knows that our only crime was witnessing about our Savior, and this must have impressed him. Maybe this impression wasn't as strong as that felt by the Philippian jailor, who converted immediately to Christianity after the earthquake. But nonetheless I clearly saw the deep emotions and spiritual struggle in the soul of my own jailor.*

Years later, after the Lord had sent a different kind of "earthquake" that released many people from the great jail of Soviet oppression, I personally met several of those jailors who now turned to us Christian believers with the same question: "Sirs, what must I do to be saved?"

But now I was bound for the camps in which I would be isolated from all relationships with the outside world except through the two censored letters I would be permitted to send each year. I would also learn by experience the well-known truth that "when a man becomes an animal, he's worse than an animal."

CHAPTER 7: Behind the Clouds—the Sun

I spent the first 18 months of my five-year term (1948 to 1953) in the corrective labor camp in Mordovia (about 400 miles east of Moscow). The remaining time I was rotated through several other camps in the Karaganda region of northern Kazakhstan.

"Corrective labor camp." I found myself smiling bitterly the more I heard that term. *How on earth,* I asked myself, *do the authorities think they'll "correct" anyone with this plan? If they're trying to "uplift" us so we'll become happy Soviet citizens, they're going about it in a strange way. What is the goal of these camps except to dehumanize us? "Well," the authorities might say, "you can't make an omelet without breaking eggs." That might work as a temporary salve to their consciences, but it doesn't do anything for the prisoners.*

And just as I began serving my term, the government implemented new and even harsher camp regulations. Each of us was assigned a number that was sewn into all of our clothing. We were totally isolated from the outside world except for the chance to mail two censored letters per year—and the stove in the censor's office was kept warm with the flames of incoming mail that he was too lazy to check. Daily we were marched out to do exhausting work, which was made even worse by our constant hunger and weariness.

Back in Latvia my mother learned where I was from the return address on my first letter. She began sending me small food packages from time to time. But even though the prison authorities didn't put a limit on food packages the way they did on letters, Mom simply couldn't spare much. Our country was reeling from the twin devastations of World War II and the socialist economic system, and in those years the majority of the population dragged out a miserable, half-starved existence. So it was a luxury for me to receive four or five small packages a year, each containing small amounts of onion and garlic, a pound of sugar, some oatmeal, and dried fruit. After the arrival of a package like that, for a few days I was delivered from the painful cramp of hunger.

One of Mom's letters brought ominous news about my brother Stephen, now in a labor camp near the Arctic Circle. "Your brother," she wrote, "is very ill."

In an earlier chapter I mentioned that when Dad was exiled to Siberia, Mom and Victor and I joined him, but there was no school for students that were Stephen's age. He'd been sent to live with my grandmother, whose home was in surroundings unfavorable for my brother's Christian upbringing.

A few years later Stephen joined the army, and for five World War II years he served as a frontline field engineer. Though almost 20 million Soviet soldiers and citizens died fighting fascism, he miraculously survived. There at the front he clearly sensed God's protecting hand, and turned his life over to Jesus. When he returned from military service in 1946, he was on fire for God—eager to speak about God and to share the gospel with everyone.

"Stephen, be careful," I continually warned him. "Dad is already in prison because of his witnessing, and you know how cautious he was."

"That's not going to stop me," Stephen said. "God's love is so real to me, I just can't keep it to myself. I'm just going to go ahead and openly speak to people about my Creator and my Savior."

"I admire your zeal, but watch out," I said. "Be as wise as a serpent and as—"

"Look, Misha," he told me flatly. "I'm a military officer. I think that my service to my country was appreciated. Haven't you seen all the medals I was awarded?"

"So?"

"So I believe I've earned the right to confess my faith in Jesus as frankly as I need to."

But as I described in a previous chapter, the government didn't see it that way, and the medal-laden Stephen and the medal-less Mikhail were arrested at the same time and with equal ruthlessness. And now came my mother's sad letter announcing his illness.

In March of 1953, after he'd finished his five-year term in a corrective-labor camp near the Far North city of Vorkuta, Stephen lost his health completely. He was transferred to a nearby settlement where he was to remain in eternal exile. Now that he'd been released from camp, Mom was permitted to see him. Only two months after her visit, at the young age of 32, my brother died a martyr's death and was buried in Vorkuta's frozen soil. His faith never wavered.

Who was guilty? I often asked myself. *Who was guilty of my brother's premature and painful end? Was it Klanov? Was it Ptakhina? Or some other spy just like them?*

It didn't really matter, after all. Neither Stephen nor I held bitterness toward those people. We knew the reality of the brutal system under which we all lived—and too often died.

In 1991, 38 years after my brother's death, the Soviet Union collapsed. A Presidential Commission on Exoneration was formed soon afterward, declaring innocent 4.5 million people, most of them posthumously. Though a pitifully tiny return for the tragedy and horror the prisons and camps had caused, this exoneration at least admitted that the former convict had been wrongly punished, and removed the stigma of "relatives of an enemy of the Soviet people" from his or her family. Exonerated people were also given the privilege of using the local public transportation system for free, and for some of them the government also helped them to provide a shelter over their heads.

Recently a group of Russian defenders of human rights laid a wreath on Stalin's grave near the Kremlin wall. To the wreath they attached a ribbon printed with the following ironic statement:

From the ones who were posthumously exonerated
To the one who was posthumously condemned.

For all of us who experienced the immorality and violence of that system, this was a good reminder that death itself does not deliver sinners and evildoers from the responsibility for their offenses. There is a righteous Judge, and we must all finally face His judgment.

Though I understood this, the fact is that to someone just into his 20s a five-year sentence is an eternity. Some days I felt as though the dismal camp routine would go on forever. The first thing in the morning armed guards counted us and then marched us away from the camp to our work assignments. At evening, when our work was over, we were counted and marched back to the camp; at the gate the guards counted us again and searched us. We were all nearly starved and infested with lice. I'll never forget the humiliating experience of being physically weakened by hunger and of having the uncontrollable urge to scratch myself.

One of my greatest hungers was for the Bible, which was denied me for the first year and a half of my sentence. But one day a parcel arrived from my mother. I was summoned to the censor's office, and stood by while he tore off the wrapper to examine the contents. There on top of the food packages perched a small, well-worn book. My heart stood still. It was a New Testament!

"What's this? A *Bible?*" the censor snarled. He grabbed the Testament's shabby cover and with one yank loosened its elderly binding, causing most of the pages to cascade all over the table. But to my delight, two of the pages glided across the table toward me and floated to the floor.

"Please, may I keep this book?" I asked, keeping my eyes on his face so that he wouldn't suspect what had just landed at my feet.

"It is not permitted!" he snapped, and swept up the tabletop pages into a little pile. As if by accident, I pushed some of the parcel's wrapping paper to the floor, covering the two precious pages that lay there. When he'd finished searching my package, he handed it to me. I bent down and retrieved the wrapping paper—with the two pages tucked securely underneath—and wrapped it around the parcel.

Once away from his office, it was all I could do to walk slowly. As I came near my barrack, I almost burst into a run, and once inside I removed the wrapping paper with trembling hands. There before me were two sacred pages from the Gospel of John. The first words I saw were part of Jesus' prayer to His followers: "Father, I want those you have given me to be with me where I am" (John 17:24, NIV).

I can't describe to you how I felt at that moment. My heart seemed about to explode. It was as though Jesus were including me in His prayer. "Misha," He seemed to say, "I don't enjoy seeing you held a prisoner in this dirty, stinky barrack. I want you to be with Me in My kingdom of goodness and love." That single beam of celestial light, reflecting from those hallowed pages, penetrated the barbed wire and the high fences of the labor camp and illuminated my life.

And there were actually some positive aspects to camp life. I learned the joy of sharing my faith with other inmates, and having a personal fellowship with God that might not have been possible on the outside.

"Mikhail," a fellow prisoner would often say, "I envy you."

"Envy me? Why?"

"Because of your faith in God."

I shrugged. "That is exactly what makes me feel that I am your debtor. From childhood my happiest privilege was to see God's image in the exemplary life of my kind parents, and to know and love His word. Even here in the gulag my anchor is the Bible."

And I wasn't speaking only of the two pages from the Gospel of John. Several times my resourceful mother tried to send me a New Testament, but each time the guards discovered it. Finally she devised a delightfully shrewd plan.

In one of her food packages she included a rather large sack of flour. Naturally the censor probed the sack from the outside and felt several hard objects. One by one he pulled out several fresh eggs, no doubt murmuring to himself, "Aha. What an ingenious mother this prisoner has, to send her son fresh eggs packed in flour!" Satisfied with his thorough search, he tied the sack shut again, not realizing that beneath the eggs, at the bottom of the sack, was a complete New Testament in German.

Now my question changed from "How can I get a Bible?" to "Where am I going to hide it?" My solution was to hide it in several different places. For a while I concealed it beneath a floorboard in the barracks. Then I slipped it under a false bottom in my painter's case. Other times I strapped it to one of my legs

77

or stuffed it into the top of one of my boots. When it was on my body I had to be very careful when leaving and entering the camp each day. But here too the Lord helped me. I noticed that some of the soldiers who searched us grew bored with their work and became quite careless. I simply stood in line for them, and avoided the diligent ones.

It's surprising what you could get away with if you knew how to get around the searchers. Of course, such knowledge doesn't come quickly. For me it came during the fourth year of my imprisonment. At one of the camps in northern Kazakhstan the other prisoners and I were marched to work at a brick factory, where I became friends with a man named Kirillov, one of the civilian employees. He was the bookkeeper, and his job was to keep track of how many bricks we produced.

We quickly learned that Kirillov deeply sympathized with our captivity, because he himself had been incarcerated for several years. So many prisoners began writing letters to their families, concealing them from the searchers and giving them to Kirillov to mail. He never refused them, even though he was risking his own freedom.

And this was how I became very useful to my fellow prisoners. Family and friends back home would have loved to have photographs of their dear ones, but of course no cameras were permitted. However, I'd gone to art school, and once the "Kirillov connection" was established, the other prisoners began asking me to make a pencil sketch or fine pen-and-ink or painted portrait of them to smuggle out. Kirillov was not only willing to mail these likenesses— he would even take them to town and get a photographer to make copies so that other relatives could see their loved ones' faces again. One prisoner— whom I had sketched in pencil—was so grateful that he gave me one of the photographic prints, which I've kept for more than 50 years.

I cherish the sweet memory of the noble Kirillov, who engaged in this dangerous game day after day. He gave me his home address so that my mother could send some books to me. When they arrived, he smuggled the books into the factory, and I was soon the happy possessor of the entire Bible and of two volumes of the *Testimonies for the Church* in German, a language Mom and Dad had encouraged me to learn so I could at least have access to Ellen White's books in that language.

Now that I had a Bible, I read it at every opportunity. Again and again I returned to the verses the Lord had directed me to a few days after my arrest in Latvia. I quote them here from the New International Version, except for the final three words, which I have italicized and which are translated directly from my Russian Bible:

"Praise our God, O peoples, let the sound of his praise be heard; he has preserved our lives and kept our feet from slipping. For you, O God, tested us; you refined us like silver. You brought us into prison and laid burdens on our backs. You let men ride over our heads; we went through fire and water, but you" *set us free* (Psalm 66:8-12, NIV).

Heavenly Father, I prayed, *I'm lying in a bunk in a labor camp barracks. Men are stacked above me and below me and around me. How will You set me free? Our Soviet system seems so immovable, so unchangeable. How will You bring the light of the gospel to our nation? I don't know how You'll do it, but I know You must have a way.*

One might think that a labor camp would be an easy place for me to share with others my hope and belief in God and His promises. But it wasn't. We were all oppressed and humiliated, discouraged and hungry. Hope was hard to come by. I did find a few friends who were interested in spiritual things, and I could tell that some were moving toward accepting Christ.

Sadly, I met bitter Christians as well, including one man whom I'll call Ivan, who had joined an Adventist offshoot movement. I felt great sorrow for him, because not only was he very critical of mainline Seventh-day Adventism, but he was also a very unhappy person. He'd been deceived by those who'd deceived themselves. Nevertheless, we met together several times and discussed our experiences.

But Heaven's amazing power occasionally broke through. One Sabbath while walking between two barracks, I saw Ivan and another man I didn't know sitting and talking together.

"Mikhail," Ivan greeted me. "Meet my friend Nicolai. He's just arrived in camp."

Nicolai and I shook hands. He looked as though he were about my age. "Nice to meet you," I said.

After a glance around to make sure no one else could hear, Ivan said to me, "Got anything to read on you?"

I glanced at Nicolai. He looked trustworthy. "Sure," I said, reaching into my pocket. "The New Testament my mother sent me."

"Read something," Ivan insisted.

Keeping the book close to my chest, I read a chapter in a low voice, translating from the German. Glancing at Nicolai from time to time, I noticed that he was staring intently at me. When I finished the chapter, I closed the book and slipped it into my pocket, not wanting to be seen by a guard who might be strolling by.

"Please continue." Nicolai's voice was low and insistent. "Read some more. Please?"

Startled, I glanced at him again. *Is this guy for real?* I wondered. *I don't usually meet up with such a thirst for the Word of God.* "Sure," I said, and pulled out the book, opened it, and continued to read.

I didn't see Nicolai again for some time. Knowing Ivan as well as I did, I suspected him of filling Nicolai full of many untruths about my church, and of trying to prevent any further contact between us. But several weeks later Nicolai and I were part of a group of prisoners that was taken to another camp. Ivan, along with his negative influence on the young man, was left behind.

The new camp was a pleasant change of pace for me because, for a while, I didn't have to do the backbreaking work I'd done in the previous location. The doctor in charge of the camp hospital, also a prisoner, learned of my artistic abilities and gave me the job of decorating the clinic with attractive and informative signs. I worked in that hospital for a couple of weeks, and had no problem getting Sabbaths off. The doctor, who was Jewish, understood and didn't object.

The second Sabbath at camp I ran across Nicolai. When he saw me, his face broke into a huge smile.

"Nicolai," I said. "What happened? You look so happy today!"

"Of course I'm happy," he said. "Let me tell you what happened. Today I refused to go on work detail, and they threw me into a punishment cell. The camp commander himself interrogated me, and I said, 'If you'll let me have Saturdays off, I'll do double work on Sunday.' He gave me a strange look, and said, 'If that's what you really want, go ahead and take today off.' So a couple of minutes ago they turned me loose!"

My mouth dropped open. "Nicolai," I said, "you're not telling me that you decided to celebrate the *Sabbath*?"

"Yes!" His smile widened even further.

"Then you are my brother," I cried, and threw my arms around him. "Today we can celebrate the Sabbath together!"

It was on that very Sabbath that he told me the amazing story that would later strengthen and encourage me in my own struggles.

Just two or three months before, Nicolai had been more than 1,000 miles away in a prison camp in the Krasnoyarsk region, cutting trees in Siberia's deep forests. He was deeply religious—that was the first thing I'd noticed in my new friend—and had been raised in the Uniate Church, an Eastern Christian church that acknowledges the pope's supremacy but retains its own distinctive spiritual, liturgical, and canonical traditions.

"I was taught never to work on the church's festival days," he told me. "But this summer when a festival day arrived, the guards forced me to march out to the forest with the rest of the prisoners. They pointed out the tree I was to fell.

"At that moment a heavy rainsquall came through, so the other prisoners hurried over and huddled under another tree. But I knelt beside the tree assigned to me. My sinfulness deeply pained me, and I prayed, 'God, please, please forgive me! When I am free from prison, I will never again do any work on any of the church festival days!' "

Nicolai told me that suddenly he was surrounded by a bright light. Thunderstruck, he saw that an angel had appeared and was flying near him. Using the young man's Ukrainian language, the angel said, "The holy day of the Lord is Sabbath."

Both the light and the angel vanished. Nicolai remained on his knees for a few moments, absolutely stunned. Then he scrambled to his feet and ran over to the other prisoners and told them what he'd just seen and heard.

"From the look on my face," Nicolai told me, "the others could tell that something amazing had happened, but they didn't know what to say. They simply shrugged their shoulders and glanced at each other."

I can't say enough how Nicolai's story encouraged me. And as we studied together during the next few months I was able to build up his faith in other ways, including sharing the three angels' messages which had been entrusted to our church.

My hospital sign-painting job was soon over, and I had to go to work in the brick factory near camp. But Nicolai was my coworker and the sharer of my travails. His Sabbath privileges were short-lived, and now every seventh day we had to struggle for time off to observe God's holy day. As I think back on those days, I thank the Lord for sending me someone whose genuine faith and dedication were such a blessing at that difficult time.

More than 50 years later I still remember a particularly ironic moment. It was Sabbath, and the guards were hunting through the camp for those who refused to work. Somehow they failed to locate Nicolai, but when they found me, they handcuffed my hands behind my back and ordered me to sit on the ground. As I sat there, the cuffs biting into my wrists, the camp loudspeaker began to play a well-known Communist patriotic song:

How wide and beautiful is our land
Where everyone can breathe so freely . . .

What a paradox, hearing those words while sitting handcuffed!

As I'm writing this, in 2007, Nicolai and his faithful and exemplary Adventist family live in the city of Vinnitsa, Ukraine. During a 2004 evangelistic crusade held by Pastor Mark Finley in Kiev, Nicolai shared this story of how the Lord had graciously opened the Sabbath truth to him.

CHAPTER 8: Man's Inhumanity to Man

One of the grim results of a political system that first teaches you that there is no God and then arbitrarily imprisons you is the ghastly despair that you feel. As a Christian I myself could look beyond the barbed wire to a glorious earth made new, but my atheist friends felt no such assurance of a loving God. Some prisoners committed suicide; others tried—often unsuccessfully—to escape.

One night during a severe winter blizzard, when the snowdrifts reached the top of the fence surrounding the camp, two of my friends tried to make a break for it. An alert guard, staring through the whipping snowflakes, thought he saw movement beyond the camp and sounded the alarm. All the prisoners were awakened and counted. My two friends were nowhere to be found. The commander sent out squads of soldiers with dogs, and after a 25-mile trek the two were eventually tracked down. After being viciously beaten, they were handcuffed and marched back to the camp. Since they could not put their hands in their pockets, their hands froze. A few days later the blackened limbs had to be amputated.

If only these men had waited a little longer! A month later the cruel dictator Stalin was dead, and though the average prisoner's camp routine remained the same for a while, nevertheless many hearts sensed a gleam of hope that somehow things eventually might change for the better. To this day, from the depths of my heart, I regret that I was unable to convince my two friends of the gospel's beauty. Or maybe they actually did see my witness about a God who hadn't forgotten us and who in due time would rescue us from bondage, and simply chose to ignore it. They gave me no sign either way.

But my faith did have an effect on others. My own prison term was coming to a close, and many other prisoners knew this. One day a man approached me in my barracks.

"Come outside with me," he said. "So no one can hear us."

Once outdoors, he fixed his eyes on me with a serious expression. "I know that you are about to be released," he said. "I also know that you are a Christian. I have a special request for you."

"I will fulfill that request if it is possible," I told him.

"I worked as an engineer in Moscow," he said, "and my family is still living there. My sentence is a long one, and I have no idea when—or even if—I will ever be reunited with my loved ones. So I want to ask you to do me a great favor. When you are released from this place, please go to a church and pray for my dear wife and children."

I blinked rapidly to keep away the tears. "I will do that, by all means." *Heavenly Father*, I prayed, *please give me just the words I need, right now, to comfort this man's needy soul.*

While I was pondering what to say, the man reached into his pocket and brought out a spoon.

"I want you to have this," he said. "You may need it in your new life outside, and it may remind you of my request."

"I will certainly do this," I said. "I respect your belief that it is important to pray within a church. But I have good news for you. I have read the Bible from one end to the other, and I have found that Jesus never said that prayers will be answered only if made in certain places. On the contrary, He specifically said that prayers in private will reach the heart of God."

He stared at me, a ray of hope in his eyes. "That is true?"

"It is," I assured him. "May I pray for you right now?"

"Here?" He glanced fearfully around to see if any guards were watching.

I took his hands in mine and started to pray, mentioning both him and his family. He began to sob, and I could feel the shudders of grief through his hands. May the Lord help each of us to remember to always pray for those who are suffering around us, and for our reunion in the great family of God's children.

One of the most chilling aspects of Soviet Communism under Stalin was that it was no respecter of persons. One day, while I was serving in the Dubravlag camp in Mordovia, I happened to watch as a new group of prisoners arrived. Among them was a man whose face seemed very familiar.

That looks like Leonid Sobinov, the world-famous operatic tenor, I thought. *But it can't be. Sobinov is dead.*

I walked up to the handsome middle-aged man. "Excuse me," I said, "is your name Sobinov?"

He glanced at me, and paused. "Yes," he finally said. "I am Boris Sobinov."

"You're Leonid's son?"

"I am."

"I can't believe that I am actually speaking with Boris Sobinov," I said. "Your father was known as the Pride of Russia. You and he performed concerts together all across the country. Your own abilities as a virtuoso pianist and composer are legendary. It is a privilege to meet you."

I wanted so badly to ask him the question "But why are you *here?*"

For some reason this gifted musician took a liking to me, and we became very close. One day he told me his tragic story. In 1917, after the Bolshevik revolution, several army officers loyal to the czar emigrated abroad, taking with them their young regimental musician, Boris Leonidovich Sobinov, then age 22 or 23. He wound up in Berlin, completed his musical education, and in the course of time rose to a professorship in the Berlin Conservatory. He and his wife had no children, so they dedicated themselves fully to music, even as World War II raged around them.

"Though I lived in Germany," he told me, "I always remained a Russian patriot. I rejoiced when the Soviets and the Allies defeated the Nazis. And when the Soviet troops entered Berlin, I greeted our liberators with outstretched arms. I befriended many of the officers, and cordially entertained them in my luxurious apartment. I took them around town to see the beautiful buildings and other sites that weren't destroyed by the bombing."

Suddenly this camaraderie came to an abrupt end. Someone high in the Soviet authority made a senseless, arbitrary, brutal decision, and one day some of Boris' officer friends knocked at his apartment door.

"Please step outside," one said.

Boris joined them outside the door. "What's going on?"

"Boris Leonidovich," one of the officers replied, "even though personally we deeply respect you, we have been ordered to place you under arrest."

Only someone like me—who'd seen this sort of thing happen repeatedly—could even begin to understand the shock of this monstrous injustice. To Boris Sobinov it was absolutely baffling.

"But why?" he stuttered. "What have I done?"

"Please come with us."

Immediately after his arrest Boris was transported back to Russia, charged with counterrevolutionary activity, and sentenced to 10 years in the camps. Imagine a sensitive musician, his mind filled with unwritten symphonies, his fingers trembling with unplayed piano concerti, sitting near an open-flame stove in Belorussia, scraping lice from his body by the handful and throwing them into the fire.

Our daily duties at Dubravlag consisted of being marched under escort to fell trees in the forest or do miscellaneous agricultural work. It pained me to watch this man's physical and mental suffering.

"I am wondering, Boris Leonidovich," I said to him one day after screwing up my courage, "if I might be permitted to ask whether you believe in God."

He shook his head. "I've always had very little in common with religion. In Germany people would ask me, 'Are you Lutheran or are you Catholic?' I would always answer, 'I'm a musician.' "

Indeed, Boris Sobinov lived by, and for, his music. Having reached dizzying heights of success as a pianist, he now considered the camp's lack of a musical instrument more agonizing than the gloomy atmosphere or heavy labor.

But one day I saw a brand-new, electrified Boris. It was as if he'd been resurrected from the dead.

"I have just heard from Cultural Development Director Devetaykin!" he told me.

At this point I should probably respond to what must be the highly raised eyebrows of many of my readers. "A cultural development center in a *Soviet labor camp?*" some might be asking.

But it's true. Many of the Stalinist camps did maintain cultural education departments, a way in which their commanders could pay lip service to the idea of reeducating incarcerated people. And Mr. Devetaykin did indeed head that department in our camp. He was responsible for providing the camp with certain Communist newspapers. (A few copies were available on a table in a small room in one of the barracks.) He was also charged with controlling and guiding us "in the proper course of Communist education," which meant that he supervised each of the prisoners' attempts to entertain themselves with music, folk songs, or poetry. In reality it was another form of depersonalization.

Startled at Boris' change of mood, I asked, "And what did Director Devetaykin say?"

"I understand from him," Boris told me in a trembling voice, "that we are to receive a piano one day soon!"

The thought of finally being able to play the piano again affected my friend deeply. He continually paced the barracks floor, wringing his hands, massaging his fingers, wondering if they were still able to play. On his face was a mixture of both happiness and concern. Day after day he waited for the good news.

But the piano never came. It seems that Director Devetaykin, instead of delivering the piano to the camp, decided to take it to his own house. Boris Sobinov was crushed.

A short time later he and some other prisoners were marched off to a work detail outside the zone. In the evening they returned, and only then did I learn that their assignment had been to scoop out the contents of the outdoor latrine pits used by the guards. It was terrible to see the expression on the face of the former Berlin Conservatory professor. He seemed utterly destroyed, crushed by the humiliation he'd had to endure.

At this point his personality changed. Usually polite and amiable, he now began to use profanity. It might be surprising for my readers to know that normally, even in the labor camps, only the most hardened cynics cursed or used filthy language in the presence of believers. Knowing I was a Christian, prisoners who slipped and used foul language normally apologized.

Boris noticed that I was astonished and saddened by the change in him, and this made him uncomfortable. One day, probably out of a desperate need to open his heart to someone, he told me in a trembling voice, "Just look! Look what they have made out of me! They have no respect for people! They have no respect for history, or culture! They have no respect even for *themselves!*"

Then, as though he wanted to justify his personality change—or maybe quiet his conscience—he told me about his youth.

"When I was a boy I had a violent nature and a very quick temper," he said. "If someone angered me, I grabbed whatever was nearby, even an expensive dish, and smashed it against the floor. But over time my wife helped change me. She is a very mellow, self-controlled, sober-minded woman, and whenever I gave way to an outburst of irritation or anger in her presence, she never responded in kind. Instead she simply looked at me with her gentle and understanding eyes, and this calmed me down and composed me. But now," he growled, "my former bad nature is returning."

He and I soon were separated, never to see each other again. For years I did not know where and how his tragic life ended, but I recently learned that Boris Leonidovich Subinov was finally "exonerated" and released from prison in 1955, a year before his death from cancer. I often think of him with sadness. How many intelligent, serious people miss the opportunity to respond to God's call and accept the gift of His grace, which is able to change our sinful nature and lead us to victory over self.

Soon I was on the move again. I and several hundred other prisoners, mostly young people, were herded into railway freight cars and transported from Dubravlag to a camp called Peschlag in northern Kazakhstan. Each car had two levels of plank beds, a small barrel with drinking water (everybody drank from the same mug), and a large barrel for physical needs. Once or twice a day the train would stop, and two of us—accompanied by guards—had to carry the barrel to a runoff ditch and dump its contents. During the stops the guards gave us each a chunk of bread and a small piece of salty fish, and then herded us first to one end of the car and then the other, while they banged on the car walls with big wooden hammers to make sure we hadn't created escape hatches.

We eventually arrived at a transit camp, where we waited for a few days while—I presume—they were preparing the necessary documents to send us to one of the many camps in that region. It was winter, and bitterly cold. Coal furnaces kept the barracks warm, but each was so overcrowded—and so filled with stench from the urine barrel—that I frequently had to walk outside in order to get a gulp of fresh air. One thing the guards couldn't hide from us was the cloudless night sky, and as I walked among the barracks I gazed upward at the blazing stars.

Heavenly Father, I prayed, *You see everything, You know everything, and You overrule all evil to the eternal good of those who trust You. You have a plan for my life.*

Always, after praying that prayer, I felt stronger. I would hurry back inside, not only because promptly at 9:00 p.m. the guards locked us in, but also because I was hoping to get a place on one of the plank beds. More than 200 prisoners were crowded into that one building, and if you dallied you'd end up lying on the cold earth floor.

But even if you were one of the lucky ones who got to sleep on the planks, it was incredibly crowded. We lay on our sides, fitted together like spoons, doomed to lie on the same side all night because if we wanted to turn over, everybody else on the plank would have to turn too. Added to this was another torture—the planks were too short. There was no way I could curl up my legs so my feet didn't have to dangle over the edge. I have remembered that nightly torment all through my life.

Finally our papers were ready, and one day—it was January of 1951—the guards, armed with rifles, arrived outside the barracks.

"Gather your belongings!" they shouted. "We are taking you to your new camp!"

Carrying our bundles, we straggled outside into the snow.

"Your new camp is 10 miles away," a guard bellowed. "We must be there by sunset. Get going! Run!"

"They're crazy," somebody muttered in a low voice. "They're not going to make us run the whole way."

But they did. And finally at twilight we staggered into our new camp area. Dimly, through weariness and sweat, I saw a few brand-new barracks. I selected one, and hurried inside out of the cold. Once we were all indoors, the guards immediately locked us in. Overstrained and sweaty from having to run while carrying our personal belongings—and from the salty fish we'd been given before that horrendous marathon began—we had just one thing on our minds: water. We searched through every corner of that barracks but found only a slop bucket with a bit of mysterious moisture in it. I was so thirsty that I actually moistened my lips with that fluid before collapsing to sleep on a plank bunk, dead to the world.

"Up! Up!" roared the voices of the guards, and I realized it was morning.

Our first job was to get our new barracks ready for occupancy. There was no running water. In fact, the water supply would be a continual problem all the time we were there. Somebody finally thought of bringing in buckets of snow and melting them near the furnace. By noon bread and cereal had arrived, and gradually we all settled into camp life routine. A week later our *banya* (bathhouse) opened, where we were allowed to wash ourselves once every 10 days. But each person received only a basin—and sometimes a half basin—of water. It doesn't take much imagination to guess how thorough our washing was.

Nights were a bit easier. We still had plank beds, but now they were two-level bunk beds for four people, two below and two above. Mattresses and pillows were both stuffed with straw, which was replenished from time to time.

We spent the rest of that winter building other new barracks. This was discouraging work. For one thing, we weren't working on worthwhile projects such as bridges or roads, but simply erecting more dwellings for future prisoners as hopeless as we were. But even more discouraging were our working conditions. Several winter months had frozen the ground, yet we had to dig holes for the new barracks' foundation posts, and our only tools were crowbars, picks, and spades. These implements rebounded off the soil as though it were metal, and each blow chipped away only tiny particles.

"Let's build a fire on top of where we have to dig," someone suggested. "Maybe that will soften the ground."

So we gathered a pile of sticks, lit it, and waited patiently while the wood flamed up and then became embers. Brushing the coals aside, we started hacking again.

"There is no difference," one of the hackers groaned. "It's still as hard as ever."

One such discouraging day I noticed another prisoner, who seemed to be about 40, behaving strangely. His face wore a look of grim despair, and he was slamming the earth with his crowbar as hard and as rapidly as he could. Though coughing and choking uncontrollably, he still kept hacking away.

"Hold on," I called to him. "You're going to kill yourself."

He glared at me. "Exactly," he growled. "That's what I'm trying to do— overstrain my heart. If I don't die, maybe they'll put me in a hospital. Maybe I'll get disabled, and they'll release me from this work."

By now there was only a short time before my own imprisonment would end. Yet tragedy and testing still lay ahead.

CHAPTER 9

We Have Nothing to Lose

Camp life got a little easier when summer came. Not only was the weather warmer, but we no longer had to stay inside the camp compound 24 hours a day. Every morning the guards shouted us up, counted us, and marched us a mile to a self-contained brick factory. Surrounded securely by barbed wire, this huge plant contained an open brick-earth mine, along with a molding shop, drying chambers, and firing furnaces. Three shifts of 200 prisoners each labored in the plant, the night shift made up of women from a nearby female labor camp. (It was comical—and sometimes tragic—during shift change to watch the men and women trying to signal each other with eye, gesture, or voice contact.)

One of my fellow brickmakers was a young man named Anatoly. He was one of several young adults who had grown up in Moscow. They were the golden youth—children of high-ranking Soviet government and Communist Party members. But Anatoly stood out still more distinctly from the others in that privileged class. His face showed a kind of inherent nobleness that the others' didn't.

Could it be that he is a believer? I wondered. But after a bit of careful conversation I found that he didn't share my religious views. To be more exact, they didn't interest him.

And I know why, I thought to myself with a sigh. *My country is so immersed in its militant godlessness that if you weren't born into a family with strong religious traditions—or if your suffering hadn't driven you to seek faith in something beyond yourself—what hope did you have?*

But Anatoly had a large and noble heart. "Your Christianity has no appeal to me," he once told me, "but you have the right to believe the way you want." And when other young men made fun of my faith in God, he always stood up for me.

Anatoly didn't talk much about himself. But gradually, mostly from others who knew him, I pieced together a little of his story.

"What did Anatoly do back in Moscow?" I asked a friend of his. "He looks and talks like one of the intelligentsia."

The friend grinned. "He was an ordinary factory worker."

"Really?" I shook my head in disbelief. "With his connections? With his high-ranking parents?"

"I'm telling you the truth. Anatoly's mom and dad belong to a small number of party members who really believe in the ideals of Communism." The friend chuckled. "Believe it or not, there are such people. These 'true believers' look around them, and they see all the corruption in the Stalinist government. And they refuse to use their own high position to benefit themselves or their families."

He nodded toward Anatoly, who stood talking with a group some distance away. "His father could have made just one phone call, or asked for a recommendation from an influential friend, and Anatoly would have had a tuition-free education in Moscow's most prestigious university. But no, Mom and Dad were true Communists, and they told him to earn his living honestly.

"And here's another strange thing," the friend continued. "You know that his mother is a high-ranking member of the Communist Party's Central Committee, right? You didn't? Well, she is. Yet she's having just as hard a time as your own mother trying to get food to her son."

"Why?" I asked. "My own mom is nearly starving, but surely Anatoly's mother has plenty of food."

"Yeah, but she's got to be careful," he said. "Remember, her son is an 'enemy of the Soviet people.' She has to show her faith in the Soviet judicial system, or they might come and imprison one of her other children too."

I didn't realize at the time that the KGB, with Stalin's approval, didn't spare even the relatives of the people closest to him. Mikhail Kalinin, president of the Soviet Union, watched helplessly as his own wife was accused of anti-Soviet propaganda and imprisoned.

So when Anatoly and I received packages from home, we always shared with each other. Once my mother sent me a little pouch of pearl barley, and I took it along with me to the brick camp the next day. During lunch Anatoly and I found a tin bucket, put some water in it, and boiled that barley on top of a coal stove. We had brought spoons with us from camp, and even though we had no salt or other flavoring, we devoured the barley, scraping every bit of it from the bucket's bottom.

One morning a little later in the summer we had started our usual mile-long hike to the brick plant. The guards, rifles at the ready, were barking their usual orders: "Don't run ahead! Don't remain behind! A step to the right, a step to the left, is considered an escape! We'll shoot without warning!"

As we hurried along, Anatoly maneuvered himself close to me. "Misha," he said in a low voice.

"What?"

"I'm going to make a break for it today."

I jerked my head around so quickly that my neck hurt. "You're going to *what?*"

His voice became a delicate whisper. "I'm going to escape. With some of the other guys."

"What are you talking about?" I hissed. "*Nobody* escapes. You know that. And if you did get away, where would you go? How could you possibly hide from the KGB?"

Anatoly shrugged, and then with a touch of irony in his voice he quoted a famous line from Karl Marx's *Communist Manifesto:* " 'We have nothing to lose but our chains.' "

Surely he's got to be kidding, I thought. *It's preposterous. He knows that. The whole idea is so impossible that I can't even wrap my mind around it. It's simply prisoner braggadocio,* I decided, *or at any rate wishful thinking.*

I was wrong.

A half hour later, I was at the molding shop collecting raw bricks. Suddenly I heard gunshots.

"Everybody! Stop your work!" the guards bellowed. "Get into formation immediately!" As we hurried to the waiting area, we heard the same orders shouted all over the plant grounds.

As our group got larger the muttering grew louder, because several eyewitnesses had arrived and were telling the story. Each day dump trucks were loaded with brick and taken out through the camp gates. But while still empty, the trucks were parked some distance away within the brick plant, far from the guards. It might seem puzzling why the empty trucks weren't guarded, but the security focus was on the possibility of prisoners escaping underneath a load of bricks once the trucks were loaded. The guards took careful precautions, including looking underneath the truck body, and thrusting metal rods down between the bricks, to prevent this from happening.

After all the eyewitness accounts had been sorted out and compared, here's the story that emerged. Four prisoners were in on the plot—Anatoly plus three friends. They had evidently carefully planned every move from every possible angle, and discovered the one weakness: the lightly guarded empty trucks. On this day it happened that several trucks arrived at once. Anatoly and his friends chose the biggest and newest-looking of the trucks, and rushed it before it was loaded. Pulling the driver out, they trampled him into submission. The three other men leaped into the cab, and Anatoly scrambled up the side of the truck and into the empty box.

The prisoner who took the wheel was an experienced driver, and he slammed the engine into gear and raced toward the closed gates. A wooden locking-bar gave way, the gates wobbled open, and the truck roared onward, swerving to avoid a heavier metal bar and almost killing a guard, who leaped aside just in time.

By now the guards had recovered from the surprise, and began firing at the escaping truck, which was heading at top speed back along the road toward the city of Karaganda, which passed very close to our prison camp. The guards stationed in the camp's watchtowers had heard the distant shots, so when they spotted the approaching dump truck—going much faster than dump trucks usually go—they correctly assumed that an escape was happening, and opened fire.

They needn't have wasted their ammunition. The crash against the first gate had punctured the truck's radiator. The water began to leak out, and by the time the truck reached the camp its engine oil had overheated. And just as the hail of gunfire from the towers reached the truck, the pistons froze for lack of lubrication, and the truck shuddered to a stop.

The three men in the cab scrambled out on the side opposite the gunfire. "Anatoly! Jump!" they shouted up at the truck box. "We can still make it!"

There was no answer.

"Anatoly! Hurry!"

No answer.

One of the men grabbed the side of the box with both hands, and pulled himself up to look. Anatoly lay sprawled on the bottom of the box, terribly wounded by the bullets from the tall towers. He'd had no place to hide.

"Come on!" his friend screamed. "We'll carry you!"

Anatoly shook his head.

"We're not leaving without you!"

"I'm dying," Anatoly said weakly. "Go."

With a final despairing glance at his comrade, the friend lowered himself to the road. He and the two others jumped the ditch and began to run across the field. But by this time the guards were pouring out of the camp. Most of them pursued the prisoners, who were soon caught, handcuffed, brought back to the camp, and thrown into the punishment cell, but several ascended the truck box and dragged the dying Anatoly down onto the road. There they took this opportunity to brutally express how they felt about this "enemy of the people," beating and kicking him mercilessly.

Eventually we prisoners were marched from the brickyard back to camp.

"Anatoly's dead," somebody told me when we arrived. "The guards are going to force us to bury him ourselves."

It would be my very first funeral.

My friend's body was riddled with bullets, and his clothes were dreadfully bloodstained. When I removed his shirt, I was shocked to see that his body was covered with bruises from the guards' angry kicks and blows.

Somebody in the camp made a coffin, and after I'd dressed him in better clothes from his suitcase, we placed Anatoly inside. Then I had an idea.

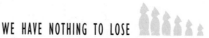

"Find me a piece of tin," I said to one of Anatoly's acquaintances.

"Why?"

"I want to put his name on it," I said. "His mother might want to bury him somewhere else."

When the tin was brought, I took a hammer and nail and tapped out Anatoly's full name into the metal with little indentations, then nailed the tin to the coffin lid. We loaded the coffin onto a horse-drawn cart, and several of us—escorted vigilantly by guards—followed the cart away from the camp zone, where we dug a grave in a patch of tough soil.

Anatoly's death stunned and depressed us all, and it wasn't until several days later that I suddenly thought of his mother. I've already mentioned that even though she was a high-ranking Communist, she was shown absolutely no favoritism. I suspected that the camp commanders would simply not inform her that her son had been killed, and that still higher-ranking authorities might have even more reason to keep this tragedy swept under the rug.

I must get a message to her, I decided. *But maybe I should try to soften the blow.* Naturally I need to bypass the camp censors somehow. So I wrote a postcard that said something like "Your son is very ill," and finally managed to smuggle it out through the kindness of a civilian brick plant worker. I intended to follow that up with another card gradually revealing more of the truth, but it's been so long ago that I honestly do not remember whether I did this.

93

CHAPTER 10

A Lovely Surprise for an Exile

I've always found it interesting that my five-year prison camp sentence ended the same month as did the life of Joseph Stalin. On March 5, 1953, Stalin died, and on March 18, along with other prisoners whose term had ended at that time, I exchanged camp life for "eternal banishment." My destination was to be the remote fishing village of Mirsikul in the Kustanai region of northern Kazakhstan. This was western Siberia, where the winter cold is severe and the population sparse.

It was a warm spring day when, after several stops at transit prisons along the way, I was told to climb into the box of an old and shabbily painted truck along with other former convicts, both men and women. Now we were free. No soldiers stood over us with guns. Instead they were riding in the cab with the driver. We were "freely" sitting on the bare floor of the truck box, and "freely" bouncing up and down and against each other along the 50 miles of road that ran across a boundless steppe of northern Kazakhstan.

Finally we arrived at Mirsikul, a settlement consisting of a few small wattle-and-daub houses and two or three clay-and-manure-plastered barracks, each with several apartments. This village was so small that it didn't even have an office for its commandant, so one of the soldiers ordered us to remain beside the truck while the other ran to hunt for that representative of the Soviet power.

Soon the soldier was back, accompanied by a short man whose dark-brown face and distinctive bearing showed us that we were going to be under the control of a member of the very friendly and hospitable Kazakhi nation. I later learned that if our arriving prisoner party hadn't been so large, he would have invited us to his own home for a tea party.

But even though at this point I didn't yet know about this hospitable practice, I could see the conflicting emotions in his face. As a man of Eastern culture, he would have liked to welcome us not only as his guests but also his future neighbors. However, his official position obliged him to keep some distance from us—and gave him a feeling of slight superiority.

So rather than take us indoors, he received us in the open, right there beside the truck. The soldier presented him with the covering letters and documents for each of us, and using Eastern politeness and diplomacy (and avoiding any offensive threats such as we'd been used to in the camps), the commandant made a short official statement that went something like this:

"According to Article So-and-so of the Criminal Code of the U.S.S.R. you are sentenced to lifelong banishment to this place. Any attempt to escape from here will be punished with 25 years' penal servitude."

Then he simply added, "On the fifteenth of each month you must come to my home in order to mark your presence here. Now you will each sign one of these papers. It contains your sentence, and your signature will be proof that you know and understand it." He held the folder with the papers in his hands, and one by one he asked us to approach. One after another we came up to him and signed away our freedom.

As I think back on that scene, with one human being holding such unquestioned sway over other human beings, I remember an anecdote that—while actually a bitterly ironic Russian joke—shows how if one lives in a society deprived of the knowledge of God, one can truly lose any sense of personal worth and dignity.

The joke went like this.

"One day in a Soviet collective agricultural farm, the party boss called a meeting of the workers. 'You farmers have failed to fulfill the state plan of agricultural production,' he told them in a loud voice. 'For this treason against the state you are condemned to execution by hanging. Do you understand this?'

"Everybody was compliantly silent. Nobody protested.

" 'Any questions?' the party boss asked.

"A farmer raised his hand.

" 'Well?' the boss barked. 'What is still not clear to you?'

" 'I understand the reason we'll be hanged,' the farmer replied. 'No problem there. My only question is about the ropes. Do we bring our own, or will they be provided?' "

As I waited for my turn to sign the sentence paper, I couldn't help staring around me. *There is no natural beauty in this place,* I thought despairingly. *No trees. Not even any bushes. The only reason anybody settles here at all is that big lake that has some fish in it.*

There was also an agricultural collective farm, and it was here I was assigned to work. But God provided some bright spots for me. Almost immediately one of the villagers introduced himself.

"My name is Behnke," he said with a thick German accent. "I'm a fisherman, and an exile like you. My family and I would like to invite you to stay with us."

Touched by his kindness, I immediately said yes, and he took me home with him. He and his wife and their five children lived in one of the village's wattle-and-daub homes, a small two-room dwelling with floors made of a mixture of clay and manure. I happened to let slip a few German words, and Behnke and his wife were overjoyed.

"You are an educated man?" my host asked.

I nodded.

"My wife and I have had no formal education," he said wistfully. "And therefore my children do not know how to read the language of my forefathers."

"In return for your kindness in giving me a place to stay," I said, "I would be happy to teach them German."

I was assigned a corner in one of the rooms, which was also used as the dining room and the children's sleeping area. At night I went fishing with my new friend, and by day I worked at the farm, in an agricultural machinery workshop. The shop foreman took a liking to me.

"You will do repair work on combines," he told me.

"I have no knowledge of mechanics," I said apologetically.

"That is no problem. I will show you how."

Kind as he was, this work definitely wasn't in my line, and I'm certain I was more trouble than help to him. *Why did he choose me for this duty?* I often wondered. Later he answered my silent question when he told me in private, "When I first saw you, I said to myself, 'I'd better take this young man under my wing.' " I can only conclude that the Lord caused him to feel that way.

It staggered me to think that this tiny village was where I would spend the rest of my life. As I've mentioned, my work was boring, and the landscape around the village was like a desert. But what depressed me most was the lack of people I could communicate with on a spiritual level. Most of the population was Kazakh, a Muslim people whose language I did not speak.

Heavenly Father, I often prayed in the tiny attic of the Behnkes' home, *I'm 26 years old. Is this what You have planned for me—permanent exile in this distant outpost? Lord, I'm so lonely.*

There on my knees, feeling like the prophet Elijah pursued by Jezebel, I told God, *I've had enough. Take my life.* Though I never entertained thoughts of suicide, it did seem that death would be the only escape from that miserable existence.

Then one day I received a parcel from my mother. I took great joy in being able to open it myself, all alone, and not under the eye of a censor. My joy doubled when I saw that the package contained a Bible. I could now read this Bible openly! If you've never been forced to read the Bible in secret and hide its presence from others, you can't possibly understand how much I enjoyed my new liberty.

And how the Lord comforted me and spoke to me through that Book. I'll never forget one Sabbath day. I was sitting near the lake reading the Gospel of

ABOVE: My grandfather Stephan Victorovich Kulakov served in Russia's first Duma (parliament). This photo is from the small book a woman attending my father's trial handed my mother during a break in the proceedings.

ABOVE: My wife's uncle Pavel Pilkh and his wife, Anna, served the Lord in Russia's Trans-Caucasus and North Caucasus regions. He was arrested in the early 1930s, sent to a hard-labor camp, and executed in 1937.

RIGHT: Family portrait, St. Petersburg, 1928. My big brother Stephen poses with calm professionalism, but I must have been wriggly, because Mom has a grip on my foot.

LEFT: A summer Sabbath afternoon in Siberia, 1936. This creek and the village to which Dad had been exiled have the same name, Krazny Klyutch, which in Old Russian means "beautiful creek." My parents and my brother Victor and I loved to sit there and enjoy the music of nature.

ABOVE: As a lieutenant in the Soviet Army during World War II, Stephen learned to trust God amid the dangers. "I am a believer in God," he finally told his superiors, "and I must worship Him on the day He established for that purpose." Indignant, the military command transferred him to the reserve forces. On his way back home he met Pastor Constantine Titorenko, who, though he had just been released from exile, was glad to clandestinely baptize my brother.

ABOVE: After Dad had been sentenced to a labor camp in the northern Komi republic—and before family visits and photographs were prohibited—my recently reconverted older brother Stephen visited him in 1947. This would be the last time they would see each other. A year later my brother and I would be arrested, and he would die in 1953.

ABOVE: In 1953 my brother Stephen, age 32, finished his labor camp sentence badly weakened, probably with tuberculosis. My mother was able to join him in his place of exile above the Arctic Circle and to care for him until his death two or three months later. Mom later told how some of his friends hacked through the permafrost to prepare his grave. In this photo one of these young men—who said that Stephen's testimony and martyr's death led him to Christ—mourns the passing of his friend.

ABOVE: G. A. Grigoryev, Russian Adventist leader for many years, warned me to beware of KGB informers planted within the church.

RIGHT: February 1948. Here you see me teaching art to a class of fifth and sixth-graders in Daugavpils, Latvia. In a month and a half the KGB would arrest me and transport me back to Ivanovo, where I'd be imprisoned, tried, and sent to the labor camps.

RIGHT: My art training came in handy while I was in a Karaganda labor camp in 1952. With photography forbidden, prisoners had me to draw their pictures which were then smuggled out by a friendly civilian and mailed to family members. Often my sketches were first taken to a photographer, who made several copies for the different relatives. I don't remember the man sketched here—I drew so many—but he gave me this copy in gratitude.

ABOVE: This is my friend and fellow labor camp prisoner Anatoly. When either of us received food packages from our mothers, we shared with the other. One tragic day at the brick factory where we worked he and some friends attempted to escape, and he was shot to death. His was the first funeral I performed. I found this precamp photo among his possessions.

LEFT: Newly released from prison camp a month or two before this was taken, I'd signed a paper saying that I would be permanently exiled to Mirsikul, Kazakhstan. I'm standing in a boat owned by my landlord and fellow exile Herr Behnke, dropping a fish into a bucket.

LEFT: Our wedding happened in wintry November, and since we had neither transportation to a photo studio nor money to spare on portraits, the camera is my old tripod-mounted one, and the photographer is Anna's younger brother Iliya, who has just removed the lens cap and is counting "one, two, three" before replacing it. Anna's cousin made this beautiful dress of a patterned material combined with natural silk and lined in pink.

ABOVE: Married for six months, Anna and I stand in front of her parents' wattle-and-daub home with their wedding gift to us, the heifer Zorka (little star). A year later Zoeka gave birth to a calf, and when we moved to Almaty we sold them for enough money to buy a humble hut in the city's outskirts.

RIGHT: After I'd been detained by the KGB in Almaty in 1959, local church leaders suggested I leave town for a while. So I spent a month with my uncle Alexander Demidov and his wife, Evdokia, in Norilsk, above the Arctic Circle. Both were exiles, Evdokia having spent eight years in forced-labor camps. She enjoyed reading this rare pre-Communist edition of the Bible and disguised it by wrapping its cover in pages from a Soviet magazine. Here I am in a later picture with this dear couple.

ABOVE: Our secret worship services and Bible studies in Kazakhstan's capital city, Almaty, and the surrounding area resulted in several baptisms. Since I wasn't yet ordained, the beloved Pastor Kazimir Korolenko conducted this clandestine 1957 baptism of 18 precious souls. Sadly, his participation in these and other baptisms led to his arrest later in the year.

LEFT: It's March 1961, and I've been brought before my first "public court" in Almaty, Kazakhstan. The pink draping on the lectern is adorned with the hammer and sickle; the grim-faced woman is chair of one of the local executive committees. The man intently watching me is acting as prosecutor. I have no attorney, but have been given a mere five minutes to answer an hour's worth of charges against me. I am reading from a pamphlet that contains some of Lenin's statements maintaining that the government should not persecute the church. In a moment the judge will silence me. Anna is in the audience, and will be severely traumatized by this "trial."

ABOVE: From 1962 to 1967 we found refuge in Kokand, Uzbekistan, from which I secretly traveled to our churches in Kazakhstan and central Asia. Seated at the table (left to right) are Michael, Peter on my lap, Pavel, my father, Maria, and my mother. Anna and Evangeline are standing. On the table is the violin I used to accompany our singing.

ABOVE: In 1964 our fifth child, Peter, was born. Since no visitors were allowed in a maternity ward Anna's aunt Agaphia helped the rest of the children get a peek at Mom and little brother through the window.

RIGHT: It's September 1966. Evangeline (left rear) holds the customary first-day-of-school bouquet for her teacher but knows that the absence of a Young Pioneers red tie will cause trouble. Beside her are Pavel and Maria, who have a kindly teacher who won't bother them about the tie. Michael, in front of Anna, is an excited first grader, while carefree little Peter grins impishly. I'm behind the camera, and have just read a few words from the Bible, prayed with them, and entrusted them into God's hands.

ABOVE: In the 1960s, though I was an underground pastor, I worked for the government as a traveling photographer, secretly visiting churches and scattered groups as I created passport photos and did other camera work. Here I'm drinking tea in a hospitable *yurta* (nomad's tent).

ABOVE: This photo was taken to honor my precious Anna's fortieth birthday. It's 1973 and we've gathered in a Chimkent, Kazakhstan, photographer's studio.
Back row (left to right): Pavel, Evangeline, Maria and Michael.
Front row: Anna, Elena (holding her doll "Dasha"), me, and Peter, who's thoughtfully watching the photographer at work.

ABOVE: In the fall of 1970, thanks to an invitation from my aunt Valentina, who lived in America, I made my first visit to the U.S.A. General Conference president Robert Pierson graciously organized a tour so that I could see many historic Adventist places, including the Ellen G. White Estate at Church headquarters. Here I'm trying to lift a Bible similar to the one the young Ellen supported while in vision.

BELOW: Though the government was adamantly against an organized Adventist Church, in 1981 we received official permission to gather delegates from Russia's central region to elect a "senior pastor," Nicolay N. Libenko (the bearded man in the center of the picture, in front of the two women in light-colored coats). Unofficially, this marked the creation of the Central Russian Conference.

RIGHT: In September 1990 I had the honor, together with Russian Orthodox patriarch Alexi II (on my left), to appear before the parliament to discuss the U.S.S.R.'s new religious legislation. We spoke carefully, for we were addressing the country's leading Communists. "If you will grant liberty to people to exercise their religious convictions," I told the legislators, "you will strengthen our citizens' feelings of patriotism." This photo is from the London *Daily Telegraph*, September 27, 1990.

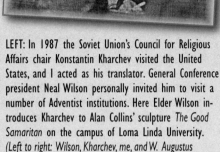

LEFT: In 1987 the Soviet Union's Council for Religious Affairs chair Konstantin Kharchev visited the United States, and I acted as his translator. General Conference president Neal Wilson personally invited him to visit a number of Adventist institutions. Here Elder Wilson introduces Kharchev to Alan Collins' sculpture *The Good Samaritan* on the campus of Loma Linda University. (Left to right: Wilson, Kharchev, me, and W. Augustus Cheatham.)

LEFT AND BELOW: The transformation of the fire-gutted abandoned school building to the Zaokski Seminary was done without cranes or other machinery because the church owned none, and the state was not permitted to grant their use for religious purposes. God miraculously intervened so that even with several workers moving heavy loads to great heights, there was not one accident during the construction.

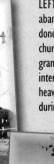

BELOW: This is more than simply a photo of men in suits. It shows an event for which I and fellow Russian Adventists had been working and praying for decades. It is 1981, and General Conference president Neal Wilson stands in front of Moscow's Sovietskaya Hotel with representatives of several Adventist groups throughout the Soviet Union—a tentative but dramatic move toward unity!

LEFT: "Anna," I said when receiving an honorary doctorate from Southwestern University, "this is *your* achievement!" "Misha," she gently corrected me, "it is the approving smile of our gracious heavenly Father, a token of His love to you and me."

RIGHT: On August 12, 2001, a generous Andrews University awarded me my second honorary doctorate. My precious children and their progeny gathered from all directions to pose in front of the Pioneer Memorial church. It looks as though Anna and I are the only ones not wearing wide grins—we're probably thinking of the days of slower camera film when, if you changed your expression during the "one, two, three" count of the exposure, your face would smear!

BELOW: It's 2003, and our youngest daughter, Elena, holds our Bible Translation Institute's *New Testament in Modern Russian.*

ABOVE: In spite of the sober photos above, I *do* know how to smile! And my smiles are broadest when I'm with my family, such as my great-granddaughter Elizabeth, whose mother is my oldest grandchild Maria, Evangeline's daughter.

John, which had always encouraged my soul. *No wonder my dad knows John's Gospel by heart from start to finish,* I remember thinking to myself. *Dad feels that to be a victorious Christian in life's struggles, he needs to abide in "the true Vine," which is a central theme of that gospel.*

That day I was reading John 13, about how Jesus had instituted the Communion service.

I have been deprived of taking Communion for a long time, I thought mournfully. *And if I stay in this place I'll continue to be deprived, of this and so much else.*

But then the words Jesus spoke to Peter sounded in my heart: "What I am doing you do not know now, but afterward you will understand" (John 13:7, RSV).

Thank You, Lord, I prayed. *Thank You for the assurance that someday I will understand.*

And this understanding wasn't long in coming. I soon found that God had a very special surprise, and a totally unexpected joy, in store for me. It's almost impossible to express the elation I felt when I learned that there was a small group of Seventh-day Adventists in a nearby village in this same region.

Heavenly Father, I prayed, *how I long to meet with these believers. But it's illegal for me to go there without official permission. Please help me!*

A traveling nurse visited our little fishing village from time to time. On one of her visits I came to her for a checkup. During her examination she said, "Tell me about yourself. Where are you from? What was your profession before you came here?"

She seemed to listen to my story with genuine interest, especially when I mentioned that I'd graduated from art school the year before I was arrested.

"*Art* school?" she asked.

"That's right."

She studied me for a moment. "We need to get you out of here, young man," she finally said. "If you're an art teacher, we need you in Semiozernoye." Semiozernoye was the district center. The name, which is a lovely sound to a Russian ear, means "seven lakes." I sighed wistfully, thinking, *Semiozernoye . . . that's where the Adventist believers are.*

A little later in the same conversation she hesitantly, almost humbly, made a request. "I live in a small apartment," she said, "and it's impossible to buy anything locally to decorate it with. I wonder—would it be possible for you to paint a picture for me?"

"Of course," I said. "My mother sent me a set of oil paints, and I'd be delighted."

When I finished the small painting and gave it to her, she was very pleased.

"In return," she said, "I've written you a prescription."

I gave her a puzzled look. "For what?"

"For a physical examination in the Semiozernoye medical center," she said with a wink. "Just take this to the commandant. He'll give you permission to go."

Imagine my joy—after months in a desert landscape—to see several clear water lakes surrounded by bushes. After feasting my eyes on the scenery for a while, I quickly located the Adventist believers. They were very happy to see me, and invited me to stay with them for a few days.

The medical center's examination was a mixed blessing. "There's nothing wrong with you, Comrade Kulakov," the doctor assured me. "You are in perfect health, and you may go back to your village."

Lord, I suppose I'd better not ask for a chronic illness! I prayed. *But if it is in Your plans for me, please open an opportunity for me to move here and find work.*

I visited the local school and asked to see the director. "I'm an art teacher," I told her.

"You're an art teacher?" she said, excitement in her voice. "We've never had an art teacher in this school, ever. I would like to hire you."

"You probably suspect my problem," I told her. "I'm an exile living in Mirsikul. I could come to Semiozernoye only because of a medical exam."

"We'll work that out," she replied. She sent me to the district manager, who was also very friendly to me.

"I want to hire you," he said, "but I'll have to get permission from the district police office." Soon I was in the office of the chief of police.

"So you're an artist, are you?" the chief asked.

"I am."

He glanced at a bare spot on his office wall. "I need a portrait of Dzerzhinsky to hang there," he told me. "Could you paint one for me?" Dzerzhinsky was the founder of the KGB.

"Certainly," I said, "if you can provide me with a photograph or two."

"Excellent," the chief said with satisfaction. "In that case I will grant you permission to relocate here." I painted the portrait, which he proudly hung on the wall, and soon I found myself teaching art at two local schools, a Russian and a Kazach. Local Adventists recommended a very inexpensive room in the house of an elderly woman.

On my way to school each day I passed the house of Sister Agaphia, one of the local Adventists. She invited me to stop in at least once a day to have a meal with her. I didn't realize that she was studying me very closely.

"Mikhail," she said one day, "did you know that there is an even larger group of Adventists in Kushmurun?"

"I didn't know that," I said. "I'd love to meet them, but you know my situation. I can't travel that far."

She nodded thoughtfully. "My niece lives there," she said. "Her name is Anna, and she has grown up in the fine Adventist family of Ivan and Maria Velgosha. I think she'll soon be coming to Semiozernoye to buy schoolbooks for herself and her younger brother."

"I look forward to meeting her," I said.

I will never forget the day I saw Agaphia's sweet, nice-looking young niece for the first time. As I write this, it's been 55 years, but my first impressions of her are still fresh, strong, and deep. I remember Anna's light step as she entered her aunt's small, tidy room. And how can I forget her nice white dress with dark blue polka dots, cut modestly but well fitting to her beautiful form?

Her dark thick hair was neatly gathered in two splendid braids, the ends of which were bound by black ribbons. The braids were crossed at the shoulder level and then gathered up again, where their ribbons were tied in a gorgeous bow at the back of her head just above her sweet little ears. All these things I noticed immediately and liked them very much. But believe me or believe me not, what impressed me most, and instantly won my heart, was the expression in her big, wide-open eyes.

You see, Anna had heard about me from her aunt, but she had no clue that I would be there that Friday evening. But as she entered the room, there I was. And that's when I saw, in those lovely eyes of hers, the confusion of an innocent, modest, and pure girl's soul. More than any words she could have said, her eyes told me that she was a sincere and humble Christian, able to love selflessly and faithfully.

The next day was the Sabbath, and we spent the whole day together. From the very first moment we met, I had made my decision. *Anna,* I said to myself, *is exactly the woman I would be happy to have as a friend and partner throughout my whole life.*

As I accompanied her to the train station I asked her to visit me again. It wasn't long before her father arrived to visit his sister Agaphia, and probably to look me over as a possible son-in-law. I liked him from the start. He was a decent, kindhearted person with a noble character—the same openness, sincerity and Christian simple-heartedness that I found so appealing in his daughter. He and Anna reminded me of the joyful comment Jesus made when seeing Nathanael. "Here is a true Israelite, in whom there is nothing false" (John 1:47, NIV). Even at age 26 I had already had many chances to observe that this humble purity was a rare virtue in this world. Among Anna's many charms, this was what determined my choice.

"Ivan Pavlovich," I told him respectfully but frankly, "I am deeply interested in Anna, and wish to ask you for her hand in marriage."

He looked me up and down. "You're an exile."

I nodded.

A small smile began to grow on his face. "But even though you're an exile, I have an idea that there would be many girls who'd be happy to travel out here and marry you."

"Thank you for your gracious words."

He stared up at a corner of the room for a moment. "I know it won't be long until your father is released from concentration camp. Why not wait until he's free, so that you can discuss this matter with him?"

He must have noticed my downcast expression, because his next words gave me courage. "But this is your own choice, of course," he said. "You may speak to Anna about this when she comes the next time."

A few days later I sent her a telegram inviting her to come for a visit. *And would you mind bringing your passport with you?* I wrote.

So on that Friday afternoon I walked to the small train stop, three miles from the village, to meet her. As I waited, I noticed that although most of the landscape was barren, nearby there was a little grove of beautiful birch trees surrounded by fresh green grass and wildflowers.

Soon a locomotive with just one carriage attached chugged to a stop beside the wooden signpost that served as the depot. Anna, the only arriving passenger, stepped from the carriage.

"Anna," I said after we greeted each other, "come over under these trees and sit down with me. That way we can talk undisturbed."

"Fine," she said, and when we were seated she gave me a puzzled look. "Could you explain why you sent me a telegram?"

Now it was my turn to look puzzled.

"I've never received a telegram in my life," she continued. "It worried me. I thought you were sick, and needed me to help you."

My mouth opened to speak, but she wasn't finished.

"And why on earth," she asked, blushing a deep red, "did you ask me to bring my passport? Surely you can understand that this was rather embarrassing."

I nodded, and my own face turned red as well, for at that time in the Soviet Union passports were a required form of identification for couples who registered their intent to be married. "Anna, please forgive me," I said, and then the words tumbled from my lips, words that will sound unusual to couples who have courted under less repressive conditions.

"Anna," I said, "you must realize that in our country the life of a Christian is filled with persecution and hardships. I don't know how much your aunt has told you about me, but my father and my elder brother are still incarcerated. My uncle Alexander is living in exile beyond the Arctic Circle."

As I say, these aren't the normal words of a suitor pressing his request. But my dear Anna looked at me with such sympathy that I gained the courage to continue.

"I tell you frankly," I said, "that I have been praying to God to send my way a girl who would be willing to share the life of a persecuted Christian. Anna," I said, summoning all my boldness yet trying to speak as tenderly as I knew how, "I see in you the one who with the help of God will be able to help me follow Jesus and serve in His cause." I took a breath and hurried on. "Anna, I ask you to accept my proposal and to marry me!"

Her eyes blinked rapidly with tears, and she looked shyly down at the flowers for a moment. She paused a long time, then finally said in a soft voice, "I will speak with my parents about this proposal."

Did my words fall on "good soil"? I wondered. *Will I get a positive answer—and soon?*

Anna and I prayed together, asking the Lord to lead in this important issue. And incidentally, 30 years later we visited that same grove together, and thanked our gracious heavenly Father for answering that prayer.

Though I knew my proposal was startlingly bold, I had no way of knowing that it was an amazing confirmation of a miracle story. That is something Anna told me later, after she had accepted my proposal.

"There have been several young non-Adventist men who have wanted to marry me," she confided. "But I've always had this deep conviction that I could be happy only if I married a man of God with whom I could share my beliefs. And I held to this conviction even though there were no young Adventist men for hundreds of miles around."

"But why are you willing to marry an exile?" I asked her. "We're doomed to live here the rest of our lives."

"Let me tell you why," she said. "After I graduated from high school, I took teacher training, and I taught in a remote country school. Once when I was back in Kushmurun visiting my parents, I saw that a wedding reception was being held right in our neighbor's yard. Their daughter, a former schoolmate of mine, had just gotten married.

"Father saw me wistfully watching the merry scene across the fence, and came out to stand beside me. He said, 'Anna, you must remember what Jesus said: "Look first for the kingdom of God and His righteousness, and the rest will be given to you."' I thought about his comforting words, and accepted his advice."

Then Anna turned and looked me fully in the eye.

"A little time went by," she said, "and one night I dreamed a dream. In that dream a very distinct voice said to me, *'Your husband is to be Mikhail Kulakov.'*"

A chill went across my back. "You heard my name in your dream?"

"I did."

"Before you even knew me?"

She nodded. "I was astonished by this," she said, "and I tried to remember if I knew anyone with that name. But there's no way I could have known it.

"A month or two after my dream, a traveling pastor came by to do a Communion service for our little group of believers, since we don't have a pastor of our own. While the preparations were being made, he asked me, 'Do you know anything about any recent Adventist exiles who might have come to this area? In Moscow we received a message from the mother of a young man who probably doesn't live too far from here. He's living in eternal banishment, and his name is Mikhail Kulakov.' When he spoke your name," Anna said to me, "I blushed and began to tremble. I had not expected this."

The more Anna told me about herself, the more certain I was that the Lord had brought us together. She and I were fortunate to meet at a moment when Russian Adventism was just starting to revive, to emerge from the years of severe persecution that followed the early 1930s, when all churches were closed and all pastors arrested. During that dark time no new Adventist literature was produced, so they treasured the old church magazines with their pictures, articles, and progress reports of the work in other parts of the world.

"Every Sabbath when I was a girl," Anna told me, "I would page through those magazines and look at pictures of other Russian Adventist groups sitting around their pastors. Mother and Father also showed me photographs of our own congregation and their pastor. I would hear my parents tell me how much they appreciated those faithful ministers of the Lord, and how they walked on foot from village to village, often in danger of losing their lives. And finally, all of them testified to their faith under persecution, many dying in labor camps or prisons.

"I felt such a deep respect for them that I thought, *How happy I would be to have such a minister for a husband.* So when I heard that you were also persecuted for serving the gospel, I accepted your proposal and was glad to join my life with yours to help you serve the Lord in His church."

CHAPTER 11: My Angel Bride

It was Friday, November 6, 1953, and I was again waiting at the little train stop near the grove of birch trees where I had asked Anna to marry me. But now, instead of pleasant green grass and beautiful flowers, I stood in deep snow. A cold, piercing wind made the below-zero temperature even more uncomfortable as I waited for the train that would take me 25 miles to Kushmurun, where Anna and I would be wed on Sunday.

I wish I had some flowers to take to my bride-to-be, I thought mournfully. *I've scoured the entire village for a bouquet, and I'm empty-handed. But I suppose they would have wilted in this cold. I have nothing to bring Anna but my love.*

And where, I wondered, glancing at my watch, *is the train? It was supposed to be here at 6:00 p.m.*

By the time it finally chugged into view it was after 8:00, and even though I had jumped up and down and done every other exercise I knew to fight off the cold, those two frozen hours had thoroughly numbed me, especially my feet. They still felt frozen when I arrived at the Kushmurun station, only to discover that my dear Anna and her younger brother had had their own patience tested because of the delay.

Finally, late in the evening, we arrived at the house of Ivan and Maria Velgosha, Anna's parents. These two dear people came from a line of hardworking Ukrainian ancestors, and before the revolution, Anna's grandpa Paul had built a spacious wooden house for his family in the nearby village. But when Stalin's Soviet government organized the village into a collective farm, Paul's house, horses, equipment—and practically everything else he'd worked so hard for, including the last of his stored wheat—were simply taken from him.

So on that Friday evening I was ushered shivering into a far humbler dwelling, a small one-story wattle-and-daub house measuring 33' x 20', divided into two rooms. Add four beds, two tables, a stove, and a few chairs, and space became scarce. Yet this was where Ivan and Maria, their two children, and Ivan's mother lived. It was also the place where between 30 and 35 Adventists worshipped each Sabbath.

And on Sunday it would be our wedding chapel—and I could have chosen no happier place to be married. The Velgosha home was filled with such an atmosphere of Christian love that we wouldn't have exchanged it for the most elegant cathedral.

"Mama, Mikhail's feet are *frozen*," Anna called out as we entered. "Pour some warm water into a bucket, quickly!"

So it was with my grateful feet immersed in a bucket of water that I was introduced to Anna's relatives and some fellow believers who lived in that small city. Loving and lovable Sister Agaphia had arrived a couple of days earlier to prepare the house for the wedding.

I've told you that as an exile my travel was limited. In fact, I'd had to get official permission to travel to Kushmurun for my wedding. I didn't know anybody in the local church except Anna's father, and therefore I didn't have a best man. Anna had her own dilemmas in finding attendants. On Sunday three of her cousins came to the wedding, but since they weren't believers, Anna didn't ask them to be attendants, because their participation in a religious ceremony might have put them in danger.

We were married on Sunday morning, November 8, 1953. Our Communist government had tried to force changes even in traditional marriage customs. Any religious rituals or folk customs, including the adorning of a bride for wedding, were considered as symbols of capitalism, and the authorities did all they could to obliterate them. Anna, however, blissfully ignored these strictures, and wore an exquisite long white dress. And although the authorities refused to allow the manufacture of the traditional "bride's crown," Anna found a woman in the village who skillfully—and secretly—crafted such crowns and sold them "under the table." But no matter what she would have worn, my precious bride was the very embodiment of heavenly purity, dignity, and tenderness.

I'd been teaching for only two months, and hadn't been able to save enough money for a new suit, so I wore a used but decent-looking one sent to me all the way from Moscow by its owner, Pastor Matsanov.

Our marriage ceremony was conducted by old Brother Konev. Just three months earlier, on a visit to Moscow, he had been ordained as a church elder so that he could serve as lay pastor to the Kushmurun believers. Our wedding—in the presence of nearly 40 people—was his first official act in his new role. He was very nervous, but tried to conceal his uneasiness by coughing every once in a while. He would also repeat some of his words or phrases twice. Like most brides and grooms, neither Anna nor I remember anything of his wedding sermon, though I suppose it was filled with words of admonition designed to guide us happily through married life.

But one thing we remember very well.

Brother Konev had reached the end of the sermon, and had read his way ponderously through the vows. We had said "*Da*" ("Yes" or "I do"), and he then pronounced us husband and wife. Then he turned to me, coughed again, and paused portentously.

"Now, Brother Mikhail," he intoned, "show to all of us how much you love your bride, Anna."

I was taken aback. *What is he talking about?* I wondered. *How can I show my love to Anna here and now?* I could feel everybody's eyes on the back of my head, waiting for me to do something. *But what?*

Out of that agonizing silence came a hoarse whisper from somebody in the crowd.

"Kiss her!"

Ah. Now I understand, I thought. So I followed that quite appropriate prompting, and took Anna in my arms and kissed her—though deep in my soul I felt that this might confuse my pure and innocent angel girl. To be frank, this wasn't our first kiss. After her third visit to me, when with passports in hand we had registered our intention to be married at the state office, we had kissed each other. But then we'd done it, not in public, but in private and with Christian modesty and the full understanding that we would not lawfully belong to each other until we had been officially and solemnly declared husband and wife.

Once the wedding service was over, we moved a few items of furniture around, and the home chapel became a wedding reception hall. Church members and Velgosha relatives (most of them nonbelievers) made delightful company, and the simple but tasty meal made everybody feel happy. Nobody hurried home, but stayed late into the night listening to or telling interesting stories and singing Christian or folk songs.

Finally the local church members (who mostly lived in families with unbelieving husbands or children) wended their way back to their dwellings. But the visiting relatives had to stay with us, because there was no train for them to take home at that time of night. In those days it was quite natural for guests to sleep in the same room with the home's owner, and on that night 15 of us would share the two rooms.

"Now," someone finally said, "we have to make an important decision."

Everybody stopped talking, and stared—then gradually began to smile. I heard a few giggles.

"What decision?" I asked, puzzled.

"Which bed our newlyweds will sleep in."

"They must sleep in Anna's bed," someone else said.

I glanced at Anna. She was blushing prettily.

"No," she said faintly.

Everybody burst out laughing. Somebody said, "But you're *married* now, Anna."

"I can't," she repeated. "I mean, not with—everybody *else* here."

105

"Come on!" someone urged.

She shook her head, immovable.

"OK, Anna," someone said, "You can sleep in the bed by yourself."

"And let Mikhail sleep on the floor?" she shot back indignantly. "Of course not! He will sleep in my bed, and *I* will sleep on the floor!"

"Impossible, Anna!" I said, aghast. "I'm not sleeping in a bed if you have to sleep on the floor!"

But my queen's decree—earnestly ratified by her relatives—was unchangeable. So on our wedding night I slept in her bed all by myself, while she and the rest of the relatives lay down on the floor.

As Anna and I look back to that happy weekend more than a half century ago, we especially remember the generosity of these dear relatives and church members. Life was tough for everyone, yet our well-wishers shared with us as bounteously as they could, providing us with several tokens of their love. Anna's parents gave us a luxurious feather bed, two big goose-down pillows, a warm blanket, and a gift that kept on giving—a young cow they'd raised themselves.

During our first months together Anna told me, "I believe that my calling is to raise godly children who will promote the spreading of the gospel." And in due time she gave birth to our first child, a baby girl. "She will grow up and help me raise our other children," Anna told me. "Let us call her Evangeline."

In the Russian Bible the word "gospel" is merely transliterated from the Greek and sounds like *Evangeliya,* but Anna had another reason for the name as well. She'd read Harriet Beecher Stowe's *Uncle Tom's Cabin* in a Russian translation, and had always been impressed by the sweetness of the little girl named Eva (Evangeline St. Clare).

My "eternal banishment" didn't last forever—only about one year. God's mighty hand was moving to change my country's political climate, and it wasn't too long after Stalin's death in 1953 that the government declared amnesty for all political prisoners serving a term of five years or less. In theory, I could now move where I wished. However, I didn't hear about this amnesty for many months, because in order to keep their labor force in place for as long as possible, the local authorities kept this emancipation quiet.

But finally word of our freedom arrived, and Anna and I, with our brand-new baby daughter, Evangeline, traveled first to visit my dad, still serving his sentence and currently imprisoned in Spassky camp near Karaganda in Kazakhstan. (After Stalin's death, close relatives were finally allowed to visit camp prisoners.) Dad remained in custody until 1956, but God was good to him, and Dad's self-taught knowledge of hydrotherapy and health principles—which made him our family doctor when I was a child—now enabled him to relieve the suffering of the other prisoners. In fact, in the last years of his captivity, the camp authorities considered Dad the camp doctor.

Saying goodbye to Dad, my family and I next visited my mother in Latvia. Mom loved Anna from the first day she met her, and appreciated the sincerity of her faith and her ability to do everything accurately.

With great seriousness my mother said to me, "Take care of her." She loved to quote the words of the well-known Russian poet Nekrasov, who lived in the time of serfdom in the country. Serfdom was almost the Russian equivalent of slavery in the United States, and in 1859, 23 million serfs lived in conditions worse than what any European peasant endured.

Nekrasov's lines that my mother quoted showed her abhorrence of what women had to go through during those terrible times when women were slaves to their husbands and sons, who themselves were slaves as well:

Three excruciating things had fallen
To the Russian women's lot:
To be a slave of her husband,
To be a slave of her son,
And to cringe to the slaves down to the grave.

Anna, in turn, was deeply impressed with my family.

"When I saw you three brothers sitting in church, all together in one pew," she told me much later, "I bowed my head and prayed, *Lord, if You bless us with more children, please grant us three sons as well, so that they too can serve you and spread the gospel.*"

Providentially, the Lord indeed gave us three sons, who are in the ministry now, plus two additional daughters, who have wonderful husbands who are also serving the Lord as ministers.

In 1955 my little family moved again. In a mountainous ravine on the outskirts of the south Kazakhstan town of Almaty was a lane called Wide Cranny Street, on which lived a number of our simple, deeply religious, and faithful Adventist believers. At that time there was no formally organized church, yet these dear people sent us a call to join them there, and we accepted. I remember them to this day: the Pavelkos, the Tchizhovs, the Frolovs, as well as Sisters Butenko and Pronevich (two widows whose Adventist pastor husbands had been martyred in camps and prisons).

Gradually others arrived from elsewhere to swell our ranks: families with the names of Misheryakov, Rybalko, and Vasilenko, and others such as a woman named Martha Samohvalova (the daughter of a former leader of our church in Russia—Genrich Lebsack) and her daughter Ruth. In spite of hardships and persecution these precious saints welcomed us with great affection, offering us their humble homes for our worship services, and sharing their last bread crumbs with all who came to worship with us from afar.

Anna and I still remember how cautious our first Sabbath worship visitors were. I've mentioned how at Stalin's death the government began to relax its restrictions, but travelers to our services in the ravine still had fresh memories of persecution. So as they arrived by bus, they would walk up the street one at a time or in pairs, so they wouldn't attract undue attention.

And those decades of persecution left a trail of other problems as well. Since there was no structured Adventist organization in Kazakhstan or in any other neighboring republics, our Moscow church leadership didn't know much about us, and we therefore couldn't rely on any kind of financial support from them.

And since our local church wasn't officially recognized by the authorities—though beginning in 1956 I'd repeatedly tried to register us—the government required me to hold a state job. Because all jobs were government jobs, I might have had Sabbath problems if I hadn't found work with other Adventists in a state construction company team who contracted for certain projects. The team—not the state—kept the time records, so they paid me for the hours I worked, but allowed me time off to visit church members and conduct other church business.

Our first three married years were hardscrabble ones. Even life's essentials, such as milk for our family, were hard to come by. But my sweet wife was so patient.

"Misha," she would say, "I praise the Lord in spite of the hardships. I am deeply convinced that it's not only our duty but our privilege to serve Him. Isn't it a blessing to see the happy faces of those who gather in the homes to worship?" And of course I agreed with her. What a gift from God to have such a faithful companion to encourage me!

In 1958 three pastors arrived in Almaty on a mission: to carry out the recommendation of our church leadership in Moscow and officially ordain me to the gospel ministry. One of these men was Kasimir Andreevich Korolenko, who secretly visited our congregation as well as other groups in the area. Unfortunately, the authorities arrested him that same year and charged him with committing an unbelievably heinous crime totally at odds with Christian teachings and lifestyle.

"Korolenko," his captors said. "You have two sons. Is that correct?"

The pastor nodded.

"And they have families?"

Pastor Korolenko nodded again.

"If you do not admit to your immoral deeds, Korolenko, we will find something with which to accuse your two sons. We will arrest them, and their families will be left without their fathers."

So to protect them, Pastor Korolenko finally admitted his "guilt" to the charges against him. But for all of those who knew him personally it was obvious that the local atheistic authorities in Tajikistan, where Korolenko lived, had manufactured these trumped-up charges to carry out the Soviet government's latest religion-crushing methods.

Shortly after his trial the church elders of those scattered Adventist groups gathered in Almaty for a meeting, and asked me to attend.

"Mikhail Petrovich Kulakov," they told me, "not only do we invest you with the responsibility of pastoring the Almaty church, but also with coordinating the Adventist work in the entire southern region of the U.S.S.R."

By doing this, they established an underground Adventist organization in Kazakhstan and the central Asia republics. And thus plunged me and my family into several years of life and work in an unforgettable crucible of testing and trial.

CHAPTER 12: Unwritten Laws

L *ord, please give me wisdom,* I prayed.

I was sitting across the desk from the commissioner of the Council for Religious Affairs at the Ministries of the U.S.S.R. in Kazakhstan, located in that republic's capital city, Almaty, and I was on a mission.

"I would like to request an official permit to openly conduct worship services," I told him.

"Very well," he said. "But in order to receive your permit, you must provide us with the names, addresses, and places of employment of all your members, and of all the nonmembers who come to visit you."

"Might I quote a line from our Soviet constitution?" I asked. " 'The church is separated from the state.' "

"Quote as much of the constitution as you wish," he said sharply. "But you know as well as I do that there are unwritten laws."

We gazed at each other in silence for moment. Finally I rose, said goodbye, and left the office. I knew the danger our members and friends would be exposed to if I agreed to his demands. So our 100-member Almaty church continued to conduct its services in secret, because we were still considered illegal.

And we soon learned that Stalin's energetic replacement, Nikita Khrushchev, was just as much of a hard-liner in matters of faith. "Christianity?" he scoffed. "We will destroy Christianity and all other religions within another two or three years." The past decades had shown that mass arrests didn't work, so new tactics were announced:

"Spread ill will toward believers among the atheistically brainwashed general population. Give local authorities freedom to follow their own whims in accomplishing this goal. Subject church leaders and active members to public humiliation and court trials in order to discourage and disillusion them."

The local commissioner didn't waste any time. Soon his officials closed our little church building on Krestyanskaya Street—which we had constructed with great sacrifice and difficulty. Again we had to meet in the homes of our congregation. But now the authorities carefully monitored these little gatherings, and shadowed the worshippers who entered.

Suddenly, if you were an Almaty church member and you opened your home to a church service, you were fined. The names of your visitors were noted, and they were later harassed where they worked. Can you imagine what it was like to invite someone to come to church with you, with both of you knowing the ordeal that might follow?

Once, apparently trying to frighten my family and me, as well as obtain evidence to arrest me, KGB agents raided our home during one of my absences and confiscated a large amount of our religious literature. Fortunately most of my books were hidden in the attic of the Lubenchenkos, kind neighbors who willingly risked their own safety in this way. May the Lord reward them and their descendants for their love and selflessness!

My daughter Evangeline still has vivid memories of those dangerous times. At my request she agreed to share some of these in the following paragraphs:

Evangeline writes:

"I remember that our worship services were conducted in the houses of our fellow believers. One Sabbath we met in one place, the next in another. Every home was very simple, but clean and neat. Even the window curtains were ironed for Sabbath.

"Each home had a supply of boards, and on Sabbath morning each plank was placed on two or three stools and covered with rugs or cloth, to form backless benches for us to sit on. Sometimes the worshippers were so numerous that benches had to be set up in two or three adjoining rooms.

"The window shutters were tightly closed to prevent our singing from being heard and reported, but when the songs were over, someone opened the windows again, and the fresh air stirred the crisply ironed curtains and refreshed the worshippers. A bucket of water, and a mug placed on a saucer, was provided for those who wished this refreshment.

"Even as a little girl I deeply appreciated the solemn reverence of those services, and the wonderful singing. At that time there were no special Sabbath school classes for children, so we sat side by side with our parents on the cloth-covered boards. During breaks we children were allowed to slip outside and play quietly. I don't remember us ever playing pranks or even screaming loudly—we all knew we must not attract the attention of the authorities.

"One Sabbath morning as we worshipped together the police suddenly knocked on the door. I watched in fascination as several members immediately surrounded the doorway in a tight semicircle, forming a human screen as other church members concealed all the Bibles and songbooks under beds and inside kitchen utensils or anywhere else they could find a hiding place.

"I'll never forget one cold, foggy evening a few years later. By now I was 6 years old and already had two brothers and a sister. My mother's mother was visiting us, so my parents had left us in her care while they held an evening worship service in the home of some church members some distance away.

"Suddenly our dog Dozor (which means 'patrol' in Russian) began barking loudly. Our front door trembled as thunderous knocks landed on it.

" 'Who is it?' Grandma called out.

" 'Open the door!' a man's voice shouted.

" 'What do you want?'

" 'We want to talk to Kulakov! Open the door!'

"The knocking continued. Somebody else began rapping on the glass of the window. Grandma said nothing, but pulled aside the curtain for a few seconds so that whoever was outside could see that there was no one in the room besides her and the children.

"This didn't satisfy our visitors. 'We want to see Kulakov! Kulakov, we know you're in there! Open the door, woman!'

" 'Mikhail Kulakov and his wife are gone,' Grandma replied firmly. 'They told me never to open the door for anyone.'

"Suddenly Grandma remembered all the Sabbath school discussion guides and songbooks we were storing in our home at that time. These had been laboriously typed on thin rice paper—several carbon copies were made with each typing—and the loose sheets had not yet been bound.

"Grandma thought, *If these men break in here and find these Bible study materials, they'll take Mikhail into custody!* So while the fists pounded on the door, she began stuffing fistfuls of the sheets into our wood stove, stirring them with the poker so that the fire would burn them faster. The other children and I stood watching as the flames hungrily licked at the thin paper.

"My little brother Pavel suddenly understood that the men outside might steal things that belonged to us. Bursting into tears, he sobbed, 'Are they going to take my colored pencils in my cornflakes box?'

"Suddenly we realized that Dozor had stopped barking.

"Grandma listened. 'They must be gone,' she finally said.

"Then we heard voices we recognized.

" 'Mama! Papa!' I cried.

"Grandma unlocked the door, and my dear parents hurried in.

" 'It's really foggy out there,' Papa said. 'We got lost. We've been wandering around far out in the pasture next door. Then we heard Dozor barking in the distance, and we knew which way to come.'

"Grandma told them what had happened, and together we thanked God for His kindness in letting the fog keep them away from home until the police had gone."

Mikhail continues with the story:

Anna and I had indeed become lost. As we carefully made our way through the mud and thick fog, we became disoriented, but when we heard Dozor's agitated barking in the distance we knew which direction to go.

By the time we got closer to the house, the fog had lifted a little. Not knowing about the visitors who'd just left, I knocked on the window. The curtain barely cracked open, and we saw the frightened face of Anna's mother. Recognizing us, she quickly opened the door and told us the story.

Then she began to cry. "I have a confession to make," she sobbed. "I was afraid that the police would break down the door and search the house. So I started burning copies of the hymnbook sheets."

To the end of her life she recalled that incident with great regret.

"I trust that the Lord will forgive me," she would say. "I decided that if these atheists took the literature away they would destroy it anyway. I just didn't want you to be arrested."

In spite of the increased police persecution, our Almaty church continued to grow, and I conducted many a nighttime baptismal service. Other Adventist congregations in the surrounding towns and villages swelled as well, especially those in areas populated by Germans who, during the war, had been deported from the Volga, Crimea, and northern Caucasus regions to Siberia and the Asian republics. In these new and unfamiliar surroundings, these dear people hungered for the Word of the Lord.

And our Almaty Adventists responded. In the late 1950s many of them fearlessly and joyfully traveled to these newly founded congregations to conduct worship services in homes such as the Kaskalen dwelling of Friedrich and Maria Stele. This family raised a son, Arthur, who consecrated himself to God and later became a prominent church leader. His own son (also named Arthur) eventually became president of the Euro-Asian Division of Seventh-day Adventists.

It's impossible to tell you how important my dear wife, Anna, has always been to my ministry. As the next chapter begins, I have invited her to share some of her recollections of what our church and our family lived through during the Khrushchev years.

CHAPTER 13: **Far Above Rubies, My Anna**

A nna Kulakov writes:

"With joy in my heart I often think of the many wonderful people we had the privilege of living, meeting, and working with. I saw so much selfless love in our brothers and sisters in Christ in those days.

"Yes, we lived with poverty and distress. Since Mikhail gave the greater portion of his time to the ministry, his meager earnings weren't enough to fully meet the needs of our rapidly growing family. Fortunately, from childhood, by their example, my careful parents taught me the very important truth that thrift is also an income. My husband appreciated this, and often thanked and encouraged me.

" 'Anna,' he would often say, 'you probably earn more money than I do.'

" 'What do you mean by this?' I asked the first time he said it.

" 'It is very simple,' he answered. 'Look at it this way. You never throw away any of our food—everything is always used. You care for every piece of clothing in such a way that it passes in our family from one child to another.'

"During our five years in Almaty our family was blessed with three more children besides Evangeline. Though I did my best to conceal our needs, our dear brothers and sisters in Christ witnessed our state of distress and often tried to ease our burden.

"How can I forget the many friends who came to see me every time I was in the maternity hospital? In those days women in maternity wards were not permitted to have visitors, but fortunately the ward was on the ground floor, and my Adventist women friends soon discovered which window was mine. They would climb up on rocks or stacks of bricks, poke their heads over the windowsill, and call to me their tender words of Christian love.

"Often a nurse would arrive in my room bearing freshly baked patties, or a small jar of preserves, or a delicious glass of raspberry juice. 'Kulakova,' she would say, using the feminine version of my last name, 'some people came and dropped these off for you. What a big family you must have!'

"Indeed, I did feel the love of the great family of God.

"As a young Adventist pastor, Mikhail often secretly visited the families of those who became interested in the Christian message. Since Stalin's death the church wasn't persecuted quite as severely as before, but there was still the constant danger that any of the pastors could be arrested and sentenced to five or 10 years in prison.

"This thought did not give me peace of mind. By the spring of 1959 we had three small children, and I was expecting a fourth. I was just 26 years old, and it was hard for me even to think that I might lose my husband and be forced to raise our four children all by myself.

"That year we witnessed an especially remarkable miracle. One day Mikhail left on the bus for the town of Issyk, where he was to give a Bible study and prepare an entire family for baptism. The Adventists in that city were so excited that these dear people were ready to join God's family. We all knew that it was not an easy decision, since in that atheistic society they were risking the loss of their close friends—and perhaps even their freedom. We kept praying that they would sense God's special encouragement.

" 'I'll probably be home earlier than usual tonight,' Mikhail told me as he left. But the evening grew later and later, and he didn't return. I sat on the bed where our three little children peacefully slept, and I couldn't stop thinking about him. *Maybe they've arrested him,* I said to myself. Those past few weeks he'd mentioned that some strange people had been watching him and following him wherever he went. Each time he spoke of these watchers, my heart ached.

" 'God,' I prayed again and again, whispering so I wouldn't wake my children, 'please protect my husband in his service for You.'

"I spent most of the following day on my knees. I could not eat; I could not work. I worried—not about myself, but about Mikhail. *If only I knew where he was,* I thought.

"The third day dawned—and no Mikhail. I left the children in the care of my mother and, together with a church member named Vera Frolova (who knew the city well, and whose husband had spent 10 years in a labor camp), walked across town to the KGB office to find out whatever I could. The building was huge and gray, with narrow windows and marble steps. I'd never been there before, and had no idea which person I should speak to, so I approached the officer on duty at the front desk.

" 'I am looking for my husband,' I told him. 'I expected him home two days ago.'

"He gave me a surprised look. 'Your husband's missing? Why come here? Why don't you go to the police?'

"I hadn't had Mikhail's experience in dealing with the authorities, so I paused in confusion. But God gave me the courage to speak openly, something I would never have done on my own.

" 'My husband is a Seventh-day Adventist pastor,' I replied. 'We know that he has been followed by KGB agents for the past several weeks. They must have arrested him and placed him somewhere in this building.'

115

"The officer, who now was listening attentively, opened a big folder and glanced down a list of names. Then he shook his head. 'Your husband is not here. Anyway, as I said, this is the wrong place to look for him. Go to the police.'

"My heart sank. I was ready to cry right there. *How terrible it is not to know,* I told myself. *If only I could communicate to Mikhail. If only we knew where he was, I would feel so much better. Heavenly Father,* I prayed, *I entrust my precious husband to You, and I beg You for his protection.*

"Vera and I then walked to police headquarters, and I put my questions to the officer there.

" 'Don't you understand, woman?' he said with a mocking grin. 'It's the same old story. Your precious husband has found himself another woman, and has left you for her.'

"I did not dare argue with him, but in my mind I was saying, *I don't care what you say about my husband. I know of his true love for me. I know his deep dedication to the Lord. What you've said to me convinces me more than ever that Mikhail has been arrested by the KGB. For some unknown reason, they want to keep his arrest a secret—maybe to keep me and the church off balance.*

"When I got home late that evening, my mother met me at the door.

" 'Mama, what is wrong?' I asked, seeing a look of concern on her face.

" 'While you were away,' she said, 'two officers brought a paper from the main KGB office. It was a summons slip, and they ordered Mikhail to come there Friday morning at 10:00 a.m. to be questioned.'

What could this mean? I asked myself. *I've always been a rather trusting person. I'm accustomed to believing in people. I've even given our atheistic government the benefit of the doubt most of the time. Did these visitors to our house tell the truth, and Mikhail isn't in the hands of the KGB? But where else could he be?*

"So Friday morning I took the summons slip to the KGB office. Once in the building, I used a telephone to contact the officer whose name was on the paper.

" 'My husband has not been home for more than three days,' I said. 'And I believe he can be nowhere else except right here in your building.' I paused, preparing to listen carefully for any hint that I was right.

" 'Since the summons was for your husband and not you,' he told me rudely, 'I refuse to speak with you.'

"Once home, I began to hear more gloomy news. One by one, the members of our Almaty church were being interrogated by the KGB. They were attempting to trick our members into giving evidence against the church, and of course against their pastor. Along with intimidation and threats of punishment, the authorities demanded that the members sign an affidavit promising to keep their summonses secret.

"But despite the warnings, immediately each of these friends came to me to give me every detail of their interrogations.

" 'We wanted to let you know these things,' they said, 'to spare you unnecessary grief, and to warn you about what the KGB is up to.'

" 'What are they asking you about?' I wanted to know.

" 'They tell us, "We just want you to confirm some facts already known to the secret service. We understand that Kulakov urges young members to refuse service in the Soviet army. We understand that he encourages parents to keep their children from attending school on Saturdays." '

" 'But don't you see their game?' my friends told me. 'It's easy to spot what they're trying to do. They're keeping your husband in secret custody while they see if they can gather testimony for charges they're trying to fabricate against him.'

"I could not eat. I could not sleep. It had been four days since I'd seen Mikhail. I was ready to give up, but again and again a heavenly hope strengthened my weak soul, as did the outpouring of compassion and support which our church family gave to my children and me. Through the open door of our tiny house at 195 Shelikhova Street many well-wishers came to offer support and comfort. As some left, others would arrive. All who came to see me shared my concern through love, encouragement, and intercessory prayer. It was a great comfort to me.

"That Sabbath I did my best to rise above my physical and mental distress so I and my children could attend the worship service in the home of one of our church members. It happened that on that very day the Sabbath school lesson dealt with Acts 12, which tells how Peter was freed from the dungeon while the believers were still in urgent prayer.

"There, surrounded by my family of believers, I asked the Lord to protect my husband and to strengthen my own faith. Others joined their prayers to mine. 'Please, Lord,' they prayed, 'please intervene! Please release this husband from prison! Please return him to his wife and small children, who have been left without a father!'

"Brother Sukhodolov concluded our prayers with the following plea, which erupted from his very heart. 'Almighty God, answer our supplications with a miracle, as You once did so long ago in behalf of Your servant the apostle Peter. Lord, You delivered Peter from prison, and we are all filled with the hope that You will do the same for our dear Pastor Mikhail.'

"I returned home through the slushy mud—it had been a snowy day— encouraged by the prayers of the faithful, yet physically very weak. Pregnant and tired, I agonized over the uncertainty of the situation my husband was in. I vividly remember how my three small children clung to me, while my parents simply sat next to me with their heads bowed.

"A bit later that afternoon some of the sisters from the church arrived to encourage me, to read God's Word with me, and to pray. 'God is my shepherd,' one of the women read earnestly, 'I shall not fear.'

"Before she had finished the verse, someone knocked loudly and forcefully on the window, calling, 'Anna! Anna! Come out! *Peter* is coming! Galya [my nickname]! Galya! Come to meet someone! *Peter is on his way!*'

"At first none of us could understand what was happening. I darted out of the house and found Sister Olya Lybenchenko standing at my window, galoshes on her bare feet. She'd come running through the mud so she could spare me any more minutes of worry, and to be the first to announce something very exciting.

" 'Go meet *Peter!*' she squealed. 'I saw him coming from the bus stop!'

"I glanced toward the steep ravine that led into our street. Sure enough, someone was making his way toward our house. Only then did I understand— she meant Mikhail! My precious husband ran toward us, and as he clasped me in his arms our three children crowded around and clung to him.

" 'Praise be to God, we cried, who even in this day performs miracles as great as He did in the days of the apostles!'

"For those four days Mikhail had indeed been kept under arrest at the KGB prison, where many charges had been leveled at him for his active missionary work. But the Lord led him through to a miraculous deliverance. Those who tried to break his spirit realized that all their efforts were without success, so they decided to set him free, at least for a while."

Mikhail continues:

With my dear, brave Anna's permission I am going to bring her story to a temporary pause so that my daughter Evangeline can give you a brief account of her own memories of that day.

Evangeline writes:

"I couldn't understand what was going on, only that Dad hadn't come home one night. My memory is imprinted with the picture of Mom's slender figure, protruding belly, and large eyes. I could clearly see the grief and anxiety on her face.

"Mom left me and the rest of the children with Grandma, and went to the home of Vera Frolova to ask her help in searching for Dad. Almost as soon as Mom was out of sight, a man I didn't know knocked on our door.

" 'Does Mikhail Kulakov live here?' he demanded.

" 'Yes,' Grandma answered, 'he lives here. But he is not at home now.'

" 'Where is he?'

"Grandma glared at him. 'He is at *your* place!' she snapped.

"I saw the man get an angry look on his face. 'Where did you get that information?' he growled. 'Why would we take him away and then come here looking for him? Here.' He produced a piece of paper. 'Give this to Kulakov. He must appear at the KGB office at 10:00 a.m. Friday morning.'

"Mom returned home sick and sad. She could not find out where Dad was and what had happened to him. Tortured by uncertainty, she spent the night in prayer. The next morning she took the summons to the KGB office, but again returned home unsuccessful. We children could feel her grief, so we silently pressed up against her. Quietly I prayed my own childish prayers to God, asking Him to help my dear mother and father.

"I'll never forget how glad we were when on Sabbath afternoon our grief was changed into great happiness. Our good neighbor, who from a distance saw our dad coming home, loudly knocked on our window and announced the good news. Dad was alive, he was free, and he was on his way home to us!"

Anna continues:

"This terrifying adventure greatly tested my trust in God, but from this experience, and many experiences thereafter, I learned well that Christ is ready to lead us through all the hardships of this earthly life, if only we do not give up hope.

"Mikhail was often gone, visiting our congregations strewn all over Kazakhstan and the central Asian republics. I clearly remember a story I heard from the Laluev sisters, who lived in Karabalty. They were the daughters of Ivan Evdokimovich Laluev, a tireless toiler in God's field. Ivan Laluey, also, was constantly harassed and persecuted, and his earthly life and ministry were eventually cut short in prison, where he died a true follower of Jesus.

"The sisters told me that on Mikhail's first visit to the Karabalty believers, the KGB became suspicious. The town was not far from a secret military installation with the mysterious name The Mailbox. It's likely that it was given this name because it was probably a secret scientific research center as well. There were several such centers, guarded by the military, and nothing was known about them besides their mailbox address.

"So as my husband was conducting a worship service in the Laluev home, the authorities arrested him and took him away for interrogation.

"Ivan Laluev and the rest of that small group were shocked. They felt responsible for not being able to protect the man who came to minister to them. Those several hours that Mikhail spent in the custody of the KGB were hours of fervent prayer by the believers. When the authorities finally released him, he returned to the Laluev home and found the family and several other church members still on their knees, still praying. The wooden floor bore the evidence of their tears.

"With this I will conclude my story, with the request that Mikhail continue with his recollections. I am afraid that much of what I remember contains too many tears, though not all were tears of sadness—many were tears of joy as well. It is hard to say which there were more of. Praise God that we have the glorious hope of a Savior who eagerly awaits to wipe away all of our tears (Revelation 21:4).

"Mikhail and I wholeheartedly agree with a beautiful stanza of one of Margaret Clarkson's hymns:

" 'O Father, you are sovereign,
The Lord of human pain,
Transmuting earthly sorrows
To gold of heavenly gain.
All evil overruling,
As none but Conqueror could,
Your love pursues its purpose—
Our souls' eternal good.' "

CHAPTER 14

At the Public Court

Mikhail writes: The longer Anna and I served the Almaty church, the more we appreciated those faithful saints, and the more interested we became in their past. During the late 1930s and early 1940s Stalin's anti-Christian forces swept through the Soviet Union with a fervor like Saul's as recorded in Acts 9:1: "breathing threats and murder against the disciples of the Lord" (NKJV).

Vera Stepanovna Butenko, who was 8 years old in 1934, remembers those times well.

"Our Almaty church had about 40 members at that time," she recalls. "I remember the glorious congregational singing led by Sister Sabina and six members of the musical Ribalko family. These people sang from their whole hearts, even during a terrible famine that lasted several years, praising God for His salvation and care. During that time our church lived out the book of Acts, having all things in common."

In 1935 the Isaac Chizhov family arrived, bringing five more singers to the congregation, which now met in a house on what was then Kirghiz Street. By 1936 the attendance had swelled to 60, and services—under the direction of Pastor Remfert—were moved to the Luchinikov home on Podgorny Street. It was easy to think that this happy experience would continue forever.

But alas—1937, that sad year in Russian history, when Stalin's religious repressions began in earnest, arrived. And Almaty's Adventists were not spared.

The blow fell during a worship service, which at that time was held on Friday evenings in the Luchinikov home. Brother Stepovoy was leading out in the service, and Pastor Remfert was about to begin his sermon. Both men stood at the pulpit under a large kerosene lamp that hung from the ceiling.

Suddenly there was a commotion, and in through the door rushed a woman brandishing a huge stick. She'd occasionally attended meetings, but had behaved in such a suspicious way that everybody had suspected her of being a provocateur from the NKVD.

The woman flew toward the pulpit, screaming, "I demand that you accept me into the membership of this church!" Then she swung the stick like a baseball bat, striking and destroying the kerosene lamp. A few men moved forward to restrain her, but she resisted them, frantically scratching her face with her fingernails and banging her head against a wall.

Three days later the local newspaper ran an inflammatory article criticizing the "sect," alleging that they severely beat and raped women. It cited this woman's scratched face and bruised head as proof. Pastor Remfert and two other church leaders, Brothers Shishkov and Rybakov, were immediately arrested. The authorities forced them to ride through the streets in an official black raven car and point out the homes of other members. Thirty-two were arrested in all, including the heads of the Butenko, Dyadichkiny, Sitnik, Stepovoy, and Goncharenko families. Only a few were able to hide themselves. All that was left of the Almaty church were a few widows and some children.

Pastor Remfert and Brothers Shishkov and Rybakov were shot. Mrs. Bazalivich, the church treasurer, vanished without a trace, and no one ever knew what happened to her. The other arrested church members were transported north to the arctic Komi Republic, where they were mixed with a huge crowd of prisoners—300 in all—and driven under guard into the deep taiga (forest). There they were given saws and axes, plus a food supply of crusts and dry fish, and left to fend for themselves. Their only water was underfoot—the heavy snow.

Someone built a huge bonfire, and in the below-zero-Fahrenheit temperatures the prisoners searched for patches of moss to use to create beds and pillows. When someone died, his or her clothing was claimed and worn by others. Twelve Adventist men died there, far from their families, and were buried by Brother Stepovoy in graves that their descendants will never find.

But even in that cruel captivity, the faithful found ways to worship. They had their "Bethel" places, just as did Jacob—solitary walks along well-traveled tundra trails where they sought fellowship and strength from God, even though they suspected that only the coming of Christ would reunite them with their beloved families.

And the Lord responded.

Late one afternoon an Adventist man named Makar Stepovoy was returning along a forest trail from a hard day's work. His legs were so tired that they were almost dragging. Suddenly, on the path ahead of him, he spotted a small bag. He stooped and picked it up, and discovered that it was filled with dried bread crusts. As his trembling fingers thrust one of the fragments into his mouth, his mind was racing.

Who, in this starving land, he wondered, *placed that bag of crusts on the trail? Maybe the crows, like those who fed Elijah?*

Another believer, Alexandr V. Frolov (the husband of Vera, who had accompanied Anna, my wife, on her visits to the authorities when the KGB were secretly holding me) told his own miracle story. He'd been arrested in 1939 and sent to a frigid region of Siberia. One winter day as he was returning from a prayer walk, he saw a roe deer standing in a snowdrift a little way ahead.

"It stood there as if it were waiting for me," he later recalled. "I happened to be carrying an axe with me, and I raised it over my head and threw it toward the animal with all my strength, killing it at one blow. At no time did the deer flinch or try to run. I buried the meat in the snow, and that was how I and another Adventist brother survived that winter. Who prepared this animal for me? Undoubtedly the One who knows all our needs!"

One cold day in March 1961 an Almaty city council official summoned me to his office.

"Mikhail Kulakov," he intoned, "by order of the city council you are to appear at a public court to answer charges that you have illegally conducted religious services."

These public courts were just the latest tactic that Nikita Khrushchev hoped would rid the Soviet Union of what he called religious prejudices. "We need to reshape the consciousness of those who are bringing to completion the building of socialism in our Soviet Union," he and other party leaders declared. "We are living in a new world of universal equality, brotherhood, and justice for all. Religion is not only 'the opium of the people,' as Marx said, but it is also an ugly hindrance on the path to our bright future. *Remember! The struggle against religion is a struggle for socialism!*"

Back then no one could imagine that 50 years later Dmitry Ageev, a participant in one of Moscow's Conferences on Human Rights, would offer this sober look backward at a dismally failed philosophy.

"Extremism," he said, "which threatens to become one of the most terrible catastrophes of the twenty-first century, is the direct result of a disdainful attitude toward the human personality and its spiritual essence, an attitude that has been ideologically consolidated and put into practice by the totalitarian regimes of the twentieth century."

But in 1961 nobody in power knew, or cared, that this might happen. Almaty's local authorities, as well as the KGB, did everything possible to eradicate Seventh-day Adventism and other faiths. And since the past decades of arrests, murders, and Siberian deportations seemed only to *increase* church membership, party directors changed their approach. "Use ideological methods in the war against religion," they commanded.

Translated, this meant attacking believers with ugly newspaper articles, dismissing them from work, and subjugating them to the so-called public courts.

"Kulakov," the council official told me, "as you get ready for your public court trial, you must be prepared for the worst. Though a public court decision is not legally binding, your case might very well go from here to criminal court, where you may be sentenced for your unlawful activities. So bring with you appropriate clothing and food for travel."

With a heavy heart I trudged home to share the news with Anna. Remembering my previous arrests and the years spent in prison, we braced ourselves for the possibility that we might be separated for years to come.

A few days later I got the summons. My public court hearing would be held in a clubhouse on the premises of a factory in which felt boots were made. Anna, trying valiantly to hide her tears from our children, packed my bag with food and some clothing, just in case. Before I left the house I picked up our fourth child, 1½-year-old Mikhail, Jr. (Michael), and held him close. Though the older children clung to me, it seemed especially painful to be separated from this helpless babe.

"Heavenly Father," I remember praying, "You did not spare Your own Son in order to save us sinners, and therefore You understand what we're going through at this moment. Sustain us, O Lord, we pray, and if possible let us not be separated. We trust You completely."

Leaving the children in the care of their grandparents, Anna and I left for the clubhouse. As you'll remember from earlier chapters, the trials of both me and my father were held in absolute secrecy, but this public court—under the new ridicule religion philosophy—would be totally different. The idea was that the people, the "representatives of the public," would be able to listen to a case openly and give their opinions on whether the accused was right or wrong.

The club was filled to capacity. Most of the people in our church's congregation sat in the audience, and the city authorities had brought in a large number of the Komsomol (Young Communist League) members to swell the crowd. These young people had been carefully coached to interrupt the proceedings with speeches and outcries designed to show hatred for religion and contempt for its believers.

After the presiding magistrate had opened the session, the government prosecutor was first to speak. In a long harangue, he did his very best to smear my name and denigrate my congregation.

"Kulakov," the magistrate finally said, "you have five minutes to respond."

Five minutes? I thought. *Is that all?* But then I had never expected fairness.

I arose and approached the platform. In my hand were two brochures that contained quotes from the works of Lenin, Soviet Communism's founder. It may surprise my readers to learn that before the Bolshevik Revolution of 1917, Lenin in his published writings severely criticized the czarist government for its persecution of non-Orthodox believers. He promised that if Communists won the victory, they would grant full religious freedom to the Russian people.

So I simply read some of these statements aloud. I read how Lenin considered laws that persecuted non-Orthodox Christians as disgraceful. " 'All these laws are most unjust and oppressive,' " I read. " 'They are imposed by force alone. Everyone should have the right not only to believe what he likes but also to propagate whatever faith he likes.' " But I'd barely had time to read two or three sentences when the presiding magistrate interrupted me.

"Look at that," he said contemptuously. "Kulakov's an old upstager. He understands how to baffle an opponent with his own weapon!"

I continued to read.

"Keep silent!" the magistrate shouted.

"Hey!" someone angrily shouted from the back row.

I glanced around, and saw that a man I didn't know had risen to his feet.

"Hey, you godless judges!" he roared, and I could hear exasperation in every vibration of his voice. "Why are you trying to make Kulakov shut up? It's his turn to speak!"

"Be quiet!" the magistrate roared back. "Police! Police! Remove that intoxicated drunk!"

Once the indignant man—who did not seem drunk at all—was gone, the Komsomol youth and others raised their voices.

"Come on!" one shouted. "Let's make this place really hot for Kulakov!"

"Yeah!" said someone else. "Exile! He deserves exile!"

"To Siberia!" a third voice called out. "*Eastern* Siberia! All the way to Kolyma!"

My precious Anna wasn't used to this kind of thing. As she listened to these shouts and threats, she prayed steadily. *Heavenly Father, whatever happens, please don't let us be separated. Even if we're deported to the scariest place in Russia, please keep us all together.* .

Suddenly the proceedings came to an abrupt end, I'm not sure why. I'm reminded of the scene in John Bunyan's *Pilgrim's Progress* when Christian was frightened by the lions, but they could not harm him because they were chained. I was released and allowed to go home. Anna was so traumatized that she could not walk alone and needed me to support her on one side while one of our dear Adventist sisters held her on the other. Fortunately the walk to our small house on Shelikhova street was only five or six blocks.

As I was writing this book, I received an intriguing "voice from the past" that reminded me of that public trial, and that convinces me that nothing happens in this world that is totally forgotten or lost without a trace.

In November 2005 the General Conference of Seventh-day Adventists received an inquiry from a Russian citizen who was trying to get in touch with me. Since his last name was the same as some of my relatives, I mentioned this in my response.

"I do not know you," I wrote. "Are you perhaps a member of my extended family?"

I had included my e-mail address in my letter, and promptly received a reply.

Allow me to introduce myself more properly. Unfortunately I must disappoint you. I am not one of your relatives, but instead I am someone from your distant past—one who had a brief conversation with you many years ago.

It must have been in the early 1960s, at the beginning of March, in Almaty. It was one of those bitter cold evenings, with frozen puddles crackling under our feet. That night a so-called public court was being held at some kind of boot factory. Under discussion was the activity of an organization you were the head of, and many rude comments were hurled in your direction.

I happened to be there among the group of Komsomol volunteers. I'd come there to help swell the crowd, but also to broaden my own views. I felt bad after the meeting, because I knew that even in a small way I had participated in a despicable "kangaroo court."

At the exit I approached you as you were leaving the building (I believe your wife was at your side).

I said, "What went on at that meeting must have been depressing for you."

You looked at me with an expression of sadness, and said, "You were there. You saw what went on."

After many years I noticed your name popping up in the mass media, and later in your capacity as leader of the Adventist Church in the U.S.S.R., and finally as the director of the Bible Translation Institute. More than once I saw you on TV, and I also remember your speech at the Supreme Soviet of the U.S.S.R.

In regard to your translation of the New Testament . . . may God's blessings accompany your noble enterprise! . . .

As I read this man's letter I remembered the words of Psalm 126:5, "Those who sow in tears shall reap in joy" (NKJV), and I thanked the Lord for giving me the opportunity to see the results of seeds that were planted 45 years ago, back in those days when we were forced to witness to our Savior's glory more by our lives than by our words.

CHAPTER 15

Division in the Church

In order to introduce you to one of the most puzzling dilemmas our Russian Adventists faced during decades of oppression—and to show you the problems it caused and how it was triumphantly resolved—I must now move back a few months before the Almaty public trial I described in the previous chapter.

It was late in the fall of 1960, and I was walking the streets of Moscow, thinking and praying deeply.

I was 33, and was just finishing my second year as leader of the underground Adventist movement in Kazakhstan and other Asian republics. My heart was not only burdened with my responsibilities, but saddened, because Pastor Korolenko, who'd held this leadership position before me, had just been sentenced to eight years in the labor camps. Every day I expected that the same thing might happen to me.

So I'd traveled to the nation's capital to meet with someone I deeply respected, a man humble in spirit and slender in figure, the elderly Steven Kulizhski, chair of the Seventh-day Adventist All-Unions Council. One of the burdens on my heart was the fact that in spite of his comprehensive-sounding title, Elder Kulizhski represented only one of two main factions of Russian Adventism. The other was headquartered in Rostov-on-Don, in the Soviet Union's southern region.

"But why would Russian Adventists split into factions?" I can hear some of my bewildered readers asking. "Wouldn't it be better to stay together in order to present a united front to the authorities?" The answer to this question shows the genius of God's plan of church organization—and the tragedies that happen when that plan can't be fully followed.

The main reason we couldn't stay united was that the government made it nearly impossible for us to communicate with each other. The Soviet state had an almost pathological fear of organizations or gatherings it did not control, and since the state owned (and monitored) all communication services such as telephones and mail, and since the only print shops were state-owned, Adventists had long ago found it virtually impossible—and quite dangerous—to try to conduct long-distance print or voice conversations about the country's growing churches.

So of course this meant that we couldn't conduct church elections. And even if we'd managed to come up with some sort of detailed working policy satisfactory to everybody, there would have been no way to implement it. With no secure means of communication, church leaders found it impossible to keep their fingers on the pulse of their far-flung churches in a nation with an area larger than Canada, the United States, Mexico, and Central America combined. Under the current repressive conditions, there was absolutely no way all of Russian Adventism could ever be "on the same page."

So the inevitable happened. KGB infiltrators within the church, as well as plain old human nature, caused leaders and lay members in one area to become suspicious of church leaders and members in another part of the work, whom they didn't know well or at all. Rumors spread and grew, and there was no way to use truth to squelch the false ones. Oh, what a difference it would have made if we'd have been able to hold regional camp meetings featuring speakers from all over the nation—as well as from the General Conference!

You can imagine how frustrated our Adventist leaders felt. Back in the terrible 1930s Pastor Grigoryev had done his best to hold the church together. By the mid-1940s, pressure from other countries had forced Stalin to grudgingly allow a little religious freedom, and along with leaders of other denominations, Grigoryev was given permission to organize a "church governing committee." However, he couldn't draw in talented Adventists from across the nation, but had to rely on those who were nearby and available—and whose appointment aroused no objections from the authorities.

"You may also publish a church paper," the state authorities said. "But you must include occasional articles that encourage your readers to be patriotic people who love their country. Let them know what we are doing to work for peace among nations and to promote the well-being of our own citizens."

Grigoryev saw no problem with this, so he put out a call to an ordained minister he thought would do a great job as editor. "We haven't had a church paper in this country since 1928," he reminded this man. "Let's make up for lost time."

But the potential editor turned out to be a rather inflexible person, and when he learned about the authorities' requests for occasional press coverage favorable to the state, he frowned. "Impossible!" he said. "This is contrary to my convictions. It would be better not to publish at all than to compromise with the system."

I knew both Grigoryev and the potential editor very well. Both were faithful Adventists, but they held sincerely different opinions on the proper methods to spread the gospel. I was saddened to see the chagrin of the old leader as he watched the opportunity to publish a church paper slip away. It would be another 35 years, and only after many applications to the government, before we would be permitted to publish again—and this time it wouldn't even be a church paper, but just a small calendar with Bible verse references.

Meanwhile, factions were beginning to form. Persecution had removed many wise, influential church leaders who might have helped safeguard unity. So after Grigoryev's death in 1952, the church split into two major groups—and several smaller ones loosely under the umbrellas of the larger. Each group fought for dominance over the other.

What was so sadly puzzling was that nobody could put a finger on the real reasons for these splits. None of these groups could be accused of repudiating Adventist doctrines. Each faction was fully certain that it was on the side of truth, protecting the church from the unfaithful followers of Jesus.

In some cases it was a matter of "majoring in minors," such as whether or not to have "open Communion" or whether to reserve the Lord's Supper only for faithful members. Again, in an open society, such questions could be openly dealt with by an established church organization whose leaders and other thinkers could provide seminars and literature. For us, this was impossible.

Also, because of government restrictions on printing, the works of Ellen G. White were scarcely available at all. It wasn't until the 1950s that members began to translate and "print" (by secretly typing multiple carbon copies) such books as *Christ's Object Lessons, The Desire of Ages, Steps to Christ,* and *Thoughts From the Mount of Blessing.* This meant that the complete, balanced truth about righteousness by faith didn't reach Russian church members until they read those rice paper translations.

Oh, how I wish we could have had early and frequent access to inspired warnings such as this: "Self-righteousness is not true righteousness, and those who cling to it will be left to take the consequences of holding a fatal deception. Many today claim to obey the commandments of God, but they have not the love of God in their hearts to flow forth to others" (*Christ's Object Lessons,* p. 279).

The Asian underground organization that I led had tried to remain neutral between the conflicting groups. I visited both centers and tried to maintain fraternal Christian relations with them.

However, on that chilly autumn day in 1960 I was walking the Moscow streets, rather than going directly to the nearby Mira Avenue apartment that housed the All-Unions Council offices, because of my own suspicions. These had been planted in my mind by some of the leaders of the Rostov-on-Don faction. "Brother Kulakov," they warned me, "some of the men who work in that office with Elder Kulizhski are unfaithful to the cause of Christ!"

Do I dare take my heavy burdens to the Mira Avenue office and share them there?
I asked myself. *If it's true that there are wolves in that office, I might bring greater
danger to the Lord's work. Instead, I'll go to Elder Kulizhski's home and meet him
there after working hours. His hospitable wife, Eugenia, will do for me what she does
for all traveling pastors even with no advance notice—feed me and provide me a place
to sleep.*

I knew the Moscow transportation system well enough to be able to time
my arrival so that I would get to Elder Kulizhski's house at the same time that
he would. The trip involved taking two buses, so I boarded the first. When I
arrived at the connecting station, I was delighted to see Elder Kulizhski himself in the crowd. He spotted me almost at the same instant, but on his face
was a mix of surprise, vexation, and anxiety.

"Mikhail! Mikhail!" he called in a greatly agitated voice. "Where have
you been?"

I hurried toward him, astonished. "What do you mean?"

"Why didn't you come to the office?"

I stared. "You couldn't have known that I was in town!"

"I didn't," he admitted. "But we needed you badly at the office today."

"Why?"

He looked around, then whispered in my ear, "Today we had a Visitor—"
And then he paused. I could almost hear the capital V in his voice, and I wouldn't
have been surprised if he'd finished the sentence by saying, "from heaven itself."

"—from the General Conference!" he finished triumphantly.

I gasped. Now I could understand his joy. "From the *General Conference?*"
I repeated. "Who? Who was it?"

He nodded. "The president himself, R. R. Figuhr! He came to our office!"

My mind was spinning. "But—the *authorities*. How did he get through
their screening?"

"You mean, how official did they allow him to be?" Elder Kulizhski again
glanced carefully around him, then continued. "They certainly knew who he
was. Last Sabbath he visited the Moscow church as a tourist. The authorities
would not permit him to preach, or even to give greetings from the front. But
they did allow him to pass a note up to the pulpit for someone to read." He
peered at an arriving bus. "This is ours," he said, and together we boarded it.
Once in our seats, he continued.

"And today Elder Figuhr took a taxi; showed up at the office!" He was
hardly able to contain his excitement. "He knew our address, and he came
right in!"

To understand Elder Kulizhski's feelings, it's really necessary to be in his shoes for a while. To have loved and served the church the way he had, and yet to be separated from its main body by the iron curtain, and to hear about Adventism in other countries only through tiny bits of hopefully credible information—no wonder this day had been one of the most thrilling in his life.

"But Mikhail, my son, we needed you today. How we *needed* you!"

"The language barrier," I guessed. I'd learned English in the labor camps, first from a Russian naval architect named Lapin who'd lived in England for 25 years. He'd been sent there by the Soviet government to study the art of shipbuilding, but when he returned home they decided he was a British spy and promptly shipped him to the camps.

Elder Kulizhski sighed and nodded. "There was so much I wanted to say to him. I wanted to share our joys and predicaments. I wanted to give him some sense of how much our church is suffering, not only from persecution but from its splits and internal fights. I wanted to pray with him. I wanted to discuss how the General Conference might help the Adventist people in this country."

"So what did you do?" I asked.

"We invited one of the women in our church to translate. But her English wasn't very good, and frankly, I didn't know her very well, so I didn't want to say too much about church problems in her presence."

But then he looked sadly into my face. "If only you'd been at the office today. He and I could have shared so many blessings if you'd been on the spot. Why on earth did you not come to see us?"

I lowered my eyes. "Because of my unpardonable suspicions," I confessed, and briefly shared them with him.

Later, after his kindly wife, Eugenia, had invited us to the table, I asked my host, "Did Pastor Figuhr have any advice for the Russian brethren?"

"He did," said Elder Kulizhski, watching me carefully, "and this might come as a surprise to you."

"Well? What did he say?"

"He suggested that we search for opportunities to develop working relations with the Soviet government."

He was right. It *was* a surprise. It would take me a full 10 years to reflect on those words before I began to see some light in them. First I had to overcome my personal prejudices and learn more about trusting the guidance of the Lord.

I received some answers to these questions when the Lord providentially opened the door to the General Conference headquarters for me in 1970. My aunt invited me to visit her in San Francisco, and the government surprisingly gave me permission to go. The General Conference leaders urged me to make a stop in Takoma Park, and it was a joy to pray together and discuss at great length the issue that especially troubled me: How, in our particular conditions, can we build our relations with the state governing body without compromising the basic tenets of our church?

Elders Robert Pierson, Theodore Carcich, Walter Beach, and others shared several helpful ideas with me. Among the materials I received was a copy of the report of the General Conference secretary, W.R. Beach, made at the General Conference session of 1970.

"the Savior attempted no civil reforms, attacked no national abuses, condemned no national enemies. Nor did He interfere with the authority or administration of those in power. He was not indifferent to the woes of men, but He knew that the remedy lay not merely in human and external measures. To be effective, the cure had to reach men individually and regenerate the heart [see *The Desire of Ages,* p. 509]. This He strove incessantly to do.

"So Seventh-day Adventists preach God's good news, not politics, not social reform. By no stretch of the imagination, much less sound biblical exegesis, could they equate anarchy in any form with the will of God. And the extension they make of their loyalty to God to government forbids any participation anywhere in so-called 'underground' movements. 'Underground' activity would be dissonant, a contradiction in terms for Seventh-day Adventists. They conspire against no one, nor do they hide underground in fear. They persist as did Jesus in public ministry and undertake its consequences. Said Jesus, 'My kingdom is not of this world' (John 18:36). Capitalism, Communism, and all theories of property are irrelevant. Adventists serve mankind, standing shoulder to shoulder with men of good will in noble endeavor. Possibly they stand closer to the oppressed, the destitute, and the poor; yet they must also speak their message to the rich and the powerful. They say, 'There is no power but of God.' Even in the bitter times of oppression, in the midst of difficulty, the stream of faith must flow stronger and deeper because of it. Though such faith may be frowned upon by the 'powers that be' in some lands, the way of Christ's messengers is to witness openly through life and word; and that is the Seventh-day Adventist way."

When I returned home with this material—and the good advice—from General Conference leadership, I must admit that I had a hard time convincing some of my colleagues that we should accept this position as the true Seventh-day Adventist way of preaching the three angels' messages to the world. So the struggle continued for more than a decade, as intolerance and lack of understanding on the part of some inhibited both the growth of the

church and the establishing of a good rapport with the society in which we lived and worked.

In 1975 the churches in the central part of Russia invited me to move from Kazakhstan to the city of Tula, 160 miles south of Moscow. Though we still weren't permitted to establish an SDA church organization for the entire country, in 1977 the Soviet government—in response to many applications from our members—gave permission to our churches in the Russian Republic to have a meeting of their representatives for the election of a "senior pastor." At that meeting, which was held in the city of Gorky, I was chosen for that position.

Simultaneously, leaders of the SDA churches in other republics of the Soviet Union entrusted me, and Pastor Nicolai Zhukaluk (the dynamic leader of our work in the Ukraine) as my associate, to coordinate the efforts of all the Seventh-day Adventists in that vast territory as we strove to regain peace in our Christian family, and brotherly cooperation in our mission.

A further step toward healing happened in 1981 when a historic meeting of all SDA Russian leaders was convened. General Conference president Neal C. Wilson was present, and because of his wise counsel at least a formal unity was achieved. But because of the Soviet government's strictures, we were still officially unorganized and therefore separated from the world church organization. Without the approval of the Council of Religious Affairs, we were not free to print a single page of our literature, or to call any meeting of pastors, or to invite foreign guests. It was only in 1990—*after 30 years of praying, pleading, and persisting*—that we were allowed to form the Euro-Asia Division of Seventh-day Adventists.

CHAPTER :16 **"The Children's Hour"**

While their father was moving across the Soviet Union doing these "grown-up" things, my precious children were growing, and learning about the world, and developing their own unique perspectives about the dramatic times in which they were living. I humbly thank my heavenly Father for the joy they brought into the lives of Anna and me, and for the courage they showed in the face of almost constant persecution at school and elsewhere.

In 1860 Henry Wadsworth Longfellow wrote a poem that must tug at the heart of every parent as it does at mine. The first stanza reads:

Between the dark and the daylight,
When the night is beginning to lower,
Comes a pause in the day's occupations,
That is known as the Children's Hour.

The poem's speaker then goes on to tell how he puts aside anything else he's doing and devotes some time totally to the children. This is what I tried to do on the far-too-few occasions when I was able to be home from my travels. I deeply appreciate how my precious ones seemed to understand and forgive my long absences.

As I was preparing this book, I asked my children to provide me with some memories of their growing-up years. Though occasionally I've inserted their accounts as part of other narratives in the book, in this chapter I draw together several stories, roughly in chronological order according to when these events took place, along with an introduction to each child.

Our daughter Evangeline, whose stories appear elsewhere in this book, was born in 1954. She holds a Master of Arts degree in religion from Andrews University and now works as a nursing home chaplain in the state of New York. She is married to Alex Romanov, an SDA minister, and together they have raised three wonderful children. One of Evangeline's daughters is married to a minister, and her son, Daniel, is a minister of the Adventist Church as well.

Our daughter Maria was born in 1958, and holds an associate degree from Miller-Motte Technical College and is a licensed certified pharmacy technician. She is a pharmacy technician in the Erlanger Hospital in Chattanooga, Tennessee, and is married to Paul Zubkov, an Adventist minister pastoring a Russian congregation at Southern University. Together they have reared three very aspiring and successful children.

Our son Peter was born in 1964. He holds a Master of Arts degree in religion from Andrews University, and was the founder and the first speaker/director of the Voice of Hope radio and television center of the Euro-Asia Division. Currently the director/speaker of the Light of Hope television ministry, he is also the senior pastor of the Lakeview SDA Church in Atlanta, Georgia.

Pavel Mikhailovich Kulakov is our first son, born in December of 1955 in the city of Almaty, Kazakhstan. He's married to Nina Avetesyan, and together they've raised two beautiful girls. (The oldest is already married and has made Anna and me great-grandparents.) Pavel (the Russian form of "Paul") is a former Euro-Asia Division ADRA* director, and holds a Master of Science degree in administration from Andrews University. Presently he's a district superintendent of the Michigan Conference and senior pastor of the SDA church in Travers City, Michigan.

Pavel writes: "God protected our lives in so many marvelous ways in those days. I still remember how every night before we went to bed we children gathered in a circle around Dad and Mom, and we all prayed.

"Most of the time, of course, we knelt with Mom alone, since our dad went on long journeys to visit one church after another, sometimes 1,000 kilometers away from home. Every time he was about to depart, we took a long time to say goodbye to him, since we never knew when, or if, we would see him again. I remember how my mother's eyes would fill with tears at his departure, because in her heart she knew that every unforeseen delay of Dad's return might mean he'd been arrested.

"In the spring of 1966 our family lived in Kokand, Uzbekistan. One day when Dad was gone, an elderly man knocked on our door.

" 'My son is an officer in the KGB,' he told us after Mom had invited him in. 'A while ago he was talking on the telephone, and I heard his side of the conversation. He said that the KGB has a huge file on Mikhail Kulakov, and that they plan to arrest him.'

"We stared at him, openmouthed.

" 'I have come to warn you,' the man continued, 'because I am deeply sympathetic toward your family, and it would distress me to see these little children deprived of their father.'

" 'But what can we do?' Mom asked.

" 'As I see it,' he replied, 'there's only one way to escape the arrest, and that is to immediately leave Kokand. In fact, it would be best to leave Uzbekistan altogether.'

"Our family quickly followed his advice, deeply grateful that God—through his human angel—had given us this warning."

Elena Mikhailovna Rudoy (nee Kulakov) is our youngest daughter, born in 1970 in Chimkent, Kazakhstan. She holds a Doctor of Medicine degree from Loma Linda University and currently works as a resident doctor in one of the hospitals in the Loma Linda area. She's married to Paul Rudoy, associate pastor of the Redlands SDA Church. They have a sweet daughter, Alexa, who is 12 years old.

"My name is Elena. I am the youngest daughter of Mikhail and Anna Kulakov, the greatest parents in the world and my heroes. I was born in Kazakhstan, but when I was 6 years old my dad was called to Russia to help build the church organization there. To me, this was as exciting as a trip to the moon! As the rest of the family packed, I pumped them for as much information as I could get.

" 'What is Russia like?'

" 'Do Russian people look different?'

" 'Will I have my own room?'

" 'Will I have friends?'

" 'Can I help you pack?'

"Finally somebody said to me in exasperation, 'Elena, if you really want to help, please stop asking all those questions.'

"Russia was very beautiful. Across the street from our house were lilac bushes, and a block away was a birch tree forest. We all loved our new home except for two things: there was no sewer system and no running water. We had to carry our water in small buckets up a steep hill from a quarter mile away.

"Our house was made of red brick, with two tiny rooms upstairs and three downstairs. I immediately began to do some mental math. *I have five brothers and sisters,* I thought, *and Dad needs to have an office for his books and his studying. That means I won't have a room of my own!* And sure enough, I had to settle for a squeaky old couch in the living room.

"However, having to sleep on the living room couch has its advantages— I was closer to the kitchen than anyone else! Like all kids, I was hungry a lot, but it wouldn't be true to say that I was starving. Mom and Dad always managed to get enough food for all six of us, but I know for sure that they often denied themselves to make sure we were well fed.

"The best food was always saved for our visitors, and since my dad had become the leader of the underground church organization, we had a lot of guests. Ministers came to see Dad from all over the country—Latvia, Moldova, Ukraine. For a long time the government didn't give us permission to have a telephone in our home, so we never knew who was coming and when.

"Sometimes the ministers would arrive, only to find that Dad was gone on a long trip, so they stayed in our house (and shared our food) until he got back. We kids never knew exactly where we would sleep at night, because it all depended on how many visitors we had. But I don't remember any of us ever complaining. We knew that this was part of our mission, and we needed to help as much as we could.

"This was an exciting time not only for my family but for all the Adventists in the Soviet Union. Our church was given a bit more freedom—albeit freedom that was closely supervised by the KGB. From the moment we moved into our house, we knew that the KGB had installed secret microphones so that they could hear what we were saying. They had also hired Slava, our next-door neighbor, full-time to keep an eye on everything that happened at our house.

"One day when I was outside playing, Slava said to me, 'Would you like to come to my house and have some gogal mogal?'

" 'What's gogal mogal?' I asked him.

" 'Come and find out. You'll like it. And you can see my pet pig, too.'

I was totally amazed. 'You have a pet *pig?*'

" 'Come and see.'

"Sure enough, he had a pet pig, and I did learn to enjoy gogal mogal, which was a dessert made of raw eggs beaten up together with sugar. Later I realized that the only reason Slava invited me over was to try to get information from me about the visitors that stayed at our house, and what they said to my dad. This was why he always told me not to tell my parents he had talked to me! But he never got much information from me. All of us kids knew not to repeat anything we overheard Dad discussing.

"Just hearing 'KGB' used to make me feel a knot in my stomach. When I refused to join the Young Communist organization, the KGB forced my school principal to punish me by lowering my grades, and they made my teacher ridicule me in front of my classmates and warn them not to be friends with me. The KGB threatened my parents that if they kept bringing me to church I would be sent to an orphanage.

THOUGH THE HEAVENS FALL

"To cheer me up, my parents got me a new dog, which we called Consul. He was a guard dog, but one day when we came home from church we found Consul's dead body by our front door. We knew that the KGB had killed him because he had tried to keep them out of our house while we were away.

"My favorite time was Friday night. Preparation for Sabbath was a big deal. We cleaned, scrubbed, swept, washed, and cooked until sunset. Then we'd all get dressed in our best clothes and sit around our dining table, which had been covered with a white cloth just for this occasion. We sang songs, read the Bible, and studied our Sabbath school lesson.

"Sabbath afternoons after church, if Dad was in town, we often went for a walk along the railroad tracks. When a train passed by, I'd always think of Dad's prison stories. One time he and a lot of other prisoners were being re-located to a different camp by train, and they were packed into the cars like cattle. When night came and they needed to sleep, the space was so small that they had to lie so close to one another that if one man moved, everybody else in the row had to move with him.

"Anytime I heard the sound of a train I could vividly imagine the bodies of the prisoners squashed together on the floor in the darkness, being taken against their will into the unknown. A passage from Psalm 23, which we'd memorized during one of our Friday night worships, would come to mind: 'Though I walk through the valley of the shadow of death, I will fear no evil; for You are with me' (verse 4, NKJV). I knew that the day might come again when my dad, or any other member of my family, might be arrested and taken into the unknown. Yet I knew that if that happened, we would not be left alone."

Daniel Alexandrovich Romanov is one of our grandchildren, son of our daughter Evangeline and her husband, Alexander. When I wrote this book, Daniel was working on his Master of Arts degree at Andrews University. He graduated in December 2007 and became an associate pastor in a church in the Georgia-Cumberland Conference (United States).

Daniel writes: "With a loud voice and great energy, my grandfather (whom I call 'Dedushka,' which is Russian for 'grandpa') captured my attention every time he told a story from the Bible. Even when I was a young boy I looked forward to family worship with Dedushka, because he always remembered us grandchildren. Sometimes he would bring out a wooden elephant, a souvenir from his travels to Africa, and complete with animal noises he would tell us the story of the Flood and of God's grace. At other times he would lead us in a passionate song service, and we loved to be a part of it.

"Now, as I follow God's calling into the ministry, my grandfather is able to share with me a deeper understanding of the Scriptures. But equally important are the lessons I learned from him as a child. During the summers I would stay with my grandparents in their apartment. Sometimes I was allowed to sleep in Dedushka's office, and I would wake up, and through sleepy eyes I would see him on his knees in prayer. I would fall back asleep, and when I woke up again my dedushka would be in the same position, still praying.

"He also taught me a deep reverence for the Bible, which I have kept to this day. He always held the Holy Book in his hands in a special way, and read it as though every word gave him power to live. I would sometimes preach my college sermons to him so he could critique them, and he reminded me that the words of God, quoted from the Bible, should be read with a special intonation, different from those I used for the rest of the sermon.

"When I was attending college, I vividly remember how diligently my grandfather worked on translating the Sacred Word of God. Once, when my grandparents stayed in our house for several months, Dedushka spent untold hours working on the translation. From early morning, when everyone was still asleep, until late at night he would sit at his table surrounded by many books and dictionaries. I could not wait until evening worship when he would take a break from his hard work and share with us some of the amazing insights that he had found.

"I dearly love my grandparents, and treasure all of the principles they have shared with me."

Michael Mikhailovich Kulakov, Jr., is our second son, born in 1959, in Almaty, Kazakhstan. He was the founder and the first president of the Zaokski Adventist University in Russia. He holds a Doctor of Philosophy degree from the University of Oxford in Great Britain, and currently teaches political science and philosophy at Columbia Union College in Maryland. He is married to Lyudmila Lyakhu, and they have two resourceful and promising children.

Michael writes: "Every morning before we left for school Mom would gather us together. 'You're going to school today,' she would say, 'and you're going to encounter opposition. Let me read you something to encourage you.' She would open her Bible and read a few verses she'd chosen. One of the passages she read most often was Galatians 6:7: 'Do not be deceived: God cannot be mocked' [NIV].

" 'There is no situation where anybody can ever insult God,' she would say. Because we were constantly mocked at school, this verse was a great encouragement to us. Our family was surrounded by KGB agents, and it was almost impossible to even breathe without their knowing it. Yet my mother never ceased to amaze me. No matter how much persecution she and Dad encountered, she remained so loving and so hopeful.

"And though he was often away, Dad was very passionate in his desire to help us understand the great controversy correctly.

" 'The only way to understand the fall of Lucifer is on a personal, relational level,' he told us. 'God is the powerful Creator of the universe, but He also has a loving and open nature which makes Him willing to share that power.'

"Before Gorbachev came to power, we Soviet citizens didn't even know what openness and freedom was all about. Everything was censored—newspapers, TV, radio, everything. That's why I'm so thankful for the uncensored education we received from our dad in the time of Khrushchev and Brezhnev.

"I received this education at home, but where I took the 'exams' was at school. Let me tell you just one story, which happened when I was 10 years old. I loved memorizing and reciting poetry, and wanted so much to take part in my school's poetry contest. And Lidiya Voinova, my teacher at the Chimkent, Kazakhstan, middle school, knew I enjoyed this. But one day she gave me some bad news.

" 'Michael,' she said, 'there's no way you can enter that poetry contest unless you start wearing the red Communist tie.'

" 'I wouldn't have a problem with the tie,' I told her, 'if it didn't mean I was connecting myself with the party of Lenin.'

" 'What's wrong with the party of Lenin?' she asked. 'Isn't it the most progressive and powerful organization in the whole world?'

"I had always been taught to be respectful to my teachers, but I now realized that I would have to disagree with Mrs. Voinova. My knees started to shake, and my lips trembled. 'But my dad says that Lenin didn't believe in God,' I said. 'And the party of Lenin killed many priests and many pastors and millions of Christians.'

"This made her angry. 'You're not supposed to even *talk* about those things,' she snapped.

" 'There is no way I can join the Communist Party,' I said.

"She shrugged. 'Then there's no way you can take part in the contest.'

"Not long afterward I was sitting in class and heard my name announced over the loudspeaker: '*Michael Kulakov must report to the principal's office.*'

"My trembling legs took me through the hallways to the office of the stern Maria Kornilovna.

" 'Michael,' she asked me, 'would you like to take part in the poetry contest? I know how much you enjoy memorizing and reading poems.'

"Before I could answer, she continued.

" 'There is one condition. Just a little red tie, and there you are. I am planning to give my support to you, and not only for the school competition. I will also nominate you for the regional competition.'

"The *regional* competition! This was a great temptation to me, and I was thinking it over when she gave me another challenge—except this time she told a lie.

" 'Your older brother Pavel doesn't have a problem wearing the Communist tie at school,' she said. 'Did you know that? Not a single problem. There is a girl who keeps it for him at school, and gives it to him in the morning to wear.'

"I felt as though I had just received a deadly shock in my body. I started to shake. I looked up into her face.

" 'There is no way that could be true,' I said. 'Pavel has never worn the red tie, and *I* will never wear the red tie!'

"The following day a miracle happened. The principal again called me to her office, and gave me an order—not an invitation, but an *order*—to take part in the poetry contest. 'And you don't have to wear the tie,' she said.

"Knowing that this would be a tough competition, I spent the next month learning and practicing all my poems. If you had awakened me in the middle of the night I could have recited them. I still remember them in Russian.

"Finally the contest day arrived. I said a little prayer: *Jesus, for Your glory and honor, only for Your glory and honor, I would like to win this competition.*

"And I won! And my mean principal nominated me to represent the school at the regional competition. She knew I was a Christian, but she didn't tell the authorities. She was hoping they wouldn't notice. That's how badly she wanted her school to win.

"Finally the day of the regional competition arrived. It was held in a huge city square crowded with thousands of parents and other people. Each school had decorated a truck with the school name, driven it to the square, and opened its sides to make it into a performance stage. The regional secretary of the Communist Party was there, in her own very luxurious mobile office, which had been built for her and driven to that square.

"Suddenly someone noticed that I wasn't wearing the red tie, and reported me.

" 'Michael Kulakov has been summoned to the office of the regional secretary of the Communist Party,' the authorities told my principal. The principal was terrified. She refused to go with me, and instead sent our arts and music teacher, the kind and angelic Svetlana Sergeevna.

141

"Just before we walked into the mobile office, this dear teacher gave me a big hug and said just one sentence I will never forget: *'Pray to your God.'*

"The regional secretary's office was beautiful, but she herself was a very sinister woman. She stared at me from the top of my head to the toes of my shoes. She'd never seen me before—but I soon discovered what she thought of Christians.

" 'Young man,' she said, 'would you like to achieve everything our great superpower country has to offer you?' She didn't let me answer, but continued. 'Would you like to go to the best university? Would you like to get the highest diploma and become one of the most successful people in this nation?'

"Again she paused. I didn't know what to say.

" 'The only way to get this success is to be a member of the party. And your little red Communist tie is the first step. Wouldn't you like to be successful? Or would you like to be like your father, an uneducated, stupid sectarian?'

"Her words pierced my heart. This woman obviously didn't know anything about my family except that we were Christians, and she had just made a grave error about my dad. I didn't stop to think what I should say. I just said what I was thinking.

" 'Excuse me,' I said, 'but you don't know anything about my father. My father speaks English and German. My father reads Hebrew and Greek. My father spent his prison sentence with some of the leading Soviet dissident scientists. My father is loving, courageous, and highly educated.'

" 'And what is more, I have another Father. And that Father is greater than any other father in the universe. So yes, I do want to be like my dad. And I want to be like my heavenly Father.'

"I wasn't looking at the regional secretary's face, but it must have worn a look of shock, to be spoken to in this way by a 10-year-old.

"The first thing she said was a very dirty word. Then she shouted, *'Out of my sight! Get out of my sight!'*

"I turned and saw that dear Svetlana Sergeevna was shaking. She gathered me into her arms and gave me a quick hug, and we hurried out.

"Well, that's the end, I thought to myself. *I won't be reciting any poetry today.*

"But instead something awesome and wonderful happened. A big man wearing a uniform came up to me and took me by the arm. 'Walk with me,' he said. 'Walk with me very quickly.' He led me rapidly through crowds of people across the square to my school's truck, and up onto its platform. 'You will now recite your poem,' he said.

"My principal nodded her agreement.

"As I took a breath, I noticed that thousands of people were facing me. I began to recite. But as I spoke, I suddenly realized that nobody was listening to my poem or how well I was reciting it. Instead, they focused their attention on the front of my shirt, where the red tie should have been.

"And then I heard a word, repeated again and again, passed from mouth to ear, louder and louder, spreading across that great throng.

" 'Christian. He's a Christian. A Christian. A Christian. He's a Christian.'

"A lump came to my throat as I realized what was happening, something far more eternally important than this regional first prize in poetry recitation (which, incidentally, I won). God was making it possible for a young boy to stand before thousands of Soviet people and testify powerfully to his faith."

★ Adventist Development and Relief Agency

CHAPTER 17: **The Ice Begins to Melt**

During the 10 years from 1960 to 1970—while I was considering the General Conference president's suggestion to seek ways to cooperate with the authorities—life went on much as usual for my family and me. The government tolerated Christianity only grudgingly, and there was always the chance that my freedom could end instantly.

We moved often in those years, and my heart goes out to my precious wife and children for the struggles and stresses they faced. My trips, of course, were anything but joyrides. While I traveled I studied. Like many other citizens of the world, I understood that a firm grasp of the English language was becoming crucial, so I enrolled in a correspondence course through the Moscow Institute of Foreign Languages, graduating in 1966. In 1969 I put this training to use in Kishinev, Moldova, where I'd been invited to translate for General Conference representative Marvin Loewen.

Through this wonderful opportunity, I became known to the leadership of the world church, and in 1970 I was invited to attend the General Conference session., Sadly, the Soviet government refused to allow me to leave the country in time for the session, but I was able to visit the United States. later that year thanks to an invitation from my aunt Valentina Popova, who lived in San Francisco.

Providentially, my visit coincided with the Annual Council of the SDA world church, and there I met and formed lifelong friendships with many wise and influential leaders such as Roland Hegstad, Robert Spangler, and Neal Wilson. It was a special privilege to discuss church-state relations with Walter Beach and Theodore Carcich. "We all know," Carcich told me, "that it takes special wisdom to carry on the work in the Socialist countries. Be sure to ask the Lord for this wisdom."

I thank God for the hours I spent in discussion and prayer with then SDA General Conference president Robert Pierson. As we parted, he told me, "We will stand with you in all your efforts to work for our church's unity in your country, and to present Adventists as law-abiding citizens."

Four years later I received a letter from Elder Carcich, who at that time was a General Conference vice president.

"I'm coming to Moscow as a tourist," he wrote. "I will be staying at the Metropol Hotel in Moscow. Would it be possible for you to meet me there?"

Delighted, I made the journey, and met this huge, enthusiastic man in his room at that grand hotel in the very center of the city. After we'd greeted each other, he guided me over to the window, which had a splendid view of Red Square and the Kremlin.

"Look! What a beautiful sight!" he said in his powerful voice. "You know, just after I arrived at this hotel, I walked over to Red Square. While I stood there in front of the Kremlin's governmental buildings, I prayed to God for your great nation, for your government, and especially for your leader, Mr. Leonid Brezhnev."

When we left the hotel to take a walk together, he told me, "I'm assuming that they have electronic 'bugs' in hotels like this. Whoever was listening, I wanted them to know that we're not their enemies, but that we are praying for them."

"It is a real pleasure to see you again," I said. "I'm guessing that you've come as more than a tourist."

He nodded. "Back at the GC we're very aware that up to this point not a single one of our world church leaders has been received by any Soviet officials."

"That's true."

"So I'm here to try to break the ice a little. I'm hoping to meet with some of the high-ranking officials about two important issues. First, I want to see if it would be possible for some Soviet Adventists to come to the General Conference session in Vienna next year. Second, I'd like to arrange an official visit for Elder Pierson to the Soviet Union."

"That would be marvelous," I said faintly, my head spinning. When the dynamic Theodore Carcich set plans in motion, he did not do things halfway.

He reached into an inside coat pocket and brought out a piece of paper. "Here is a letter from the General Conference to the Soviet government about these matters," he said. "Would you mind reading it over? I'd like your advice about the way it expresses our wishes—and also about the best way to get this letter to the proper authorities."

I took the letter and began to read. "Oh no," I said, "you can't say *that*."

"Can't say what?"

"Look at this sentence." I pointed to a line. "It talks about Elder Pierson as 'a chief shepherd of the flock.' "

"What's wrong with that?"

I chuckled. "Remember, some of the people reading this letter are going to pounce on anything they can manufacture an objection about, in order to prevent the GC having its way. I can imagine an official reading that line and deliberately taking it literally. He'll say, 'Does this mean that Pierson thinks of Soviet Adventists as *sheep*? That's insulting!'"

Carcich roared with laughter. "OK, we'll change that. Duncan Eva wrote this letter, and when I get back home I'll tell him that from now on the only letters he writes are to the queen of England!"

After some more fine-tuning, we agreed that I would prepare a Russian translation of the letter to present to the officials along with the original.

"Elder Carcich, there's something else you need to know," I said.

"What's that?"

"Remember when I visited GC headquarters a few years ago? When I returned here, I had a meeting with the U.S.S.R. Council for Religious Affairs. I was quite respectfully received, and they were pleased to hear my report about the cordial welcome I was shown at the GC offices."

"Good, good."

"But at my most recent visit to this council I found them very annoyed."

"Annoyed? What about?"

"One of our General Conference leaders visited Kyrgyzstan as a tourist recently," I said, and mentioned the leader's name. "He gave a talk to the Adventist church in the city of Frunze [now Bishkek], and told the congregation about some of the adroit and evasive methods missionaries are using to win souls for Christ in countries in which the preaching of the gospel is not allowed."

"And the KGB was listening," Elder Carcich said.

I nodded. "They were. And the local authorities considered this not only subversive but a violation of state law, and reported it to Moscow."

"So they may be trying to accuse us of something we didn't even intend," Carcich said thoughtfully. "What would you suggest?"

"It would probably be best," I said, "if I went to the council alone and tried to make an appointment for you."

The two of us returned to the Metropol Hotel, and on our knees we implored the Lord to guide us and to make Elder Carcich's overtures successful. This time neither of us worried about the hidden microphones, because we wanted any listeners to know that we really were sincere in our faith in God, and in our desire to bring them a testimony of His love, as well as establish good working relationships with them. I knew that the government suspected that some visitors came to their country pretending to be Christians but with other agendas entirely. Our hosts needed to know that Elder Carcich had no hidden reasons for being there, so we decided it was much better to be very open about our Christian goals rather than leave our hosts in doubt.

And God answered our prayers.

"Elder Carcich," I later reported, "you have been invited to meet with some of the highest-level officials of the Council for Religious Affairs."

CHAPTER 18

A Few Good Men

"Who knows whether you have come to the kingdom for such a time as this?" Mordecai asked Esther (Esther 4:14, NKJV).

I could have said the same thing about Elder Theodore Carcich as I watched this great man in action the day he (and I as his translator) met with the Council for Religious Affairs. Though council chair Kuroyedov himself was not in his office that day, Carcich and I were received into a spacious office by Kuroyedov's first deputy and a group of departmental leaders. As we sat down at a huge table, we discovered that in front of each person had been placed a hospitable bottle containing a soft drink.

But I don't like the look on the deputy's face, I told myself as we were seated. *He's staring at Elder Carcich with a sour expression. His eyes are gloomy and his brows are knitted.*

Carcich, who fortunately could generate enough enthusiasm to counter a gloomy deputy plus a whole roomful of other people, wasn't fazed.

"I am deeply honored and delighted," he boomed, "at the privilege of meeting with such an imposing team of important state officials. Thank you for your gracious welcome."

Next he launched into rhapsodies about all the wonderful things he had seen in Moscow since his arrival. He mentioned his prayer at Red Square, and then gracefully turned to the reason he had come.

"I appreciate the opportunity," he said, "as a vice president of the world church of Seventh-day Adventists, to negotiate with you some issues of mutual interest. I assure you that the church I represent teaches its members everywhere to be law-abiding citizens, and—"

"Oh, come now, Mr. Carcich," the deputy interrupted him contemptuously.

For the next 12 years, until Gorbachev's *perestroika* (reconstruction), I would hear exactly that tone of voice used to all other visitors from the General Conference. This was because the KGB had firmly resolved not to establish any relationship with the headquarters of our world church. They recognized very clearly that if the worldwide Adventist Church's organizational principles got a foothold, its scattered and loosely connected churches would suddenly become subordinate to a headquarters located in the Soviet Union's archenemy, the United States of America. This was unthinkable. So in an effort to keep us at a distance, they refused even to use common politeness, but instead chose to foster an atmosphere of tension. Thus the deputy's chilly *"Oh, come now,* Mr. Carcich."

Startled, Elder Carcich broke off midsentence. "Yes?"

"A few months ago," the deputy growled, "one of the workers of your Seventh-day Adventist General Conference visited the believers in the southern part of the USSR. And while speaking in a church there, he allowed himself to say certain things that the Soviet people don't like to hear."

Elder Carcich was a large man, and he could use every inch of his frame for full dramatic effect. He'd heard about this incident from me, but still he drew back in amazement, his face showing shock and remorse.

After a short pause, he hushed the volume of his huge voice and asked humbly, "May I know what this man said?"

The deputy sat in stony silence.

Once Carcich realized he wasn't going to be given an answer, he clutched his head with both hands, and shook it back and forth.

"Oh, I am so sorry!" he moaned. "On behalf of the General Conference I do apologize for those remarks. Please, please allow me to assure you that this happened unintentionally, and only because we don't know each other very well. Now that we are better acquainted, it will never happen again!"

Theodore Carcich's wonderful ability to charm even the most hostile people bore fruit that day. As I translated for him, I was interested to observe the deep impression he made on those key administrators of church affairs in that atheistic country. Whatever they may have thought of this American, they gave him permission to occupy the pulpit in our Moscow church that Sabbath to bring greetings from the General Conference and from fellow believers all around the world.

It was a long greeting—25 to 30 minutes! He, of course, made many pleasant remarks about the Soviet government, but the greatest encouragement came when he told these Russian Adventists how beloved they were by God and by His children in other countries across the planet.

His talk—fully reported to the KGB, of course—convinced the authorities that even though they might not *like* this loud and eccentric good-natured man, they needed to at least factor him into the equation. So for the next several weeks he and I visited many churches in other cities, where he freely preached the gospel of Jesus Christ.

It wasn't that the authorities had come to trust him. That would have been like the leopard of Jeremiah 13:23 changing its spots! It was simply that they had begun to realize that they could no longer simply ignore the Adventist world church as they'd tried to do before, but would need to pursue their policies on a more subtle and camouflaged level.

Elder Carcich's visit resulted in some additional concessions as well. Russian Adventists were gradually allowed to establish regular contacts with the General Conference, and to actually attend GC sessions (beginning with the following year's convocation at Vienna). Foreign Adventist leaders, though still required to visit only as tourists, were permitted to speak in our churches. The government even allowed Pastor N. Zhukalyuk and me to become members of the General Conference Committee.

I remember studying Theodore Carcich and trying to analyze some of his seemingly extravagant actions and words—so different from the way I myself might have approached the same challenges. I think I now have a better understanding of the words of Paul, who said, "I have become all things to all men, that I might by all means save some" (1 Corinthians 9:22, NKJV).

Communists and Communism were a puzzle even to Russian Christians. I remember conversations I'd had with my father (who'd spent 10 years in the labor camps) and my uncle Alexander Demidov (who'd spent a total of 30 years in the camps and in exile). Once these men were released and could move about freely, we met often to study and pray and talk.

"The early Russian Adventist pioneers—the ones who saw the revolution begin and the czar fall—didn't think the Communists would stay in power very long," they told me. " 'Just a few more years,' these pioneers said, 'and the Soviet power will be extinct.' But this regime was allowed far more time than anybody expected."

"Communism *will* fall," Uncle Alexander assured me. "But God is not in a hurry. He's giving Satan the time he needs to develop all the thinkable—and unthinkable—ways of life and systems of government that try to exist without God. But in time the whole universe will see the inadequacy of these ideologies, and all these regimes will collapse."

"And the work of saving perishing souls shouldn't stop," my dad chimed in. "We need to ask the Holy Spirit to show us the way and to give us wisdom and power to fulfill our tasks effectively."

And as we studied and talked and prayed, God began to reveal clearly to us that despite the heartless functionaries in all Soviet governmental offices, including the Council for Religious Affairs and even the KGB, there were a few Nicodemuses and Gamaliels.

The more contact I had with the government, the more of these precious people I discovered. From 1970 on, I visited the Council for Religious Affairs quite often. Among other items, my agenda of questions went something like this:

May we restore a nationwide system of Adventist Church organization?

May we establish a school to train church workers?

May we have official approval to send invitations to foreign guests for this or that function we are planning?

May we print church hymnals and calendars? (Church papers and newsletters were forbidden, but occasionally the council allowed churches to print calendars with Bible references on them.)

You can't imagine how thrilled I was to discover, in the council and in other government offices, men and women who really wanted to assist us. Actually, most of these cooperative people were not helping us because they were unfaithful to their duties or because they were Christians. It's simply that some had more foresight than their bosses. They either understood that "what's good for the believer is good for the state," or they were genuinely kind and friendly human beings, eager to help. A few, however, did have a sharp spiritual hunger, and even privately studied the Bible with us in order to overcome their atheistic education. Even now I must be cautious in giving their names, but in eternity we will meet many such Russian men and women.

One time I was at my house near Moscow. It was the middle of the night, and I was in a deep sleep when I awoke to loud knocking on the door. I can imagine that anyone would be startled by a midnight knock, but when you're an Adventist pastor in the Soviet Union and you've already spent several years in the camps, your heart behaves very abnormally at the sound of knuckles striking door panels.

I slipped out of bed and walked cautiously to the door. *Is this the KGB?* I wondered. *Am I bound for the camps again? Or into exile?*

It was none of those. It was Alexander (I will give only his first name), a good friend of mine who had worked in an influential government post for several years.

"Sorry to wake you," he whispered.

I swallowed, trying to regain my composure. "Alexander! Please come in."

"No," he hissed. "You come outside."

"What's wrong?" I asked, stepping through the doorway.

"Nothing," he said, whispering so delicately that even the most sensitive microphone bug wouldn't have picked up his words. "But I must be quick. Nobody knows I'm here. Remember those applications you brought into our office requesting permission to send some of your young men abroad so that they could attend a theological seminary?"

"I remember. Your boss denied the request."

Alexander nodded. "I know. But he just went on vacation. So as quickly as you can, fill out new applications, and I'll get someone to sign them."

Many other such stories happened, and I'll have to save them to tell when we get to heaven. But please allow me to say a few words with love and gratitude about one special friend of mine.

Early in 1985 I was surprised to receive an invitation to the very inner office of the new chair of the Council for Religious Affairs, Mr. Konstantin Kharchev. *This is highly unusual,* I remember thinking. *No previous chair ever did me the honor of having me to his private office.*

At my first meeting with Kharchev I realized immediately that now I would be dealing with an extraordinary leader with a fresh outlook. I was amazed to discover how freely he expressed his critical attitude toward past persecutions.

"So," he said with an ironic smile, "they thought they could use prisons and labor camps to prove to you that there is no God?"

During that first conversation I repeated a request I'd often asked the council. "We really do need an officially recognized church organization," I said. He and I both knew that this was exactly what the KBG did *not* want, but he didn't allude to this.

Instead, he said, "Look. Why don't you just go ahead and build your organization on a 'gentlemen's agreement' basis?" I took the hint, and from that point on our U.S.S.R. church organization began to exist in a semiofficial status.

In 1986 Kharchev and I, along with a group of about 270 representatives of the USSR community, traveled to Chautauqua, New York, to attend the huge Conference of Public Diplomacy held there. When General Conference president Neal Wilson learned about Kharchev's visit, he immediately invited him to visit some of our U.S. Adventist institutions. Kharchev decided he could spare enough time to travel to the Adventist Media Center and Loma Linda Medical Center, and I was privileged to accompany him as translator, even performing this duty on a telephone conversation Kharchev had with Senator Richard Lugar.

Konstantin Kharchev was very much impressed by everything he saw, and said to me over and over, "All this we must do in the U.S.S.R."

But the most interesting thing (to me) happened on our way back to Moscow. We were booked on the same Lufthansa flight, he in first class and I in economy. We had our tickets in hand, and I was helping him check his luggage. Suddenly the woman airline employee helping us came around to our side of the counter.

"Would you mind stepping away for a moment?" she politely asked me. "I need to speak to this man."

I glanced at Kharchev. *His English skills are probably able to handle this,* I decided, and stepped a few feet away while they had a brief conversation. Kharchev later told me that she said to him, "We have an empty seat next to yours in first class. If you'd like, I could give it to the man who's accompanying you."

Kharchev instantly agreed. This was a night flight, 11 hours nonstop to Moscow, but neither Kharchev nor I slept a wink. Instead we took advantage of this wonderful opportunity to share our hearts with each other. Finally, as the plane began to descend through the morning skies toward Sheremetyevo International Airport, Konstantin Kharchev turned to me.

"From now on," he said, "you are my spiritual father. Please tell me how I can help you in what you are doing for God and the people in the U.S.S.R."

And over the next several years, as our church was building its seminary, its publishing house, and its media center—and was establishing its lines of organization—the help of that courageous and noble man was invaluable.

The Midnight Translator
and the Exiled "Prophet"

Dear Reader: I think you'll agree, after reading her breathtaking story, that doing justice to the life of Alla Shtabinskaya, who single-handedly accomplished so much for our church, would require a book of its own.

It was a clear spring Moscow day in 1952. A teenage girl named Alla Shtabinskaya was standing in a long line at a grocery store. As the line inched forward, her attention was caught by an elderly woman working her way down the row of shoppers.

What's she doing? Alla wondered. *She's behaving strangely.*

Step by step the little *babushka* (grandmother) eased closer, and now Alla could see that she was handing a tiny slip of paper to each person, acting calmly and casually so she wouldn't attract attention. Finally she came to Alla, quickly slipped one of the papers into the girl's palm, and turned to someone else.

Alla unfolded the slip and saw the neatly handwritten address of a meeting place as well as days and times of worship services.

"This awakened within me a sense of joyful curiosity," Alla recalled later. "Though only 15, I was already searching for the meaning of life, for like millions of other Russian soldiers, my father had died during the Second World War."

A few weeks later Alla and her mother tracked down the paper's address and discovered that they were entering Moscow's one and only Seventh-day Adventist church. They began attending regularly, and it wasn't long before both mother and daughter expressed their desire to be baptized and become members.

Alla's mother was soon baptized and welcomed into membership, but Alla had to wait. "I'm sorry," the pastor told her apologetically, "but according to the Soviet laws that regulate religious organizations, it's illegal for me to baptize minors. You'll have to wait until you're 18."

But this didn't discourage Alla. She continued to attend worship services at the church she'd come to love.

"From that point on," she recalls, "the authorities had us shadowed. They even moved a KGB informer into the apartment next to ours. Anyone behind that wall could hear us talking or reading, so to have any privacy at all we either had to whisper or write notes to each other. Only in the open air could we talk freely without fear."

And the persecution didn't stop there. The Communist government was determined that Christians not advance to higher educational levels, so they informed Alla's high school administrators that she'd become a believer in God, and ordered her teachers to lower the girl's grades so that she wouldn't be able to graduate.

But this didn't deter Alla in the least.

"How can I learn more about the Bible?" she asked her pastor. "I really want a much deeper knowledge of God's truth."

The man paused, and then spoke the words that would not only change Alla's life but bless a generation of Adventist believers. "You know," he said thoughtfully, "there's an immense amount of spiritual literature available in the English language."

Suddenly Alla's heart flamed with a burning desire to master English to a "proficiency" level. She began dreaming of becoming a professional translator of religious literature. *I want to make my input into the spiritual enlightenment of Russian society,* she thought.

Through an amazing series of miracles Alla managed to overcome a multitude of obstacles in order to study English at Moscow's prestigious Pedagogical Institute of Foreign Languages. She spent four years within the walls of that university, and perhaps the most thrilling miracle is that she retained her faith, because the Communist Party had turned every institution of higher learning into an atheist factory.

Providentially, Alla had a key ally on her side. She was convinced that God opened the heart of the dean of the English Language Department, for in her travels abroad that precious woman had learned something about Seventh-day Adventists. And the dean put her own teaching position at risk by concealing Alla's religious convictions from the administration.

But in Alla's fifth year a new dean was appointed, and the truth came out. To their horror, the administrators realized that all along they'd been educating a professed believer. Dreadfully embarrassed—and anxious to redeem their integrity in the eyes of the party bosses—they immediately implemented harsh, oppressive measures against the young Christian girl. The story has it that in 1959, just before her final exams, both the university and the Moscow city council decided to "take her on." Their goal was to try to break Alla's faith by threatening to deny her her well-earned degree.

"I was called before an assembly of city council representatives," she recalled later, "then the Communist Party Regional Committee, and then the Komsomol Committee. They tried to humiliate, intimidate, and ridicule me, pressuring me to change my mind and denounce my faith in God.

"Later on, officers of the KGB, the Ministry of Internal Affairs, and the

Criminal Investigation Department interrogated me in my home and also at the language institute. Then I was summoned to 'Petrovka 38' [a KGB office], where they treated me very rudely. Using threats, they tried to turn me into their secret informer in order to 'flush out' other Adventist believers.

"However, I always steadfastly refused. I knew that this harassment was arranged by the university administration, because it happened just before my final exams in an attempt to keep me from receiving my degree. Yet my Seventh-day Adventist pastors always lifted me up in their prayers, and that only strengthened my resolve to be faithful.

"Once, on a summer morning, two militiamen showed up at our house. Without introducing themselves or showing any documents, they put me under arrest and brought me to a militia station. What they wanted was to get hold of my passport and tear it up (something they did to many believers), so that it would become invalid. This would have made my stay in Moscow impossible."

In those days every citizen of the Soviet Union had to be registered in the local police/militia office at the place of his or her residence, and this registration was marked in the passport. It was illegal everywhere to live outside one's registered area, and it was impossible to reside in Moscow unless one were a permanent resident (which Alla was) or had received an invitation from the highest levels of government.

In Alla's case the police were trying to deprive her of the opportunity to continue to live in the capital city. If she surrendered or lost her Moscow passport, she would have to leave, and then go through the tedious process of getting a new one. The authorities would of course make sure that the police denied her request, and she would therefore be compelled to leave Moscow for good.

"However," Alla said, "I knew what they were after, and refused to give them the passport. After many hours of threats, they released me to walk home alone in the dark of night."

Finally—and this is the official version—Alla and her mother "lost" their permit to live in Moscow, and opted "voluntarily" to move to the city of Tomsk, in Siberia. Yet eventually, more than 1,700 miles east of Moscow, this persistent young Christian achieved her goal. There in Tomsk she completed her English studies and received her degree. Now she had the tools to fulfill her dream of translating religious literature into the Russian language.

And the amazed and grateful leadership of the underground Adventist churches quickly supplied her with English copies of books such as *Prophets and Kings, The Story of Redemption, The Desire of Ages,* and many others. And so this brilliant young adult set to work.

Alla's years of training had ingrained within her the highest standards. "I worked very hard," she wrote to me later, "and mostly at night. I lived under constant fear of being arrested by the authorities for my 'subversive activities.' With pen in hand I would translate an entire book, carefully considering every word."

And then she faced an even greater challenge. In order to avoid errors, she refused to delegate the initial typing to anyone else. However, she lived in an apartment with thin walls, and the incessant clatter of typewriter keys was sure to arouse her neighbors' suspicions.

"So I soundproofed my printing operation as best I could," she says. "I placed an electric desk lamp close to the typewriter, and then covered everything with several blankets. After turning on the radio to conceal the sound of the keys, I would put my hands and my head under this heavy tent, and type for hours in this hunched-over position. The lamp created an enormous amount of heat, like a sauna, and I frequently had to pop my head out for a breath of fresh air before diving underneath to work again."

Living in such extreme conditions, and in constant fear of arrest, each day she labored to the point of exhaustion, never considering her own health. What motivated Alla to continue this fatiguing and dangerous work?

"I lived among people who looked for happiness in drunkenness, debauchery, and criminal conduct," she always responded when asked. "I received a call from the Lord to give them literature that would sober them up and clear their thinking."

This took faith, of course. While most Soviet citizens—along with the entire rest of the world—assumed that Communism would continue its grip on power indefinitely, Christians such as Alla believed that somehow things would change. "Faith," its been said, "is waiting to see what God will do," and the faithful believed in the ultimate triumph of good over evil, and in the fulfillment of Christ's promise that "this gospel of the kingdom shall be preached in all the world for a witness unto all nations; and then shall the end come" (Matthew 24:14). They assumed that God, in His time and by His means, would remove the iron curtain and finally open up the immense Soviet Union for the proclamation of the gospel.

Alla Shtabinskaya passed to her rest in July 2004, at age 67. A year later her 92-year-old mother followed her to the grave.

Another such pillar of faith—a faith that not only survives the present but glimpses a brighter future—was Alexander M. Demidov. Back in chapter 2 I told the story of how in the late 1920s he edited the Adventist magazine *The Voice of Truth* until the state-monopolized presses refused to print it.

In 1930 Alexander was arrested and "isolated from society" for this "crime." He spent the next 30 years in Stalin's prisons and labor camps. Sometime around 1960 I was able to locate him. He was still in exile, living beyond the Arctic Circle in the city of Noril'sk, at a latitude comparable to Barrow, Alaska, or the northern tip of Norway.

It was the time of year when the sun was never seen, and he and I stepped out of his small, stuffy apartment into a city street submerged in the perpetual polar night. In the distance, against the backdrop of the dark sky, we could see an array of brightly lit radio and television towers.

"Do you see those antennas?" Alexander asked, pointing at them.

"I do."

"You can be sure, my friend," he said, "that the time is coming when this very equipment, erected by the Communists to spread propaganda about their ideology, will be used by God to proclaim His everlasting gospel!"

I was of course overjoyed at his words, but at the same time stunned by the great faith of this man, who could turn his back on 30 years' imprisonment and exile and look forward with such certainty to a bright and free tomorrow.

And when the years had passed and the government control over the mass media had ended, I was able to witness this prophecy's fulfillment personally. The day came when the leadership of our church signed contracts with the new owners of those very same radio and TV stations, allowing us the use of the airwaves to spread the gospel!

Another fulfillment of this confident prophecy happened in the major Siberian city of Novosibirsk. In 1991 General Conference vice president Kenneth Mittleider accompanied my son Peter (founder of Russia's first-ever Christian Media Center) and me on a tour of a powerful radio station. "Only a few years ago," the station manager told us, "these transmitters were used to jam international broadcasts like the BBC and Voice of America."

But we three Adventists were there to sign a contract that would allow us to use those same towers to proclaim the three angels' messages all across Asia. God's clock had struck, the once-strong iron curtain rotted to shreds, and our church was ready. How true are these words of the wise and courageous Coretta Scott King when she wrote, "There is a spirit and a need and a man at the beginning of every great human advance. Every one of these must be right for that particular moment of history, or nothing happens."

The First Protestant
CHAPTER 20: Seminary in Russia

To tell the story of the founding of our Adventist ministerial training seminary in Russia—a "first" for Protestantism—I've depended heavily on material in the book *God's Soviet Miracles,*[1] by my son Michael Kulakov, Jr., the school's founder and first president. What follows (until I resume the story) are his words, carefully revised and condensed for this chapter.

Michael Kulakov: "Even though Mikhail Gorbachev's perestroika was bringing fresh optimism into Soviet society, the Communist Party still held a strong grip on every aspect of Russian life. However, Adventist pastoral education was happening in a clandestine way, and 'underground schools' existed in several areas of the country. For 10 years (1975-1985) before Gorbachev came to power, my father had been writing letters to the Soviet authorities about pastoral education needs. To avoid a direct clash with the Communist antireligious program, he dared not breathe a word about enrolling new pastoral candidates, but merely requested permission to give proper education to those men who already were working in Adventist churches as lay pastors.

"What we needed was a school, and we kept up a constant, polite, but insistent stream of correspondence. How many applications, appeals, petitions, and other epistolary masterpieces do you think it might take to get a yes answer from the Soviet bureaucratic maze—for something as unheard-of as a Christian school? On March 12, 1986, our seventy-sixth letter of request for a religious correspondence school—all we dared ask for at first—lay on the desk of the Council for Religious Affairs.

"The government's response was typical. Even though we'd asked permission to acquire property, their return letter said, 'We cannot allow you to begin your religious correspondence school because you have no place in which to do so.'

"However, Religious Affairs council chairman Konstantin Kharchev was far more open to change than his predecessors had been. He could see sense in our arguments that when a denomination's ministers are well educated, the state benefits as well as the church.

"Soon we heard good news from Yevlampii A. Tarasov, the council's chair of the Department for Protestant Churches: 'You may construct a small building adjacent to your church in Tula.' Tula, just south of Moscow, was where our church leadership resided. The government had refused to allow Adventism to be headquartered in Moscow.

"But the Tula city fathers—old party veterans seasoned in the Stalin era—objected vigorously.

" 'We will never in the world permit a religious school to be founded in Tula!' they growled. 'We are a "hero city;" a city of Red veterans!'

"Yevlampii Tarasov, following the instruction of his chief, Konstantin Kharchev, hurried down to Tula to try to turn the tide. We later heard from sympathetic observers that a real battle had broken out at this meeting.

" 'We don't want to hear anything about this Christian-sect school!' the city fathers roared. 'Not in a city so rich in glorious revolutionary traditions!'

"There was nothing left for us to do but look for something outside the city limits. An old Orthodox church—more ruins than anything—caught our eye, but it turned out that for many years local Orthodox believers had been petitioning for its use. The last thing we wanted was for the authorities to give us this building against the local population's wishes, and thereby stir up ill will. So we backed off.

"Several other possibilities came to our attention, but each provoked some sort of official backlash. A small private home with a plot of land was 'too close to Tula,' said the authorities. 'What's more, it's right along the Moscow-Tula rail line, and would be too public.' Another site was too close to the country estate of Leo Tolstoy, and would presumably offend the sainted memory of that national hero. We proposed more sites, and the answer was always 'Too close. Too close to Tula.'

" 'What's the matter? Do we give off an unpleasant odor?' one of our group finally demanded. The truth, of course, was that authorities wanted to keep us out of sight because our growing church gave the lie to one of Communism's core beliefs: 'Under socialism, religion is dying away.'

"But the Lord had a plan.

"August 22, 1986, will remain in our memories as the day God revealed that plan to us, answering our prayers directly and tangibly. Here's how it happened.

"Our study of area maps had told us that the farther out we got from Tula, the farther we'd be from rail and road lines that would give us the necessary direct connection to Moscow.

" 'So let's try for *closer* to Moscow,' we decided.

"Then a sympathetic government official got in touch with us. 'Why don't you see if there are some possibilities in Zaokski?' he suggested.

"We didn't want to get our hopes up, but Zaokski would indeed be ideal, and this official head-nod gave us courage. Zaokski was slightly less than 80 miles from Moscow and a major highway passed nearby. It also had both rail and telephone lines. As a bonus, it bordered on a Russian national park, and was perhaps the most beautiful and picturesque region in the greater Moscow area.

"So on August 22 I invited my relatives Vitya and Anya to join me in the car, and we set off on our search. But after traveling far and wide throughout the entire Zaokski settlement, we felt close to despair. *We'll have to go back empty-handed,* I thought. *There's nothing—absolutely nothing—suitable!*

"We lingered as long we could, but finally decided to bow to the inevitable. On our way toward the main highway, the entire settlement behind us, we drove over a railroad crossing. Just over the tracks was a street that ran parallel to the rails.

"I'd remembered this street as we'd arrived, but had paid no attention to it. Now I turned onto it. Typical little country homes—small, wooden, and rather dilapidated—were strung out along the road.

"Suddenly the road ended. And there, beyond rows of tall old poplars we saw the remains of a large three-story building with yawning gaps for windows.

" 'It looks to me as if we've found it!' I shouted.

"Tumbling from the car, I ran toward the old building. Inside, a couple of boys sat on the piles of debris and wreckage, laughing and talking beside a fire. When they saw us, they grew quiet and stared curiously.

" 'Hi, kids,' I said.

" 'Hi,' they said cautiously.

" 'What did this building used to be?' I asked. 'Do you know? What was here?'

" 'A school,' one of them said.

" 'Who owns the building now?'

"One of the kids smirked. 'What difference does it make? It no use to anyone!'

" 'So nobody's planning to do anything with it?' I asked. "Like restore it or something?'

" 'Of course not. It was ruined a long time ago.'

" 'So what happened?' I asked. 'A fire?'

" 'You'd learn a lot more if you asked Ivan Ivanovich," one of the kids said. "Over in that house. He used to be the director of the school. He can tell you every detail.'

"At my knock on the house door, an elderly gentleman appeared, wearing thick-lensed glasses. When he found out that I was interested in the history of the old school, he sat down on a bench, and after unhurriedly lighting a cigarette he began his story.

" 'This school was built in the thirties,' he said, 'using the "people's construction method"—volunteers that worked on the construction after their regular day's work was finished. But after the war the town kept growing, and soon outgrew my school. We needed a gym, but since the town was expanding away from us rather than toward us, a brand-new school with a gym was built closer to the center of population.

" 'After that, the town council didn't know what to do with this building, so it fell into disrepair.' Ivan Ivanovich chuckled bitterly. 'And then one night a fire broke out. And even though the fire department was only a little more than a mile away, the flames burned for three days and consumed everything except the four brick walls. And then the city council gave everybody permission to dismantle the walls for building materials.'

"The old schoolmaster glanced over his shoulder at the building, which showed no signs of dismantling. 'Alas,' he chortled, 'that brickwork had been made to last. Those bricks and mortar had been cemented together by some method known only to those who did it, and nobody could budge a single brick!'

"After our visit with Ivan we immediately drove to the regional office of architectural planning, and discovered to our surprise that, on the maps, the building did not exist at all! In its place, planners had drawn neat little squares, plots for future private homes. However, the heavenly Architect had a different plan—and He brought it to pass! 'No,' we sang as we sped homeward that night, 'no one can keep us from teaching God's truth!'

Mikhail's narrative resumes: That evening I heard my son Michael's car pull into our small backyard, and I went out to greet him. His eyes aglow with excitement, he threw his arms around my neck.

"Dad," he exclaimed triumphantly, "God has answered our prayers today!"

There would be many long months of bureaucratic obstacles to overcome, but each victory would provide confirmation that the ruined school building was the very place God had envisioned for His seminary. In a wonderful way He used our influential friends in Moscow and Tula to overcome the obstacles. Those great men, just as Cyrus in antiquity, were employed for God as instruments of His favor for His people.

And on January 27, 1987, for the first time in its 70-year existence, our atheistic government granted an official permit to the Seventh-day Adventist Church, not only for the construction of its spiritual center and a seminary, but also setting aside a considerable section of land in a village near Moscow.

Was this a miracle, or *what?*

Yet serious challenges lay ahead. Any of my readers who live in a democracy, which permits free enterprise, cannot have any true concept of these challenges. Since there were no private construction companies, our center had to be figured into the government's current five-year program, and planned that many years ahead. Ordering building materials itself might take years, since each and every order for work or materials had to be first approved by the government.

But God is unstoppable. He brought my son and his coworkers in contact with many influential people whose names we are not at liberty to reveal—because many among them risked their own positions by their desire to please God and help our church.

Construction permits were granted, but building would be impossible without volunteers. Who knows how everything would have come together without construction foreman Vasilii Novosad? Without him, it's likely that the seminary could never have been constructed in as short a time as it was. Novosad was a terrific example of a servant of God. Not only was he tall, lively, smiling, and charming (and easy to work with), but without any complaint he spent a half year apart from his family working on the school. He slept with the construction workers, working day and night in the frosty cold. He had no vehicle of his own, yet to carry out his construction duties he traveled back and forth from Tula and other places on commuter trains, and even as a hitchhiker.

Construction began in March, and the weather was still frigid. The first job was to construct a sleeping shed on the second floor of the half-destroyed building for the laborers. The first night there the stove didn't work, and finally the men asked Novosad to stop his useless "smoking" with the stove, and everybody went to sleep in the cold.

From the first day onward almost all our Zaokski neighbors showed great sympathy, responsiveness, and hospitality. Women from nearby homes brought milk, potatoes, eggs, and bread to the workers. They inquired after our health, and lent us work jackets.

"Build a church here," many urged us. "We will definitely come and join you in prayer to God. Make God's work here stronger. We're so happy that we're going to have a church right here in Zaokski." These encouraging words, spoken with sincerity and warmth, motivated us to even greater perseverance.

Soon a large group of construction workers arrived from the Ukraine. "We will be working at the construction site for two weeks, at no expense to the denomination," they announced. And this set the pattern for the entire building project. Again and again volunteers came for two weeks or a month at a time and essentially carried out the construction. No one took pay for his or her efforts.

At the very beginning of the construction our church leadership sent a letter to church members laying out the plans and goals of the college, and requesting volunteers to take part, where possible, in physically helping to build or in financially supporting this great cause. The response was unbelievable. Within two or three months believers throughout the country had raised what for us was an enormous amount of money—nearly a half million rubles. Volunteers trekked to Zaokski not only from Russia itself but also from central Asia, the Caucasus, the Ukraine, Moldova, Byelorussia, and the Baltic republics. Families used their vacation time to come to the campus. They pitched their tents to live in, and Mom, Dad, and the kids all helped with the construction.

During those memorable days—from March 1986 to December 1988—our church was solidly united in heart and soul, standing shoulder to shoulder to accomplish a task. It was a powerful example of how Adventist people, moved by the Holy Spirit and inspired by each other, are capable of accomplishing great deeds for the sake of Christ.

On December 2, 1988, we attended the grand opening of the campus complex where both the seminary and the administrative center of our church organization were located.

In *God's Soviet Miracles,* my son Michael says, "We are very fortunate to have a gigantic new educational complex, named after Garwin McNeilus, a great Adventist visionary from Minnesota who dedicated his business to the Lord. Through the great help and inspiration of Garwin and [his wife] Marilee McNeilus, we were able to develop many crucial areas of the seminary's work, including our farm and our housing for married students. Without their help, we would not have been able . . . to build this new complex that will house over 200 students, along with married faculty, and will contain a floor of large, spacious classrooms and a cafeteria where we will be able to feed over 300 people at a time. We have laid the foundation for the three-story library, and with their help, we are proceeding with construction."[2]

It was providential also that at that time Elder Neal C. Wilson established a special Soviet Affairs Office at the SDA General Conference offices near Washington, D.C. He put a very talented and dedicated couple, Elder and Mrs. Harold F. Otis, in charge of that office. They were excited by the opportunities opening up in Russia, and were willing to do anything to help the church there.

During the years 1992 through 2005, 1,550 students of theology graduated from the seminary.

Before I conclude my story of how God led in establishing our Zaokski educational center, I'd like to tell you a thrilling story.

One day I was visiting our church in the city of Frunze (now Bishkek), the capital city of Kyrgyzstan. I had just stepped off a public transportation bus when I heard a woman's voice calling my name, addressing me in the usual respectful Russian way by using my first name and my father's name.

"Mikhail Petrovich!"

I stopped and turned.

"Do you recognize me?" the woman asked.

I do, I thought to myself. *I saw this lady in the Frunze church. And from the look on her face, she seems agitated about something*

"My name is Galena Vdovina," she said urgently, and after the usual polite words of greeting, she came to the point.

"I'm a single mother, and I have only one child, a daughter named Irena," she said. "I am delighted to say that she is growing in her love for Jesus. Here is the problem. She has just graduated from high school, and that means that she must either continue her education, which as you know is nearly impossible for a Christian believer, or to go to work at one of the state factories."

I nodded, and could sense what her next words would be. It was a familiar plight of Adventist and other Christian parents.

"So I've sent her to a big state company, where she is now learning a profession," Galena continued. "And you know as well as I do that the atheists there will do everything thinkable—and unthinkable—to destroy her faith in God. Would you please pray with me for my daughter Irena?"

"I would be delighted to," I told her. "Let's step through that alleyway there." There under the shadow of a big tree, away from the hum of the busy street, we presented this matter to our gracious Savior. Galena's deeply emotional supplication impressed me. I remember thinking, *I am witnessing a mother's struggle for her beloved child.*

An energetic young man named Valery was working at that same company, which manufactured heavy machinery. He was also the leader of the factory's chapter of Komsomol, an atheist youth organization that was a stepping-stone to membership in the privileged Communist Party.

Valery's job at the plant was to educate the younger workers in the principles of Communism. One morning he was approached by a superintendent.

"Comrade Valery," the superintendent said, "I want to let you know about one of our new employees. Her name is Irena Vdovina. She's a young woman, and from what I hear she belongs to some strange, weird religious sect. This means that either we have to see that she drops those connections or else we fire her. Otherwise," he added with a finger across his throat, "our own heads may roll. You'd better get on it right away."

"Right. I'll talk with her today if possible."

Valery had his secretary deliver a note summoning Irena to his office at 5:00 p.m. But it was he who was the more nervous of the two. *I've never met a real live sectarian before,* he mused. *What's she going to be like?* He was actually biting his nails in nervousness when a slender, gracious, pleasant-looking young woman entered his office.

"Please sit down, Irena," he said. "You may call me Valery. Tell me something about your background, and your outlook on life."

As the young woman began to speak Valery found himself impressed with the way she handled herself. *She's obviously well read,* he decided, *and well educated, too. She doesn't fit what I'd always thought a sectarian would be like. I'd imagined that they were all backward cave dwellers. Well, I guess I'd better cut to the chase.*

He cleared his throat. "Irena," he said, "I understand you profess a belief in God. Why could you ever imagine that a Deity exists?"

She looked him in the eye. "Valery, have you yourself ever read a Bible?"

He blinked. "No."

"Have you ever attended a church meeting?"

"I never have."

Irena smiled. "I will be happy to continue my conversation with you about God and religion if you will take time to read the Bible for yourself so that we can intelligently discuss its content."

He shrugged. "Sounds logical to me," he said. "I'll do it." Then he paused in slight embarrassment. "But where am I going to be able to find a Bible?"

"My mother would be happy to lend you one. She could also help you become familiar with it."

"That would be very kind of her."

Soon Valery was enjoying the warm Christian atmosphere of the Vdovina home. The more the three of them discussed God and the Bible, the more sense and wisdom he saw in the arguments of his educator.

"Valery," Irena finally said, "you really need to attend one of our meetings."

And not long afterward the young Komsomol leader found himself in an Adventist gathering. *I'm impressed,* he told himself. *These people are sincere, and their reasoning is excellent. I like their common sense. And I like how neatly they dress!*

Now the "monkey" was on Valery's back. His own intellect and education were being challenged, so he asked for more literature, more information. Since it wasn't legal to print Adventist books, they had to be secretly typed and so were quite hard to come by. If the average Adventist even got a chance to borrow a book, he or she was lucky to receive a tenth-carbon copy of an onion-skin-paper, hand-bound, typewritten manuscript. But church members did their best to supply Valery with books on creation and evolution, the inspiration of the Bible, and other illegally translated books.

The young Communist took notes and compiled material, matching argument against argument. *The more I study,* he told himself, *the more I'm convinced that there is wisdom, light, and meaning in the teachings of the Bible. And now that I know this, I don't feel I can perform my Komsomol work at the company.*

So one morning he gave notice to his party leadership that as a convinced Christian he could no longer remain a member of the Communist Party. This shocked the Kyrgyzstan party bosses, and they didn't want to accept his decision. However, in spite of their threats and enticements, he wholeheartedly accepted Christ as his Savior, and through baptism became a member of the Seventh-day Adventist Church.

And these events led Valery to another life-changing decision: he asked Irena to be his wife. Today they have two sons, Alexei and Maxim. Irena personally told me how proud she was on the day in 1986 that Valery enrolled in the Tula correspondence course for ministerial training.

My son Michael remembers another special day in Valery's life.

"In November 1990," Michael says, "when I stood on the platform of the Zaokski Seminary chapel, a lump came into my throat. During the graduation ceremony that day I handed Valery—the former ideologist of the Communist Party—his diploma from this Seventh-day Adventist institution."

And it was for people such as Valery—people with inquisitive minds who readily and humbly acknowledge their delusions and mistaken ways, and who receive Christ's truth in order to take it to others—that this seminary in Zaokski, by the grace of God, was miraculously established.

---

[1] Mikhail Kulakov, Jr., *God's Soviet Miracles* (Boise, Idaho: Pacific Press Pub. Assn., 1993).
[2] *Ibid.*, p. 126.

CHAPTER 21: God Opened the Doors

The iron curtain.

Churchill inserted that famous phrase into modern culture in an address at Westminster College in Fulton, Missouri, in March 1946. It's not clear whether he was consciously echoing H.G. Wells' use of "iron curtain" in a 1904 book entitled *The Food of the Gods,* but it's an apt way of describing the Soviet Union's harsh and desperate attempt to seal itself off from influences it feared.

But though from outside the iron curtain may have seemed as grim and impenetrable as before, on the inside it was rusting badly. On March 11, 1985, Mikhail Gorbachev came to power in the Soviet Union, and the man with the mark on his brow and the open, approachable expression announced a startling motto:

We will show the world that Socialism has a human face.

Actually, Gorbachev wasn't the first to see the need to do this. Even in Leonid Brezhnev's government were leaders who understood that sooner or later they must somehow demonstrate to the outside world that the Soviet Union wasn't completely deaf to the requests of their citizens who believed in God. And one day this "human face" turned—voluntarily or not—and smiled in our direction.

I still remember how stunned we Adventists were when in early 1980 a message arrived from the Council for Religious Affairs: "The Seventh-day Adventist Church is allowed to place an order with government printers for a quantity of 10,000 Bibles."

Ten thousand Bibles? I remember thinking, *From Soviet presses?* My mind went back to Alla Shtabinskaya's midnight typewriter and her aching wrists, and its 10 onion-skin and nine carbon sheets rolled tightly under the platen. I remembered many other one-person printing presses besides her. I remembered the reverent way we handled and preserved the Scriptures produced by such loving labor.

And now this avalanche, this Niagara, of Holy Writ coming our way! You may be surprised at the first question that came to our minds: Wherever are we going to *store* them? Since for decades our church had been "underground," we had no official headquarters, no warehouse. Fortunately, the Moscow Baptists allowed us to store half the Bible order on their limited premises, and a kindly Tula church elder named Alex Romanov and his wife,

Lena, gladly agreed to store most of the other half in their home (though it took up most of their living space) and to be responsible for distributing them.

I stored the remainder in the attic of my house. My son Peter, then 16, helped me carry the bulky books upstairs. The next day he carried one of the Bibles to his school, and in front of the teacher and the entire class he turned to the first page.

"Look!" he told them. "This Bible was published by the Seventh-day Adventist Church, and printed on Soviet government presses!"

Then came 1991. Like a colossus with feet of clay, the Soviet empire crumbled into pieces. Communism's totalitarian grip, which had held our citizens hostage for 70 years, loosened before the winds of democracy.

But those of us who'd experienced persecution and harassment for our faith couldn't expect that this amazing freedom of conscience would last long.

"We need to seize the moment," we told each other. "We need to plant new congregations and build new churches. We need to present a positive Adventist image to the general public." The latter was extremely important, since for centuries Russia had cultivated exactly the opposite attitude toward any Protestant churches on its soil.

As I look back on our desperate struggles to take advantage of these God-given opportunities, I see that we succeeded in some areas, and in others we unfortunately left things undone.

But God in His great mercy continued to astonish us. After years of cruel repression and adversity, Russian Adventism couldn't rally to its feet quickly enough to preach the gospel on its own. What a blessing it was to appeal to the worldwide church for help in preaching the gospel! The response was overwhelming. Hundreds of evangelists from many parts of the world offered their wholehearted support. Meetings were held all across the vast territory of the Soviet Union, and thousands came out of the darkness of unbelief and atheism to accept Jesus Christ as their Lord and Savior.

The year 1991 was only three months old when the Ruler of heaven swung wide the gates of the Kremlin and beckoned us inside. Here's how it happened.

Moscow's Kremlin—the symbol of Russian power—is recognized as one of the most marvelous architectural structures in the world. Constructed of red brick, its formidably high tooth-notched walls contain 20 towers and many luxurious palaces that serve as offices for top government officials. The Kremlin inspired such fear in those years that once when I visited Moscow for underground pastoral gatherings and happened to walk past the Kremlin walls, another pastor told me, "Don't even *look* in the direction of the walls or the towers—you might be suspected of spying!"

During Nikita Khrushchev's rule, a new palace was built within those walls. Completed in 1961, the Palace of Congresses was considered to be one of the finest in the world. It could seat up to 6,000 people, and was designed to accommodate Communist Party conventions and other major cultural events that trumpeted the greatness and unshakable stability of the Soviet state.

As this palace was being built, Khrushchev was riding high. In the two years prior to the start of construction, the U.S.S.R. had scored a series of devastating firsts in the space race: the first intercontinental ballistic missile, the first satellite, the first animal to enter earth's orbit. As the palace foundation was laid, a Russian spacecraft circled the moon, taking pictures of the far side.

It may partly have been these triumphs that gave Nikita Khrushchev the confidence to boast, as the Palace of Congresses was rising from the ground, "Within two years the Soviets will forever do away with the cancer of religion!"

What would that energetic leader have done had he known that 30 years later his empire would crumble, and the walls of that very Kremlin Palace would resound with the voice of an Adventist evangelist preaching about the second coming of Jesus?

What happened was that Adventist businessman Garwin McNeilus got word that a Korean missionary had rented the palace for a three-day evangelistic crusade. He quickly got in touch with us and promised us his financial support if we would make arrangements to rent it.

Again God used His men to accomplish His ends, proving to believers and unbelievers alike that nothing is impossible with Him. If there are people thirsting to hear the message of salvation, and if there are messengers willing to take it to them, God will open any doors.

By the grace of God such a messenger was found for the palace. He would bear the great honor—and the equally great responsibility—of proclaiming the heaven-inspired messages in one of the Soviet empire's most public places. This man of God was none other than Pastor Mark Finley.

And one of our goals, a goal Mark earnestly shared, was to place a Bible in the hand of everyone who attended at least four of the 11 lectures. And guess which vehicles were used to transport the thousands of Bibles. *Soviet military trucks!* And those who drove them, and those who unloaded them, were Soviet soldiers! Thousands of people witnessed the arrival of these trucks. Some within the crowd exclaimed loudly, "Look! They're bringing Bibles inside the Kremlin! Look, look! Military trucks full of Bibles are entering the Kremlin!" Others silently stood and wept.

I'm going to quote—with careful condensation because of space requirements—the words of my dear friend, Pastor Nikolai A. Zhukalyuk. Here are his impressions of that historic crusade in March 1991:

Pastor Zhukalyuk writes: "As I approached the great Trinity Gates of the Moscow Kremlin, crowds of people had already gathered around the checkpoints, even though it was still 30 minutes before the start of the evangelistic program. These people had obtained tickets—which allowed them to attend all 11 of Mark Finley's sermons—at a nearby Kremlin office. Now they were presenting the tickets to the guards. Soon a flood of 6,000 people was swallowed up inside the foyer of the Palace of Congresses.

"In the huge cloakroom Adventist ministers from all over Russia were handing out Bibles to those who had attended the first four sessions. The day before, all these helpers had been carefully instructed by Mark Finley.

" 'Distribute the Bibles promptly,' he had said, 'and don't forget to give each person a friendly smile. A smile is one of the conditions for you to participate in this program! All right, everybody, let's practice. Smile for me.'

"A lot of us had indeed forgotten how to smile. Some of the ministers attempted to produce something that resembled a smile. Others gazed at the stacks of Bibles they would be distributing. *How scarce this treasure used to be only a few short years ago,* they seemed to be thinking. *It's difficult to believe that now this book is being given away for free.* Others seemed to be immersed in memories of their own, and I saw not a few eyes moist with tears of joy.

"As each night's program began, not a single empty seat was to be found on the main floor or in the balconies. Many on the outside literally begged the ushers to allow them at least a place to stand. On my way into the auditorium I walked shoulder to shoulder with people who, with trembling hands, kept turning and turning the blessed pages of the Bibles they had just received.

"In the large auditorium all around me were seated ordinary helpers, young people, who for the first time in their lives found themselves inside the famed auditorium they'd read about in their school textbooks. Devout elderly men and women reverently made the sign of the cross as they entered. Those with disabilities were there on crutches and in wheelchairs. Homemakers sat side by side with soldiers. In short, here was an honest cross section of the entire population of Moscow and its suburbs.

"*These are the true owners of this marvelous auditorium,* I thought to myself. *Their calluses, their blood, sweat, and tears, built this palace. And now, finally, they have a chance to enter its walls and to listen to the most necessary and most everlastingly important news they will ever hear.*

"And finally the tall, engaging 35-year-old evangelist Mark Finley appeared, along with his translator, Peter Kulakov. People broke out in long-lasting applause, even though applause was not the reason he had come.

"After greeting the assembly, Pastor Finley said, 'Please raise your Bibles. Please hold them high.'

"Thousands of Bibles, like banners of a new era heralding liberty of the Spirit, began to flutter upward, raised by the hands of grateful listeners. Again, I could not help remembering watching televised Communist Party conventions, in which thousands in these same seats had waved their red booklets as they cast their ballots. Could this really be that same auditorium? Was I dreaming?

" 'Let me remind you,' Pastor Finley said earnestly, 'that you can't expect any help from your Bible if you leave it on a shelf to collect dust. If you decide to sell it, you will lose a lot. The writings of this book must become the experiences of your personal lives.' "

Mikhail's reminiscences resume: Let me add my own recollections to the apt and dramatic words of Nikolai Zhukalyuk. To me, the most significant phenomenon of that event was not only that God saw fit to allow us access to one of the best and largest auditoriums in the center of Moscow, but also that *atheism was powerless in the presence of a people who had become interested in faith in God.* During Mark Finley's entire series that 6,000-seat auditorium was filled *twice daily,* without a single empty seat. People were hungry to hear the Word of God, hungry to enter a place in which they could be taught about Him and learn to pray to Him.

My eldest son, Pavel, remembers that not everyone was overjoyed at Mark Finley's presence.

"All the major TV news channels showed the interminable stream of people passing through the Kremlin's gate," Pavel says. "But in the background, viewers could also see a line of Russian Nationalists holding protest signs. The Nationalists suspected that every American evangelistic series was a U.S. expansionist plot, and the message on one of the signs is still fresh in my mind. At the time, George H. W. Bush was America's leader and his last name rhymes with the Russian word *dush,* which means 'soul.' So on the sign someone had written *BUSH NE TRON NASHIKH DUSH!* which means 'Bush, keep away from our souls!' However, when God opened the Kremlin gates, nothing—not even shouting protesters—could stop the streams of those who were eager to hear His Word."

My dear daughter Evangeline was especially proud of her younger brother Peter:

Evangeline writes: "I'll admit it. It felt good to see my youngest brother, Peter, whom I once babysat with great love, now standing with Mark Finley and translating his inspired sermons in this enormous Kremlin palace.

"Thousands of people had come to this majestic room to listen to these

171

sermons. Peter, though young at that time, was doing a great job of translation. He spoke in such a lively way, with much feeling and great conviction.

" 'Peter,' I asked him, 'aren't you nervous standing there in front of this sea of people?'

" 'No,' he answered. 'I love to translate for Mark Finley. I do it with great joy and courage, which is given to me by my Lord.'

"Then he paused. 'Actually, there was one difficult moment. As I was standing on the platform, I saw our parents making their way between the rows in this auditorium where 6,000 people were about to hear God's Word. My voice cracked, and my heart nearly stopped. I always knew my parents had lived for this very moment. They had always believed this time would eventually come, and for many years they prayed and labored for it, and were ready to give their lives for it. And it has come—and they have seen it!' "

Mikhail's reminiscences continue: One night as I was sitting in the auditorium, I witnessed a scene that deeply moved me. The entire auditorium was filled to capacity, and security guards had begun to close the doors.

"There is no more room!" the guards told those that still waited outside. "The auditorium is filled! There is no more room!"

I could hear a struggle beyond the doors, and several people pushed their way through. Among them was an elderly man, his hair disheveled from the struggle, tears streaming down his face.

"Why?" he asked the guards. "What are you closing those doors for? *Why?* For 70 years *they've* been shutting the door on God, and now *you're* trying to do the same!"

Those anguished words still ring in my ears to this day, impelling me to pray that Russia's doors might remain open for the proclamation of the gospel.

Only eternity will reveal to us the full significance of what happened within the palace's walls during that dramatic week and a half. However, we can say confidently that the gospel is being preached for a sign unto all the nations—and it's happening even where the devil and the state attempted to shut the door in its face. We thank God that in Moscow and its suburbs there are now 27 Adventist congregations, with 3,410 members.

Yet even with the taste of unbridled freedom in their mouths, some of the people still couldn't "get it." I'll give you an example.

In the 1990s I held the post of the secretary of the Russian chapter of the International Religious Liberty Association (IRLA). Early in 1993 I was invited to participate in a nationally televised debate. The topic was the free exercise of religion in today's Russia. At one point we were discussing whether to allow groups such as the Jehovah's Witnesses to proselytize.

"No," several participants said. "We're deeply concerned about allowing that foreign sect to corrupt our young people's minds."

One of the panel members, who represented certain religious forces in Russia, put me on the spot.

"What do *you* think?" this representative asked bluntly, turning to me. "Do you believe it's OK for our society to tolerate this sect's propaganda?"

I patiently elaborated the IRLA's position. "We believe that every faith should have the right to freely express its beliefs," I replied, "and that its hearers have the right to judge for themselves how to respond. I may disagree with the Jehovah's Witnesses' teachings, but Jesus Christ and human history both clearly teach that he who would make his own liberty secure must guard from oppression even those who disagree with him."

At this, someone sitting at my side swiveled to face me, his face distorted by fierce anger. "If I had a gun on me right now," he snarled, "I would kill you on the spot!"

CHAPTER 22: "Give Them Something to Eat"

On a Palestine hillside two millennia ago Jesus said something to His disciples that has sounded in my mind for years. Raising His voice above the chatter of thousands of hungry people, He said to His friends, "You give them something to eat" (Matthew 14:16, NKJV; Mark 6:37, NKJV; Luke 9:13, NKJV).

I've put the "you" in italics because Matthew, Mark, and Luke also emphasize that word. Under the Holy Spirit's direction they could have simply written "Give them something to eat," because in the Greek language that they used, the word "you" isn't grammatically necessary. But when it's present, it's *emphatic*. And in all three parallel passages, Jesus adds the *you*.

In this book I've told you stories about how faithful Russian Seventh-day Adventist Christians prayed and worked for opportunities to share their own nourishing faith in an atheist culture. But all of us understood very clearly that behind any of our kindly human words and unselfish acts was a more potent Food, the Holy Scriptures, which is as necessary for spiritual progress as bread is for physical growth. I've described how many of us sat at our typewriters acting as one-person printing presses, braving the threats of reprisals from the authorities while pounding out copies of the venerable Russian Bible one keystroke at a time.

Maybe that's the reason I've had, since I was a very young man, the dream of translating the Bible into current contemporary Russian. You may not be aware that until the present time, there's been only one generally available Russian Bible translation, called the Synodal Version. I wish I could tell you that this version is crystal-clear and easy to understand, but with all due respect to those who prepared it, the general opinion of those who read it agrees with that given by Professor I. Yevseyev, chair of the Russian Bible Commission.

In a 1917 address to Russian Orthodox Church officials, he admitted that "the Synodal translation of the Bible completed in 1875 . . . urgently requires revision, or still better, complete replacement." Further, he pointed out, "it does not follow consistently the original text. . . . [But] a much more serious problem is its literary backwardness. The language . . . is heavy, outdated, artificially approximated to the Slavonic, and one century behind the literary language."

In addition, Russian, just as every other language, has gone through so much change that modern readers find parts of the Synodal version incomprehensible.

Take the word *soblaznitsya*, for example. It used to mean "offend," as in Christ's statement "Blessed is he, whosoever shall not be offended in me" (Matthew 11:6). Today's Russian reader—one not schooled in ancient Slavonic—understands this verse to say, "Blessed is he who is not *attracted* to me." This is not Matthew's meaning at all!

Another Russian word, *pochil*, used to mean "rested," as in "God ended his work . . . ; and he rested" (Genesis 2:2). But instead, a newcomer to the Russian Bible is startled to see, "God ended his work . . . ; and he *died*." Reading this passage and nothing else, someone who believed in the "God is dead" movement of a few years ago might imagine he'd found confirmation in the old Synodal Version!

Some of these distortions cast truly serious aspersions on God and His character. Though the Bible tells us that a loving Father God must sometimes discipline His children, the Synodal Version calls Him a "severe chastiser" (Ezekiel 7:9). And Genesis 5:22 says that righteous Enoch walked not *with* God but *under* Him. Unfortunately, the list of similar distortions could be continued endlessly, building a picture of God that a spiritually starved nation has sometimes found unsavory. No faith-seeker should have to travel such a rocky path to reach the Savior.

And opinion polls show the result. In a recent survey 30 percent of Russian citizens say that they own Bibles (the old translation, of course), but only half say that they've tried to read it. And most of those who've tried confess that they didn't understand much of what they read.

This is why for several years I and a number of others have been prayerfully engaged in preparing a new Russian translation of the Bible. "Why," we asked ourselves, "should millions of Russian-speaking people remain deprived of an accurate rendering of the richness and dynamism of the Holy Scriptures?"

In 1992 I resigned from my church leadership positions, asking my brethren to give me the opportunity of fulfilling this dream of my life. In 1993 the Bible Translation Institute was organized in Zaokski as an institution of the Euro-Asian Division of the Seventh-day Adventist Church. From the start, our goal was to achieve accuracy in translation and clarity and ease of reading. Using Greek—and later Hebrew and Aramaic for the Old Testament—we have sought to prepare a Russian version suitable for public and ecclesiastical reading and liturgical usage, as well as for personal study, preaching, teaching, and memorization. To achieve these goals, we are in continuous consultation with foreign and local scholars from different religious backgrounds.

In 2000 the state publishing house in Mozhaysk printed our *New Testament in Modern Russian*. And in the same breath I must immediately mention the many devoted Adventists believers whose cordial involvement made it possible for us to prepare the translation of the New Testament (and later the New Testament and the book of Psalms) into modern Russian, and to print it.

My good friend the late pastor Robert Spangler was the man who, even before we'd talked about this together, clearly saw the need for this translation. When he learned that all my life I had been dreaming and readying myself for this task, he gave me the following advice:

"Mikhail," he said soberly, "I will raise funds for this work, but on only one condition. Promise me that as you work on this project you will follow the example of the English historian Edward Gibbon as he wrote *The Decline and Fall of the Roman Empire*. In order not to be distracted from writing, he shaved the hair off half his head!"

"Bob," I replied, my face as sober as his, "I will do my best." And we both burst into laughter.

But under our mirth we were both dead serious. And thanks to efforts of Pastor Robert Spangler and the Adventist Theological Society in the U.S.A., and Pastor Austin Fletcher in Australia, many of our faithful Adventist believers contributed to the translation of the New Testament and Psalms.

My dear friend Bill Iles, Adventist businessman and administrator, willingly paid all the expenses for the printing of the New Testament's first edition. And when the time came to print the New Testament and Psalms in one volume, God found, in the small Wisconsin village of Arpin, a man with a wonderful vision of the needs of God's work around the world—Arnold Gratias.

I use the word "vision" deliberately, because at age 16 Arnold had lost both his eyes in an accident. Yet this did not embitter him toward his Creator. Instead, his love for the Lord led him to develop a real estate business to raise funds for the preaching of the gospel in his native country as well as in other parts of the world.

I was introduced to Arnold and his (at the time) seriously ill wife in their very humble home. When he learned that for a dollar and a half we could print one copy of the New Testament to give someone in Russia the Word of God he said to me, "Here is my check for 30,000 such books." This made me feel very humble as I saw the leading of the Lord in this project.

I am happy to say that, to the glory of our Lord, *The New Testament in Modern Russian* was well accepted by the Russian public as a work done—as noted in the newspapers—"carefully" and "responsibly." We still continue to receive letters of gratitude and approval, such as this one from prominent Bible translator Ar'ye Olman.

"Being tired of reading poor renditions of the ancient texts, I was pleasantly surprised by such an excellent translation of the Psalms. It is not only lucid and true to the original, but also retains the poetic style of the Hebrew text! You have indeed succeeded in conveying the authentic atmosphere of the biblical passages."

Ar'ye Olman
Research Fellow, Bar-Ilan University, Israel
Professor, Center for Judaic Studies and Jewish Civilization
Fellow of the Institute for Asian and African Studies at Moscow State University
Former member of the Jerusalem Bible Translation Project

Our institute was greatly encouraged when the leadership of the interdenominational society Friends of Sacred Scripture asked us to allow them to use some parts of our Bible translation in their publications for children. When I saw the result, a book called *The Gospel of Luke,* I and the rest of the institute team were extremely pleased and grateful to God for the opportunity to help spread His Word.

Even as our New Testament was being published we were at work on the book of Psalms, and in 2002 printed the two in one volume. Currently a staff of five scholars (the majority from the Russian Orthodox faith) and I are hard at work on the Old Testament. If you'd like to see several pie charts that describe the stages of our translation progress, and read other details about the Bible Translation Institute, you're welcome to visit us at www.russianbible.org.

Since this project is one of my chief joys, I could go on and on, wearying you with details about the complexities of translation, but I won't. Instead, let me tell you a story that not only gives a tragic picture of some of the common problems of today's Russian society but also shows how the entrance of God's Word—in this case, our Bible Translation Institute New Testament—gives light (Psalm 119:130).

As I mentioned, once our translation was off the press, we began receiving letters of appreciation. One of these was from Anya Parinova, a physical education instructor we knew while we lived in Russia.

"I can no longer resist my desire to express my gratitude to you," she wrote, "for your great work for the glory of God—your translation of the New Testament. Please read the following true story, which involves very dear and close friends of mine. Then, at times when you feel dead tired, as though your last ounce of energy is spent, with no more strength left to carry on this great task of translation, be assured that your work is not in vain in the eyes of God."

Anya told us about her cousin Lily, whom she considered closer than her own sister. "Lily is an incredible person," Anya wrote me. "Having observed her over many years, I am beginning to understand the Bible words, 'the law written on the heart.' "

Lily and her husband, Rashid, had two girls, Katya and Nadya. A couple of decades earlier Lily and her daughters had become ill and had to spend several weeks in the local hospital. In the next room was a quiet little orphan girl named Olya. Attracted by the two little girls close to her age, 5-year-old Olya began to visit them, sometimes to play and sometimes just to talk. And eventually this lonely waif could bear it no longer. She knew that soon her new friends would be discharged.

"Mommy," she said, raising tearful cheeks to Lily, "I want to live with you!"

Heartbroken, Lily held the little girl close. *As much as I'd love to, this would be impossible,* she told herself. *Rashid and I and our girls live in a tiny apartment, and there are times we don't have enough food money for ourselves. To bring another child into these circumstances would be cruel.*

Lily and her daughters were discharged at the end of the month. But as "Mommy" tried to resume her usual routine, she had no peace. Always before her she saw that tearful little face and heard those heart-wrenching words. So she checked with the Social Service Department to see what the chances were that they could adopt Olya.

"Sorry," she was told. "There's absolutely no way you can adopt this child and care for her. Olya has a serious kidney disease. Apparently her mother gave her vodka in early childhood to keep her from crying. She's the state's responsibility."

A while later Lily stopped by the hospital hoping to have a quiet chat with Olya's doctor. But Olya caught sight of her, bounded forward, and flung herself face down on the floor, both hands clutching Lily's legs.

"I will not let you go!" the girl sobbed. "Not until they allow me to live with you—my mommy and my sisters!"

Two doctors and three nurses came running to help, but they could not unclench her little fingers without the risk of breaking them. For the longest time they tried to persuade the little girl to let go, but she was adamant. Finally the staff relented. The little 5-year-old had conquered the system and won herself a family.

"There is no sweeter, gentler, more thoughtful child," Lily told her cousin Anya as the years went by. "Olya is my joy and my consolation."

The girls grew up, Olya growing into an uncommonly beautiful young woman. Anya, who had recently accepted the Lord as her Savior and joined the Adventist Church, visited the family from time to time. But when she spoke of what the Bible said about her newfound friend Jesus, Lily's husband—normally a gracious, friendly man—gave back only sarcasm and irony. He made fun of both Anya and the Book she treasured, and this ridicule caused her a lot of hurt.

"But even more than that," Anya wrote in her letter, "I feared for Rashid and his family. Such arrogance toward the Word of God frightened me. Even when I decided to remain quiet about my faith, Rashid continued his mockery of the Bible. All this from a man with a good education, a strong intellect, and a splendid mind! In our discussions he somehow always managed to come out the victor."

Suddenly, as unexpected as lightning from a clear, blue sky, misfortune struck their home. Returning from work one day, Rashid entered an elevator, and two men crowded in with him. Some time later he was discovered with multiple stab wounds and severe trauma to his skull.

Police investigators eventually discovered that Rashid was the victim of a contract killing gone wrong. The innocent man happened to closely resemble a gang's targeted villain. Miraculously, Rashid lived, but the trauma to his head cost him his eyesight, and the severe damage suffered by his liver and pancreas caused him to develop serious diabetes.

"I've done all I can for you," his doctor finally told him. "Your fate will be decided by how well you are cared for."

And here was where Olya's marvelous persistence again manifested itself. Ignoring her own need for sleep, she became "Daddy's" nurse. Sometimes Lily had to practically pull her away from the sufferer's bedside. Nighttimes were especially hard for Rashid, and Olya simply would not let anyone else take care of him.

Lily, her own health weakened by sleepless nights, became seriously ill, and Olya somehow found extra strength to care for her. "If it hadn't been for Olya," Lily would say afterward, "neither Rashid nor I would have survived."

Time passed, and miraculously Rashid began to regain his eyesight, and his mind became more lucid. Though still an invalid, he now began providing for his family by working as a tutor in physics and math.

"Many times," Anya wrote me, "I observed how kindly his daughters treated their father. Rashid's hands shook terribly, and it was difficult for him to pour tea into his cup without spilling it. But somehow a widemouthed cup would always end up beside his plate so he could pour his tea without embarrassment. I saw many other examples of the barely noticeable 'little things' of which love is made."

And Rashid responded to this tender care with heroics of his own. Once he spent an entire hour tracing four words on a greeting card ("Lily, I love you") in honor of his wife's fiftieth birthday. Every one of the letters was perfectly straight. No one could believe that the trembling hand of Rashid had written it.

But suddenly tragedy struck again. Olya began behaving strangely and acting lethargic. Items disappeared from the apartment. Like thunder on a sunny day, the truth came home: *drug addiction.* A new life-or-death struggle began. The man she'd been dating had introduced her to the needle, and soon a blood test showed she'd been infected with the hepatitis C virus. Since this disease is both incurable and infectious, Olya took her doctor's advice and moved out on her own. Fortunately, she had a place to stay, for her biological mother, who had died of alcoholism at 28, had left her apartment to her daughter.

"What was most agonizing to me," Anya told me in her letter, "was watching the once strong-willed Olya simply give up without a fight when her disease flared up. The only thing that brought her through was that Lily always managed to be nearby no matter what."

Olya's illness hit Rashid the hardest. To think of the girl who'd been his brave little nurse now reduced to this condition—and he unable to help—caused him great agony. But exactly at that time a barely noticeable miracle began to happen in his life.

"At one point," Anya's letter continued, "my schedule allowed me to spend several weeks with the family. Rashid and I took daily walks, and talked for hours at a time. I carefully brought up the subject of faith in God, doing my best to address his questions and doubts in a logical way, to suit his usual manner of thinking. A few traces of his former sarcastic arrogance remained, but they were minimal."

Two months later, after she'd returned home, Anya received a letter from him. After the usual greetings and sharing of news, Rashid's next lines amazed her.

"Recently I was reading the New Testament," he wrote, "and I thought with gratitude about your Bible Translation Institute. In the past I could never understand the Bible. It made no sense. This new translation, however, seems to convey just as much of the spirit of the meaning as it does the letter. Also, the type in this edition is larger and therefore easier for me to read, for which I am also very grateful."

Anya concluded her letter to me with these words:

"Remember that none of your work is in vain. Remember that, in time, thousands of proud Rashids will bow before the majesty of the Lord, saying, 'This is our God, in whom we have trusted!' "

Certainly such responses encourage us tremendously as we see the urgent need to spread an accurate and readable Word of God, especially since Russian

readers such as Rashid are weaned and raised on such literary giants as Pushkin, Dostoyevsky, Tolstoy, Lermontov, Turgenev, and others.

This we try to accomplish, and are gladdened when responses attest that we are on the right track. May the Lord continue to give us His guidance and blessing, so that in response to Jesus' command "Give them something to eat" (Matthew 14:16, NKJV) we can provide a readable and enjoyable Bible for the Russian people!

CHAPTER 23: Light and Salt in the World

Taking a new step, uttering a new word, is what people fear most.
—Fyodor Dostoyevsky

The year was 1989. My son Michael and I were seated in the elegant office of Vadim Viktorovich Bakatin, the Soviet Union's newly appointed minister of internal affairs. We were about to ask him an important question, and we were hoping he would say yes.

A year, two years, five years earlier we wouldn't have had the ghost of a chance of even setting eyes on the interior of this august office, let alone hope for a nod of approval from his predecessor. But things were changing. Though it would be a little more than two years before the iron curtain would crumble, the Communist Party and the KGB were beginning to lose their grip on the nation.

And high in government circles several progressive and democratically minded leaders were watching how the Adventist Church acted out its faith. They liked what they saw. Among them were Council for Religious Affairs chair, Konstantin Kharchev and renowned Soviet children's writer and the creator of the Russian Children's Foundation Albert Likhanov. These men believed that we Adventists could do our country a great service with our exemplary way of life (strikingly different from the lifestyle of an average Russian) and our emphasis on welfare ministry.

So our friends in high places set up this meeting with Minister Bakatin, and had evidently filled him full of facts about our church's extremely active charitable projects in the Tula region south of Moscow.

Mr. Bakatin received us cordially and graciously, and as his secretary poured each of us a cup of aromatic tea he mentioned his delight with our work in the Tula region. I hadn't, of course, been expecting the same frigid reception Theodore Carcich and I had received from other officials several years before, but Michael and I were amazed at such warmth and friendliness from someone so powerful.

Finally we felt it appropriate to come to the point.

"We would deeply appreciate it," I said, "if your office would grant us permission to begin a prison ministry."

An expression of great joy lit up his face. "That would be *excellent*," he said. "I definitely agree with you, and I deeply appreciate your offer to help the Soviet society in this way."

I remember sitting there almost numb with amazement at how much had changed for Adventism and the rest of Christianity in my country.

Later, as we were leaving his office, Minister Bakatin made a comment that stayed in my mind.

"You know," he said, "this is the first time in my life that I have had a chance to meet with pastors from any denomination."

The following week, upon his direct order, across the entire span of the Soviet Union our congregations received permission to visit inmates inside the labor-corrective institutions. Now we could minister to their emotional, social, and spiritual needs by establishing one-on-one friendships. And so we did, sharing the riches and the joy of our Christian experience with them.

That visit with a high state official—a man raised as an atheist and a Communist, yet who sensed the potential of Christians to morally impact labor-correction inmates—drove me to my knees. "Lord," I prayed, "what is a really effective, and truly Christian, way of revealing the love of God to people who are ignorant of it?" As I pondered the crying material and spiritual needs of my country, I was tortured by the question: *What is it that will convince the minds and convert the souls of these people? What needs to happen so that they will accept deep in their hearts the divine truths of the three angels' messages?*

As I searched for answer, I turned prayerfully to Scripture. One verse that spoke powerfully to me was Psalm 119:68, TEV: "How good you are—how kind! Teach me your commands." This verse helped me see more clearly than ever the true sequence of God's dealings with us humans. *First He reveals His goodness. Only then does He teach us what He expects from us.*

Sadly, in my own country God and His will and His ways had been nearly erased from the minds of three generations. But even this attempted forcible ejection of God worked for good, because it awoke in many hearts a voracious hunger for the Almighty. And as the hungry reached out for the bread of life, their hearts bonded to those who had worked so hard and so long and so bravely to provide it.

First God reveals His goodness, and only then does He teach us what He expects from us.

I believe that an inspired author may have had this in mind when she said:

"From the beginning it has been God's plan that through His church shall be reflected to the world His fullness and His sufficiency" (Ellen G. White, *The Acts of the Apostles, p. 9*). "The unselfish labor of Christians in the past should be to us an object lesson and an inspiration. The members of God's church are to be zealous of good works, separating from worldly ambition and walking in the footsteps of Him who went about doing good. With hearts filled with sympathy and compassion, they are to minister to those in need of help, bringing to sinners a knowledge of the Savior's love. Such work calls for laborious effort, but it brings a rich reward. Those who engage in it with sincerity of purpose will see souls won to the Savior, for the influence that attends the practical carrying out of the divine commission is irresistible" (*ibid.,* pp. 109, 110).

In light of these inspired words, it's easy to understand why "Christ spent more time in healing than in teaching" (Ellen G. White, in *Gospel Herald,* May 1, 1908).

When I think of "the unselfish labor of Christians in the past," my mind goes back to such Russian Adventist trailblazers as Henry Loebsack, Michael O. Demidov, Yan Wilson, Grigory Grigoryev, Pavel Swiridoff, Pavel Pilch, and of course my parents, Peter and Maria Kulakov.

Defying danger, these pioneers unswervingly put God's interests first in their lives. Their one clear goal—impossible to dislodge from their hearts—was to proclaim the last message of invitation and merciful warning over Russia's huge expanses, urging people to prepare to meet their Savior in the air.

They lived with a bright vision of the future, their souls thrilled by a sense of its reality. The challenges and complexities of what lay ahead were, to them, probably no more distinct and definite than our own future is to us. Yet their faith in the certainty of God's promises was so strong as to stir up all the noble energies of their being in the endeavor to save their fellow men. Each consciously or subconsciously took the following passage from Paul as their life principle:

"But I do not count my life of any value to myself, if only I may finish my course and the ministry that I received from the Lord Jesus, to testify to the good news of God's grace" (Acts 20:24, NRSV).

These pioneers were a hardy breed. The thought of a weekly day off or even a vacation never entered their minds. Actually, as I look back at them from the present day I can see that in some cases they may have gone to extremes in their zeal to disseminate the three angels' messages. For example, Henry Loebsack, who led Russian Adventism until 1934, often voiced his strong suspicions that any overweight preacher—in that era when pastors had to do a lot of walking—wasn't diligent enough in seeking converts and visiting members. (Elder Loebsack himself, whether through exercise or heredity, was a very thin man!)

In those days preachers usually didn't own homes but lived in modest rented apartments that were always open for guests—guests who felt they had the right to visit their pastors day or night without appointment. Adventists, in those days, never used hotels. They knew that each and every pastor would give them lodging for the night, a meal to eat, and even his own outer clothing to sleep in if there weren't extra blankets.

This spirit, I believe, was the reason for the remarkable church growth in those difficult times. Their hearts were energized by the inspired words of God's messenger: "Russia, the home of millions upon millions, whose souls are as precious in the sight of God as our own, who know nothing of the special truths for this time" (Ellen G. White, *Evangelism,* p. 408).

But though the pioneers did their best, their work was halted for a time. By 1935, with the exception of two, our entire force of ordained ministers— 150 in all—were incarcerated by Stalin's regime. Along with them more than 3,000 active members were arrested, and most were sent into exile. With one notable exception, all of our churches were closed. One Adventist church was left in Moscow as a showcase for the West.

Yet these little churches survived, worshipping secretly in private homes. Bound by genuine love and a common cause, those left behind prayed for their leaders in prison and for their exiled members, and even tried to help the incarcerated in spite of their own needs. The severest persecution broke neither the spirit of the church nor the courage of its members. Quite to the contrary, it bonded the church even closer together.

However—and here we begin to turn some really sad pages in this history of our church in Russia—Satan put an even uglier plan B into effect. He'd tried to destroy the church from outside, and had failed. So he began to attack from within.

Paradoxically, this inner turmoil happened just as the Second World War came to an end. Under pressure from Western allies and for other reasons, Stalin's government began to gradually change its attitude toward the churches. All religious organizations in the Soviet Union began to be given a bit more freedom to worship, though under the strict control of the authorities. Pastor Grigoryev, as the recognized leader of Russian Adventism, was allowed to reestablish some form of organization.

This wasn't easy. Most of our experienced leaders had died in prisons and labor camps, and there was no school to train new pastors. Besides that, we weren't permitted to have any contact with our world headquarters. This isn't the place for me to describe the long and painful process of restoring church organization throughout the Soviet Union. I will just say that it is a great misfortune that so much time, effort, and most of all precious souls were lost while we tried to settle our differences. Whenever our group of leaders got together and tried to decide anything—whether about evangelism or anything else—these divisions would rear up again and prevent a good Christian spirit of cooperation, no matter what they were trying to accomplish jointly.

Now disagreements are a natural part of working together, and different points of view are critical to the creative and problem-solving processes. But when differing opinions clash, and when those who disagree don't behave in the spirit of brotherly love, it causes needless pain and wastes valuable time and energy.

We need to learn how to maintain clear lines of communication. We need, in the spirit of Christ, to help ourselves and others remember that it is human to err, and that our only safety is in the guidance of the Lord. With those sad experiences behind us, together let us pray and think about how urgently and efficiently we need to help fulfill the gospel commission. I pray that all of us will forever remember the precious warning of God's messenger: "The sin that is most nearly hopeless and incurable is pride of opinion, self-conceit. This stands in the way of all growth" (Ellen G. White, *Testimonies for the Church,* vol. 7, pp. 199, 200).

Now I'm going to move into rather daring territory.

If you know anything at all about recent Russian history, you know that when the Soviet Union's huge atheistic Communist regime collapsed, the doors of unprecedented evangelistic opportunity flew wide open. And you probably know, too, that now Russia is changing again. Obstacles of a totally different nature have already closed some doors. Nationalism is on the rise, and religious intolerance toward minorities—preached by those who use Russian Orthodoxy for political gain—is becoming a new sad reality. As Russia's wealth increases, and as it is again becoming a major political power to be reckoned with, anti-Western moods and hostility toward foreign institutions and foreign missionaries are alarming.

My question is two-pronged:

Did we use those open-door opportunities to the fullest?

And as some doors are closing, are we properly positioned to fulfill our mission in more difficult times?

Don't get me wrong. I thank the Lord for the foreign missionaries that arrived to help us during those delirious first years of freedom, the wonderfully generous people who came from the United States, Europe, and Australia to help proclaim the Adventist message to the people of our country. I had the privilege of leading the Euro-Asian Division at that time, and how can I not be overwhelmed with gratitude?

In fact, two of my closest Bible Translation Institute associates, Ivan Lobanov and Marina Opiyar, both distinguished graduates of Russian universities, were converts of those crusades. Like many other young men and women, they were first attracted to the evangelistic meetings because they provided a chance to finally hear native English-speakers use the language that they were taught in their Russian schools. And their interest in English led to their interest in the gospel of Jesus Christ.

And from 1990 to 1994 Adventist membership tripled from 34,000 to 99,000. But with a former-U.S.S.R.-wide population of 290 million, that's a mere beginning—only one Adventist per 3,000 people. Incidentally, during the same period the Pentecostals increased their membership by 25 times.

So what I'm saying is that I appreciate the blessings we received during those years when Russia and the other countries of the Euro-Asia Division were open for evangelism. *But it is my deep conviction—and the great grief of my heart—that we did not fully explore and utilize the opportunities given us by God.*

And I will say very frankly that, to my great dismay, the deep discord between two wings of the church (of which I spoke earlier in this book) reared—and still rears—its ugly head from time to time. This was one of the major obstacles when we gathered in joint deliberations for prayer and collective counsel seeking. I still remember Elder Bob Spangler, on his last visit to Russia in 1996, sharing with me his concerns about the results of our efforts. "I'd hoped that at least a half million souls would be baptized following these campaigns," he said sadly.

I totally agreed with him. And that's why I dare to suggest that we search for new approaches to evangelism, new avenues that are so desperately needed in a country such as Russia, which is again heading toward an authoritarian way of life of a different nature.

I believe that to reach the population with God's message, we must be dissatisfied with the status quo and to take a new bold step forward. We have to establish long-lasting ties of friendship with key people in the society in which we are called to be "light and salt." We cannot exert a permanent influence upon our society unless we have those deep, genuine ties of friendship with, and therefore a positive influence on, those who shape public opinion.

And the Bible proves my point through the lives of its most shining examples. Joseph, who rose from a slave to second in command in Egypt, enjoyed the deepest respect and trust of the pagan pharaoh. Solomon, who turned his youthful heart toward the God of wisdom, caused Sheba's proud queen to enthusiastically exalt this God. Daniel, though absolutely uncompromising when it came to a "thus saith the Lord," enjoyed the trust of royalty in Babylon and the subsequent kingdoms. All of these Bible heroes stood tall for the God of heaven in the eyes of those with national influence.

To me, Paul's words to the Corinthians ring with even deeper meaning now: "I have become all things to all people, that I might by all means save some" (1 Corinthians 9:22, NRSV).

How closely he must have identified with those to whom he preached Christ! Certainly there's always a danger that we Adventists might water down our distinct witness, *but it is no less dangerous to barricade ourselves from those we are called to serve.* Only by avoiding both of these extremes will we be able to fulfill the commission Jesus gave us.

I ask you to gaze with me at two current Russian crises. The first is the government's inability to solve political and social problems, to fight crime and alcoholism, corruption and terrorism. The second is the chilling trend to suppress human rights and religious freedom, this time in order to preserve Russia's sovereignty and cultural uniqueness. Can Russian Adventists remain satisfied with the results of our ministry there as they see new forms of sophisticated heavy-handedness descending again? Hasn't the time come to prayerfully search for some new approaches to society's crying needs in these radically new conditions?

Wouldn't it be helpful for us to cast a new glance at the inspired description of Jesus' way of reaching people whom He came to save? "He [Jesus] was in sympathy with humanity in all its varied joys and sorrows. He identified himself with all,—with the weak and helpless, the lowly, the needy, and the afflicted" (Ellen G. White, *Counsels to Parents, Teachers, and Students,* p. 178). If Jesus, for the success of His mission, identified Himself (identified in the sense of being involved or closely associated) with all who needed His help, *can we count on success in our work without personally following Him in this respect as well?*

Back in chapter 20 I related a brief history of how our Zaokski seminary (which has recently been granted university status) was begun. Now let me give you some important background that proves the point I'm trying to make.

How was it that half a decade before the collapse of Communism the Soviet Union gave us, in addition to the tiny lot on which the gutted school stood, large lots of land free of charge? It can have been none other than divine Providence. While my son Michael was searching for property on which to build a seminary, he came across a state orphanage in crisis located in a village near Zaokski. His heart was touched, and he organized a group of people to help enlarge and repair its facilities. This worked a remarkable change in public opinion, and in return, the government opened up those extra acres, which have made all the difference to our school.

Then, once we'd begun our ministry in not only orphanages but prisons and hospitals, the government soon learned about what we were doing— without any PR campaigns on our part. Those among the authorities who were initially suspicious and hostile toward our plans to build, together with our American friends, a publishing house and a clinic in Moscow now became interested and supportive.

Our church received public recognition and prominence because we became known as a people deeply interested in the welfare of our fellow citizens. National newspapers, magazines, radio, and television reported about these first steps of the Adventist Church. And later, during the crucial transition into the "new Russia," many foresighted statesmen looked favorably on our church—*because we had made conscious efforts to identify with the needs and best interests of the citizens.* The country's new leaders, during Gorbachev's and Yeltsin's time, recognized that in a country with such religious diversity it was necessary that all faiths should be equal before the law. And our Adventist believers were able to demonstrate how a church can be very useful to keep balance among the country's social forces.

Can you imagine how positively breathtaking it was for me—someone who'd spent months in prison under investigation, then years in a labor camp—to be invited in 1990 (along with the Russian Orthodox patriarch) to speak before the Supreme Soviet of the U.S.S.R. during debates and hearings on the new law relating to freedom of conscience? During that time my articles on the subject of religious liberty were readily printed in the leading Russian newspapers. I, among others, was also received by the president and courageous reformer Mikhail Gorbachev to discuss questions about how the church should relate to the state.

And shortly afterward the throb of nightly evangelism began all across our nation. Practically all our outreach efforts were aimed at planning and conducting these campaigns. I reflect often on what has and has not been done, and what could have been done better. By their style and content, those programs did not take into account the intellectuals and opinion shapers, but were predominantly aimed at the average working people. And sadly, even among those who responded, we lost so many—primarily, perhaps, because they did not see that we genuinely cared for their needs and the wider needs of the community.

Here's what we, in my humble opinion, should have done. At that time, with our rather unique opportunities to influence public opinion by our witness—supported by our hearty ministry to the needs of our people—*we should have much more vigorously stood for eternal values and religious freedom.*

Unfortunately, that didn't happen. Somehow we didn't fully appreciate Ellen White's words: "Christ's method alone will give true success in reaching the people. The Savior mingled with men as one who desired their good. He showed His sympathy for them, ministered to their needs, and won their confidence. Then He bade them, 'Follow Me' " *(The Ministry of Healing,* p. 143).

This is what I would suggest, not only for my country of Russia but for every country and every culture. Along with preaching "the gospel of the kingdom," I believe we need to develop a four-pronged strategy:

We must strongly defend religious liberty.
We must in earnest serve the crying needs of our society.
We must be involved in the ministry of peacemaking and reconciliation.
We must speak for social justice.

While in Russia opportunities for traditional evangelistic efforts are being choked off, certain forces are trying to squeeze my country—again—into attitudes of nationalism and intolerance. And it's presumptuous for us to try to protect our right of religious freedom without caring for the rights and the needs of others, and without involving wider circles of society!

Fortunately, there are those in governmental leadership who share our understanding that the progress and prosperity of that nation—and every other nation—is indivisibly linked to the liberty of conscience and religion. Others in Christian and non-Christian religious organizations echo our concerns, and are willing to cooperate with us in our endeavors to serve the people of our country. As we work together with these good-hearted people we should follow the wise, inspired counsel:

"Our ministers should seek to come near to the ministers of other denominations. Pray for and with these men, for whom Christ is interceding. A solemn responsibility is theirs. As Christ's messengers we should manifest a deep, earnest interest in these shepherds of the flock" (Ellen G. White, *Testimonies for the Church,* vol. 6, p. 78).

I pray that by God's grace our relationships with other Christians will be marked by warm respect. We must accept them as brothers and sisters in the Lord, and then we will be able, when the right opportunity arises, to tell them of the things we believe they need to know. I'm sure we will be taught by God's Spirit to know the proper time to reveal which Bible truth.

And when—neither interfering with politics nor watering down our distinctiveness—we become so well acquainted with key people in our society that they count us as real friends, we will be able to accomplish much for the Lord. This, of course, will demand some serious stretching of our human and financial resources.

As people hear our united voices protesting such social evils as corruption, the sexual slave trade, drug abuse, and others, and as they see that we—following the example of the Savior, who spent His time healing the sick and feeding the hungry—are trying by all possible means to help our neighbors in their struggle for a peaceful and healthy life, the respect of the public for our church will increase immensely. How otherwise can we fulfill the task the Lord has put upon us if not by being a genuine model, an inspiration, and a resource for society in its spiritual and constitutional reconstruction?

The minds and hearts of others will be opened to us when they come to know us as loving and caring Christians, as people who are able to listen and to conduct an open and honest dialogue in the spirit of our meek Master. And it's good to know that in all of these important and delicate issues we can constantly rely on the guidance of the Lord. He is leading His humble followers to the final triumph, which is ours in the Lord Jesus Christ.

One day 50 years ago I conducted a worship service in a private home in one of the foothill gorges on the very outskirts of Almaty, Kazakhstan. Members of our church were there, as well as other friends of God's Word.

One of our members had brought with him one of his relatives, a member of the Komsomol, the Communist youth organization. This was the first time this young man had ever heard about the Savior of the world. The meeting ended, and he stood at the door about to leave. Suddenly he turned and asked me point-blank, "Are you sure that everything you have just read from the Bible is the actual truth?"

"Yes," I said.

He stared at me, puzzled. "If this is all true," he sputtered, "then why aren't you shouting this from every rooftop, and ringing it from every bell in the country?"

Everything I have ever done in my life, and everything that I have ever written, was and still is motivated by the desire to fulfill the command of our Lord so that I will never have to hear—or answer—that question!

ANOTHER AMAZING STORY OF GOD'S LEADING

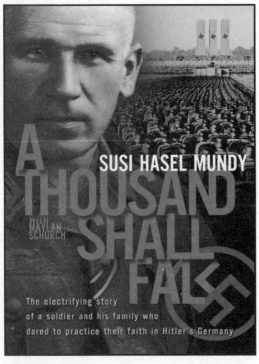

A Thousand Shall Fall

Susi Hasel Mundy

They saw God work miracle after miracle to save them from certain disaster. As thousands around them fell victim to the horrors of war, they were borne up on angels' wings—sometimes quite literally. This is the true story of one family who chose to be faithful whatever the cost. 0-8280-1561-9. Paperback, 172 pages.

3 WAYS TO SHOP

• Visit your local ABC
• Call 1-800-765-6955
• www.AdventistBookCenter.com

REVIEW AND HERALD®
PUBLISHING ASSOCIATION